Defining
Noah Webster

A Spiritual Biography

K. Alan Snyder

Allegiance Press, Inc.
WASHINGTON, D.C.

Defining Noah Webster: A Spiritual Biography
by K. Alan Snyder

Printed in the United States of America

Library of Congress Control Number: 2002105260
ISBN 1-591600-55-3

Unless otherwise indicated, Bible quotations are taken from the
King James Version.

Allegiance Press
11350 Random Hills Road
Suite 800
Fairfax, VA 22030
(703) 279-6511

To order additional copies, call 1-866-909-BOOK (2665).

Dedication

I can do no better than Noah Webster who, in the preface to his American Dictionary of the English Language, wrote: "To that great and benevolent Being, who, during the preparation of this work, has sustained a feeble constitution, amidst obstacles and toils, disappointments, infirmities and depression; who has . . . given me strength and resolution to bring the work to a close, I would present the tribute of my most grateful acknowledgements. And if the talent which he entrusted to my care, has not been put to the most profitable use in His service, I hope . . . that any misapplication of it may be graciously forgiven."

Acknowledgements

I wish to express appreciation to Dr. Roger Brown of The American University, who served as my mentor as I pursued a doctorate and helped clear up intellectual ambiguities for me in the preparation of this manuscript. I am particularly indebted to him for encouraging me to make the connection between Webster and Common Sense Philosophy. I also wish to thank two other American University professors, Dr. Alan Kraut and Dr. Charles McLaughlin, for questions they raised and the comments they made as part of my dissertation committee.

Certainly I must acknowledge my wife, Jan, who sometimes wondered if I ever would figure out what I was going to be when I grew up, and Laura and Daniel, who should be excused if they concluded that their father was married to a microfilm reader and a computer terminal. I love them all and hope they will come away from this experience with at least a deeper appreciation of the demands of scholarly pursuits.

For this revised edition, I acknowledge a debt of gratitude to Tom Freiling of Allegiance Press who believed that this work was worth republishing.

Foreword

The schooling of the Founding Fathers was full of stories from Greek and Roman history and legend where heroes were bigger than life. There have been seasons when the Founders themselves were portrayed as legends. While such heroes may inspire us at a certain level, it is hard to sustain the inspiration for most readers who are painfully aware of their own imperfection.

Many have taken to the opposite extreme in the past two decades. The founders are painted in a monochrome shade of evil—misogynist, racist, white elitist, who would have polluted the environment had they only had access to gas-guzzling SUVs.

We should know better than to gravitate to either version of history. History was made by real people who rarely come in the form of the cardboard caricature of legend or villain. And, thank goodness, the truth is far more interesting than the alternatives.

Dr. Alan Snyder makes the man Noah Webster come alive in this fine account of the life work of this influential member of the generation of the American founding. Far from a unidimensional analysis, we see Webster as a complex, seemingly contradictory personality. He is passionate for the cause of American liberty as a youth, yet impetuously declares the experiment a dismal failure in recurring moments of depression. Webster embraces all the moral rigor of his Puritan upbringing, yet is tantalized by the Enlightenment and its elevation of reason. He is driven, yet unfocused. Self-doubting, yet proud. And yet this long season of contradiction fades when Webster experiences a genuine conversion in mid-life.

There is no doubting the importance that education played in the life of Noah Webster. In turn, he had a monumental impact on American education with his famous *Blue Backed Speller* and landmark dictionary, among many other publications.

It was from his own years at Yale that Webster developed his inclination to value reason above religious faith. He viewed education as the key to the long-term success of the young Republic.

In the early days of his career, Webster embraced cultural Christianity while effectively denying its life-changing character that comes from true faith. His effort to reconcile some role of Christianity with his elevated view of Reason appears to be the central reason that Webster was so conflicted in his own life.

Snyder guides the reader through these facts to true insight, helping us understand how these warring concepts had predictable outcomes in the early seasons of Webster's career.

Many historians might fail to understand the difference between a sense of religious duty that makes a man attempt to live a morally upright life and true religious faith. Webster certainly understood the difference. Snyder brings us Webster's own words and clear objective analysis, which is the historian's key tool, to help us all to see the material impact his 1808 conversion had on his life and career.

History that tells us what happened stops short of fulfilling the real desire of the reader. We want to know why men acted and why their actions mattered.

Alan Snyder's *Defining Noah Webster* represents history at the highest and most interesting level. We understand this significant founder in both his own motivation and why his impact on the nation, particularly upon education, was so long lasting.

Toward the end of his life, Noah Webster wrote:

> Truth is the end to which all learning should be directed. We want truth in literature; we want truth in science; we want truth in politics; we want truth in morals; we want truth in religion; we want truth in everything. To gain truth in learning & science, we want accurate scholars for teachers; to gain truth in politics, we want great statesmen, & men of pure integrity; to gain truth in religion, we want the scriptures in language that conveys the exact sense of the inspired writers, & which every reader can understand.

In short, truth is everything that is valuable in theory or practice; & without it, nothing either in theory or practice is of any value.

Alan Snyder shares Noah Webster's passion for the Truth. Webster was complex man who overcame his inner struggles. But Snyder does not fail to show us the big truth about such a triumph. Noah Webster found that the power to overcome comes not from within but from the One described in Scripture as the Way, the Truth, and the Life.

Michael P. Farris
President, Patrick Henry College

Table of Contents

Preface to the Revised Edition

Noah Webster fascinates me. He has for years. That is why I chose him as my doctoral dissertation topic. So many of my interests converged in his person: his influence on early American education, his involvement with the political scene in America's early decades, and his Christian conversion in mid-life. All of these made him an attractive study.

Others apparently agreed. An academic press accepted the dissertation for publication in 1990. While I was gratified by the acceptance, I was dismayed by the price tag on the book. I know it kept people from purchasing it who otherwise would have profited from the contents. Now I am pleased to see it back in the marketplace of ideas where it belongs—at a far better price, thanks to Allegiance Press.

I have kept the main title—*Defining Noah Webster*—but have altered the subtitle. The old subtitle—*Mind and Morals in the Early Republic*—while descriptive, seems too stilted now. The new subtitle—*A Spiritual Biography*—expresses better what I aim to provide in these pages.

In revising the book, I removed a few errors that sneaked past not only the author, but also the dissertation committee and the first publisher. Additionally, I carefully considered what was really essential to tell the story and excised some other portions of the earlier work, in the hope that it will be more streamlined and acceptable for a general audience.

So, here it is—a "new" spiritual biography of Noah Webster. I pray that it will end up in the hands of those who will receive the greatest benefit from it.

Introduction

An examination of America's pursuit of intellectual and moral excellence in the post-revolutionary world must necessarily include the man who was America's premier educator for its first half-century of independence. Born and bred a Connecticut Congregationalist, Noah Webster early manifested a love of learning and a desire to share his learning that marked him as a molder and shaper of public opinion. He was a Yale graduate during the stormy revolutionary years and then became an entrepreneurial schoolmaster during the 1780s. In that capacity, he compiled the first textbooks designed to establish American education as a home-grown product, less reliant on British imports and European educational fashions. His devotion to education was constant throughout a long career that included stints as a lawyer, as editor of a magazine and a newspaper, and, finally, as the unequalled lexicographer of his time.

Webster makes an outstanding subject of study not only because he was the premier educator, but also because his writings never divorced the intellectual and the moral. He aimed constantly for moral and intellectual uplift and for the changes in manners and habits that would accompany such an uplift. Some of his texts for schools became standards, especially his Speller, and they all were decidedly moralistic in tone and geared toward proper personal bearing in society.

Besides his textbooks, Webster's moralism also found expression in publications such as *The Prompter*, *The Effects of Slavery*, *Letters to a Young Gentleman Commencing His Education*, and *The Value of the Bible*. *The Prompter* was a book of common sense sayings in the manner of Benjamin Franklin's *Poor Richard's Almanac*, in which Webster satirized prevalent vices. The work against slavery was designed primarily to warn against the effects of the system on morals and individual industry. *Letters to a Young Gentleman* centered on the application of the Ten Commandments to private and public conduct, the divine nature of the Bible, and the personal character of America's ancestors. *The Value of the Bible* was an apologetic for the Christian religion and was written for instruction in families and schools, another indication of his attempt to inculcate specific values in children.

Some of Webster's other writings focused more on intellectual inquiry and the advancement of human knowledge. His *Dissertations on the English Language* was the publication of a series of lectures he gave throughout the country in the 1780s. Its purpose was to encourage the development of a unique American language derived, but separated from, that of England. In 1798, Webster revealed the breadth of his interests by publishing *A Brief History of Epidemic and Pestilential Diseases*, a publication rather advanced for its time. *Elements of Useful Knowledge*, another in a steady stream of school texts, ranged through a vast number of subjects from the solar system and the origins of man, to the history of America, to discussions of the arts, customs, and education. Another text, *Biography for the Use of Schools*, consisted of sketches of classical authors, Biblical men of faith, and all manner of political and literary luminaries. His 1832 *History of the United States* made the case for the Christian basis for American republican government. One of his last works, *A Manual of Useful Studies*, branched into the fields of logic, rhetoric, composition, architecture, geology, and biology. In all of the above, Webster had the elevation of the nation's intellectual level as his goal.

Most of Webster's works cannot be classified as solely moral or intellectual because he viewed the two as inextricably bound together. When he penned *The Revolution in France*, for instance, he deplored France's moral decline, but in the context of how it would halt the advance of man's intellectual achievements. The subtitle of *A Collection of Essays and Fugitiv Writings* (with its title bearing one mark of his proposed spelling changes) manifests this intertwining: *On Moral, Historical, Political, and Literary Subjects*. There are also his Fourth of July orations, which are classic appeals to both fields of interest. And, of course, Webster's famous dictionary, his greatest legacy, revealed his concerns just by the wording of the definitions and the quotations he chose for examples. His definition of education, taken from the original 1828 edition, was quite broad, emphasizing both intellect and morality. He even included a moral commentary in his definition:

> That series of instruction and discipline which is intended to enlighten the understanding, correct the temper, and form the manners and habits of youth, and fit them for usefulness in their future stations. To give children a good education in manners, arts and science, is important; to give them a religious education is indispensable; and an immense responsibility rests on parents and guardians who neglect these duties.[1]

Webster also has one additional feature that makes him a unique subject of research: his 1808 conversion to Edwardsean Calvinism. Although a Congregationalist all of his life, he was more concerned with outward forms before 1808. After his personal affirmation of faith, there was a shift in emphasis in his attempts to influence America intellectually and morally. He increasingly viewed intellectual uplift as a result of spiritual and moral regeneration, and his concern for propriety became decidedly Biblically oriented. The 1808 conversion was a watershed in his own moral and intellectual development and provides a demarcation line for the comparison of Webster's early thought with the reflections of the more mature Webster of his later years.

The first scholarly treatment of Noah Webster was an 1883 biography by Horace Scudder that drew the ire of one of Webster's granddaughters.[2] Scudder's biography, declared Emily Ellsworth Fowler Ford, did a grave disservice to the memory of her grandfather in that it aimed "to discolor his character, to belittle his work as well as his aims, and to make him out an egoist of persistent self-conceit in his career." She sought to "defend his character," to "justify his aims," and to "bring the facts of his life against the one-sided judgment of his latest biographer." She was particularly concerned to reveal his Christian character in private life and to show how his "justice, benevolence and sympathy so endeared him to his family and friends."[3] The fruit of her labor, *Notes on the Life of Noah Webster*, was a two-volume work that performed an invaluable service in the collection and publication of a great number of Webster's private correspondences. This work was followed in 1936 by a new comprehensive biography written by Harry R. Warfel, who later also published a book of Webster's letters.[4] Warfel's treatment of Webster illuminated his role as America's first national schoolmaster and was more sympathetic to Webster's character than Scudder's biography.

Warfel's work remained the definitive word on Webster until 1980, when historian Richard Rollins offered a new interpretation of the educator's character.[5] Rollins approached Webster from an entirely different perspective, a perspective that revealed certain presuppositions, or the grid through which Rollins saw the world. His study depended primarily on psychological models in the hope of discovering why Webster latched onto Federalist ideology and then succumbed to a conversion experience. Religion, in Rollins's worldview, appeared to be little more than a method of social control, and he surmised that Webster converted in order to salvage some sense of control in a world that was collapsing around him. This interpretation leaves little room for the intellectual aspects of religious belief and portrays Webster as someone always on the verge of neurosis. Webster, concluded Rollins, was transformed from a libertarian democrat into an antilibertarian reactionary, and his religion provided the mechanism to make the transformation complete. The emphasis on social control, although it does not negate the sincerity of religious belief, does tend to stress a fixation with order and control almost to the exclusion of personal liberty, an emphasis that appears incongruous not only with the historical setting of early national America, but also with Webster's personal philosophy and level of influence in that society. Another short Webster biography, authored by Richard J. Moss, used Rollins's interpretation for its basis and offered nothing new to scholarly discussion.[6]

A more balanced view of Webster's character can be seen in E. Jennifer Monaghan's analysis of the famous Webster Speller, but her concentration on that one aspect of Webster's work did not draw attention to the intertwining of intellectual and moral concerns.[7] A more recent work by Harlow Giles Unger, *Noah Webster: The Life and Times of an American Patriot,* paints a sympathetic portrait of Webster, and is comprehensive in its treatment of the times in which he lived, yet seems to regard Webster's conversion experience as marginal in its effect on his thinking.[8]

This current study offers a reevaluation of the life and thought of Noah Webster, particularly in the twin concerns of the intellectual and moral development of individuals and of the new American nation. It seeks to elucidate Webster's worldview and how it affected his thinking, writing, and proposed remedies for the moral ills and intellectual inconsistencies he perceived in his country. The Webster conversion forms the centerpiece of the study. I assume the validity of Webster's conversion experience. Indeed, I hold the view—my personal presupposition—that religious beliefs form the foundation for a person's intellectual perceptions and moral stances. I also agree with Noah Webster that intellectual and moral issues touch upon all aspects of life, and have a particular impact on government, whether that government is of self, a family, or a nation.

---

[1] Noah Webster, *An American Dictionary of the English Language* (New York: Sherman Converse, 1828; reprint ed., Anaheim, CA: Foundation for American Christian Education, 1967).

[2] Horace E. Scudder, *Noah Webster* (Boston: Houghton Mifflin Co., 1883).

[3] Emily Ellsworth Fowler Ford, comp., Emily Ellsworth Ford Skeel, ed., *Notes on the Life of Noah Webster*, 2 vols. (New York: Burt Franklin, 1912; reprint ed., 1971), 1:vi.

[4] Harry R. Warfel, *Noah Webster: Schoolmaster to America* (Macmillan, 1936; reprint ed., New York: Octagon, 1966).

[5] Richard M. Rollins, *The Long Journey of Noah Webster* (University of Pennsylvania Press, 1980).

[6] Richard J. Moss, *Noah Webster* (Boston: Twayne Publishers, 1984).

[7] E. Jennifer Monaghan, *A Common Heritage: Noah Webster?s Blue-Back Speller* (Hamden, CT: Archon Books, 1983).

[8] Harlow Giles Unger, *Noah Webster: The Life and Times of an American Patriot* (New York: John Wiley & Sons, 1998).

CHAPTER 1 ·

Roots:
Spiritual Foundations

N oah Webster, Jr., born in West Hartford, Connecticut in 1758, was nurtured in a part of colonial America that maintained a strong connection with its religious and moral roots, while it joined in the intellectual debate over the legal and political rights of British colonists. A further ingredient of the moral and intellectual climate was the young Webster's personal inclination toward intellectual activity, an inclination that diverted him from the farming life chosen by most of his family and community. He lived in the community but never was an integral part of it. His thoughts centered on booklearning, his ambitions went beyond mere husbandry, and he sought to make a name for himself as America received its first taste of independence. Webster grew up with America. He searched for his identity while America searched for the same, suffered a similar disillusionment after the first flush of independence had passed, and matured even as the United States found a mature and settled government.

Religion was a staple in Webster's upbringing. His ancestors were part of the Great Migration from England in the 1620s and 1630s, including both Pilgrim Separatists and Puritans. William Bradford, Separatist governor of Plymouth Colony for thirty-five years, and an original settler from the Mayflower, was in a direct line with him through his mother, Mercy Steele. On his father's side, Webster could trace an unbroken chain of Puritan forbears. John Webster of Warwickshire, England, was one of the sturdy band of Puritan settlers who arrived in Massachusetts in the early 1630s. When the Rev. Thomas Hooker decided to start a new colony further south, John Webster was among the original settlers. He became a leader of the new colony of Connecticut and obtained the governorship in 1656.

John Webster's descendants continued to play active roles in their communities, both in Connecticut and in Massachusetts, throughout the last half of the seventeenth and early part of the eighteenth centuries. The first Noah Webster was born at Hartford on 25 March 1722, the son of Daniel Webster and Miriam Cooke. Although his letters reveal a man of little formal schooling, he had intelligence and took an active role in the Fourth Church of Hartford, eventually being elected Deacon, a position of some stature in colonial Connecticut. When he was appointed a Justice of the Peace from 1781 until 1796, his reputation in the community was established because he had attained high rank in both church and state. He was entitled to be called either Deacon Webster or Squire Webster. He took another title, that of Senior, when Noah Webster, Jr., was born in 1758.

The Puritanism that led John Webster to emigrate to the new world settled all questions on the basis of Biblical authority. It was a heady religion that dreamed of erecting a city on a hill. The Puritans were a covenanted people, covenanted with God and with each other. In Massachusetts and Connecticut, the Puritan founders established Congregational churches. Throughout the entire colonial era and into the nineteenth century, Congregationalism was the recognized religion in both states. This "establishment" was irksome to dissenting Baptists, Quakers, and others, yet its contours were fluid as both states tackled the issue of how to deal with those who chose another form of Christian worship. Historian Thomas J. Curry, in a detailed study of liberty of conscience in colonial and revolutionary America, notes that "from 1727 on both Massachusetts and Connecticut devised systems whereby Baptists and Quakers were exempted from paying ministerial taxes and Anglicans' contributions went for the support of their own ministers."[1] Congregationalism remained the official denomination of Connecticut until 1818; Massachusetts continued its establishment until 1833.

Congregationalism was the *form* that Christian religion took in Connecticut; the *spirit* of the faith, however, always was subject to change. John Winthrop, the first governor of Massachusetts, had warned his listeners about the dangers of breaking covenant with God, and his warnings were repeated and embellished by multitudes of Puritan divines in later decades. The common perception of the age was that the religious fervor of the New Englanders had declined after the passing of the founding generation. The jeremiad appeal—a warning against apostasy and a promise of the renewal of the covenant if the people would revive their flagging faithfulness—became a common Puritan sermonizing technique.

Whether or not the perception of decline was accurate, Connecticut joined with the rest of the colonies in experiencing the Great Awakening, the apex of which was reached in the early 1740s with the arrival of itinerant preacher George Whitefield. Both Whitefield and Gilbert Tennant preached to the students at Yale, Tennant a number of times. But the denominational split over the methods used by the Awakeners affected Connecticut as deeply as any colony. By 1745, student David Brainerd, later the subject of a biography written by Jonathan Edwards, had been expelled for following Tennant to Milford without permission of the authorities, and Yale president Thomas Clap had issued a "Declaration" against Whitefield.[2] Despite the controversies, the colony had been stirred, and the advocates of revival continued to have an influence on the religious atmosphere.

By the time Noah, Jr., entered the world in 1758, the Awakening was more than a decade removed. The Fourth Church, which the Webster family attended, was not known for its high state of religious fervor. The Rev. Nathan Perkins of Fourth Church recalled that the church was in a poor state when he arrived in the early 1770s. Lack of religious conviction prevailed, he could find only one young person interested in spiritual matters, and new converts were virtually nonexistent.[3] The young Webster's church experience probably did not draw his attention to spiritual pursuits.

Home life, though, was a counterbalance to the spiritual poverty of Fourth Church. Noah, Sr., and Mercy provided a highly religious and moral tone for their family. Webster later recalled that he had been "educated in the religious principles of the first planters of

New England" and that his father, mother, and most of his relatives, on both sides of the family, were "pious" people.[4] This religious concern is expressed in a 1782 letter written by his father when he admonishes his son:

> I wish to have you serve your generation & do good in the world & be useful & may so behave as to gain the esteem of all virtuous people that are acquainted with you & gain a comfortable subsistence, but especially that you may so live as to obtain the favor of Almighty God & his grace in this world & a Saving interest in the merits of Jesus Christ, without which no man can be happy.[5]

The religious emphasis in the family also is evidenced in correspondence from his two brothers, Charles and Abraham. Charles, writing to Noah in 1796, sermonizes:

> Now in this mutable & busy world how happy are we if we can calmly and dispassionately stop, & make a silent pause, & Look within our selves and see how it is with us, how it stands between our souls and our God, whether we have experienced a conformity to thee will of the Lord, . . . and dear Brother (I have nothing but good will to thee in writing so) the call is to thee I believe from the Saviour at times, & has been in seasons past, to leave the honors of the world, & go work in my vineyard.[6]

As the letter indicates, Charles was concerned with Noah's spiritual condition. Noah himself confirmed that he had not held completely to the religious heritage of his family when he announced later, in 1808, that he had been converted.

Besides the religious emphasis, the elder Websters communicated a sense of tradition to their children. Noah and his brothers and sisters were reared on their heritage. The impressions made on Noah, Jr., were to last throughout his life. In his 77th year, he completed a compilation of the Webster Genealogy and sent copies to each of his own children. To his son he wrote,

I have sent you some papers respecting our family for
private use. I wish all my children and grand children to
keep a copy each. This is done for the purpose of preserving the history of the family, which I think every family
should do.[7]

Growing up in the Webster household, then, meant a strong sense
of family tradition, careful attention to religious duties, and, of
course, the hard work of daily farm chores. Even though Noah, Jr.,
retained a keen appreciation for husbandry to the end of his long
life, it was quite obvious that the role of farmer was not to be his
primary occupation. His preference for intellectual pursuits was
unique to the family. Older brother Abraham followed in his
father's footsteps, ultimately moving to New York to establish his
farm. Charles, four years Noah's junior, became a businessman.
Only Noah had a thirst for booklearning.

Connecticut, like Massachusetts, manifested an interest in education quite early in its history. Included in the colony's first law code
of 1650 were provisions requiring parents and masters to teach children three essentials: the principles of the Christian faith through
the catechism; the ability to read English; and instruction in a trade.
Comments a historian of Connecticut education, "The stress upon
vocationalism, Christianity, and morality remained features of
Connecticut legislation on education throughout the colonial
period."[8] The requirement for the teaching of the catechism in
schools continued as a Connecticut law until 1821.[9]

If education had to be reduced to the minimum level, reading and
the catechism were usually the courses of study retained.[10] Religion
and morality were stressed because it was believed that preparation
for eternal life also would prepare one for usefulness in the temporal world. No division of secular and sacred was countenanced or
even considered. Education was carried on in a variety of schools:
the traditional grammar school with its emphasis on Latin; the
English school, which concentrated on the mastery of the colony's
native tongue; and the many private schools that had begun to flourish early in the century.[11] Primary education, which would be
comparable to nursery schools and kindergartens today, was carried
on usually by dame schools run by housewives or spinsters who

charged a nominal fee to teach young children the alphabet. Such schools served an important function in colonial and early national New England because they provided the path for admission to the grammar schools.[12]

Webster attended West Hartford's grammar school in the irregular fashion of the day, usually in the winter and whenever else he was not needed on the farm. He received the basic catechism and reading instruction, as well as writing, arithmetic, and spelling, all accomplished with very few schoolbooks. Webster commented that he used only a spelling book (the Dilworth Speller that eventually he replaced with his own), a Psalter, and a Bible in his grammar school education. Often, he was too occupied on his father's farm to maintain any consistency in his learning. By the time he was fourteen, he was imploring his father to allow him to prepare for college. The elder Webster held off these pleadings because of the heavy financial obligation that a Yale education would entail.[13] When, however, it became apparent that his namesake was more apt to take his Latin grammar into the fields than attend to routine chores, he relented.[14]

Preparation for college in Webster's day usually meant finding an individual who could tutor the prospective collegian privately. And in most instances that tutor would be the town's Congregational minister. It was no different in Webster's case; in the autumn of 1772 he began his classical studies under the watchful eye of the Rev. Nathan Perkins.

By September 1774, Webster had secured from Perkins a certificate testifying to his character and to his intellectual attainments and was ready for admission to Yale. He was accepted readily as part of the new freshman class. His father's concerns about finances were realized when the family farm was mortgaged to meet the expenses of this advanced education. The younger Webster never was able to pay back his father and when, in 1790, Noah, Sr., determined that he could not repay the debt, he sold the family farm. Noah, Jr., tried to help his father financially, but he had enough trouble supporting himself and could not forestall loss of the farm.[15] Failure to provide adequate help to his father caused him great personal pain. As he wrote at that time to brother-in-law James Greenleaf, "I have a father in distress & could I see him relieved I should be under no apprehensions to myself."[16] Again, in a later letter to the same individual, Webster declared,

> My fathers affairs give me more trouble than my own. He owes a large sum & has just had an attachment laid upon his estate. He cannot raise the money, & the probability is, he must, in his old age, be driven into the new settlements in a reduced situation. This wounds me deeply.[17]

Webster's parents had made a great sacrifice for their son's educational ambitions. The sacrifice was not made without considerable concern, yet it appears to have been made willingly. The senior Webster stayed abreast of his son's progress while he was at school, and often visited and escorted him home.

The College Years

Yale College was one of nine colleges in the colonies in 1774. Established in 1701, Yale was intended to be a training ground for ministers. Those who did not choose the ministry would take a Christian education into whatever profession they entered. Webster attended Yale in the midst of the political debate over the rights of British colonists. It was a time of tremendous intellectual stimulation for a mind such as Webster's, and the curriculum was heavily laced with political and governmental overtones.

College curriculum in the colonial era was slow to change. Throughout this period, Yale freshmen concentrated on Latin, a little Greek New Testament, and arithmetic, while sophomores added logic, geography, algebra, geometry, and rhetoric to their regimen, and juniors took on trigonometry and an introduction to natural philosophy (a mixture of biology, geology, astronomy, and physics) in addition to the ever-present Latin and Greek. Seniors focused on metaphysics and ethics (moral philosophy), spending less time in class and more in individual study. All students studied divinity, usually on Saturdays. One innovation begun during Webster's stay was the inclusion of English grammar and literature for sophomores and juniors. History also was introduced.[18]

The content of the courses incorporated some of the new knowledge espoused in the Enlightenment, yet all information was utilized to support traditional Christian belief and practice. Natural philosophy used Benjamin Martin's *Philosophical Grammar* and *Philosophia Brittanica*, texts based on Newtonian concepts. The metaphysics and ethics courses for seniors employed John Locke's *Essay on Human Understanding* and William Wollaston's *The Religion of Nature Delineated*, as the students tackled the problem of how to reconcile the Enlightenment's faith in human reason with Calvinist theology. The courses were open to new speculations, but always with a view to subsume all ideas under a Calvinistic theological umbrella. This ongoing Reformed posture can be seen in the catechism read by underclassmen and the more difficult senior readings, *Abridgement of Christian Divinity* by Johannes Wollebius and *Medulla Theologiae* by English Calvinist William Ames.[19]

Yale in the revolutionary era also began to draw on the Scottish Common Sense philosophy. This philosophy later was the key to what one historian calls the Didactic Enlightenment, which was a nineteenth-century formulation of new rational arguments for science, progress, intellectual freedom, and republicanism that fit into America's Biblical culture.[20] Lord Kames's *Elements of Criticism* and James Beattie's *Essay on the Nature and Immutability of Truth* were Scottish texts that were part of a student's course of study even before Webster entered the college.[21] The latter had as its subtitle, _In Opposition to Sophistry and Scepticism_, and was based on the Common Sense reflections of another Scottish philosopher, Thomas Reid.[22]

Reid (1710-1796) initially was regent at King's College, Aberdeen, and then successor to Adam Smith in moral philosophy at Glasgow. He began his philosophical speculations in response to what he considered to be the errors of Bishop Berkeley and David Hume. Reid believed that Berkeley had denied common sense with his assertion that the external world was a product of man's mind and subsequently had opened the way for Hume's skepticism toward the trustworthiness of man's reasoning powers. Reid insisted that there were certain self-evident truths—or intuitive beliefs—that formed the basis for all principles of morality, science, and religion. These truths included the trustworthiness of man's reasoning ability, the reality of the external world, and the sure knowledge of one's own existence.[23] The Common Sense philosophy, with its dismissal of Hume's skepticism and its affirmation of God-given, self-evident truths held great appeal for American religious leaders and educators who sought to put belief in God upon a sound rational basis as well as upon Biblical revelation.

The man credited with inaugurating Common Sense moral philosophy in American colleges is the Rev. John Witherspoon, who emigrated from Scotland in 1768 to take the reins of the College of New Jersey. Witherspoon, a devoted disciple of Reid, believed that the Common Sense philosophy was the perfect intellectual framework for espousing a Christian view of the individual's relationship with God and his complementary responsibilities in society. For Witherspoon, and for many people he influenced, political philosophy was part of moral philosophy. Political philosophy had its foundations in morality, which, in turn, rested on the law of nature, a law equated with the law of God.[24]

Recent scholarship on the influence of Common Sense philosophy shows the pervasiveness of Common Sense among the intellectual elite of the founding generation. One historian, Daniel Howe, makes specific reference to one aspect of the philosophy that he terms faculty psychology, i.e., "the study of the human powers."[25] Human nature, according to faculty psychology, is comprised of mechanical, animal, and rational powers. The mechanical, according to Reid, can be reduced to *instinct* and *habit*; the animal, which humans share with all other living creatures, he calls *appetites*, and lists as *hunger, thirst, and lust*. Reason takes priority as the rational power that is supposed to tame and direct the appetites and desires. It, in turn, is guided by the conscience, which Reid considers to be the moral faculty implanted by God.[26] It is Howe's contention that *The Federalist*—the quintessential explanation of Early National American constitutional thought—is guided by the faculty psychology of the Common Sense School. He considers faculty psychology, though, to be a secularized version of a Christian explanation of human nature.[27]

Thomas Reid and John Witherspoon, however, would have protested any explanation of their teachings as "secularized." Reid declared,

Common Sense and Reason have both one Author; that

Almighty Author in all whose other works we observe a consistency, uniformity, and beauty. . . . There must, therefore, be some order and consistency in the human faculties.[28]

Witherspoon certainly saw no dichotomy between his moral philosophy and his Christian faith as he taught his students,

The noble and eminent improvements in natural philosophy, which have been made since the end of the last century, have been far from hurting the interest of religion; on the contrary, they have greatly promoted it. Why should it not be the same with moral philosophy, which is indeed nothing else but the knowledge of human nature? . . . I do not know anything that serves more for the support of religion than to see from the different and opposing systems of philosophers, that there is nothing certain in their schemes, but what is coincident with the word of God.[29]

Lawrence Cremin, eminent historian of American education, perceived the same religious foundation in the moral philosophy courses, and the link with revolutionary discussions of government and politics when he mentioned, "there was no missing the burning relevance of the central question, What political arrangements are ethically desirable in light of the laws of nature and the teachings of God?"[30] It was through Scottish Common Sense that Webster would learn to think in terms of human faculties and their powers, and their application to the political and moral spheres. Yet in no way was Common Sense viewed as antithetical to Biblical beliefs. It constituted, instead, a rational means for explaining the truths of revelation.[31]

Disputations and declamations were highlights of the junior and senior years. Memorized recitation, which was the normal technique in course work, often could be boring. In the disputations and declamations, students had an opportunity to do some original thinking and speaking. Syllogistic disputations were in Latin, but a forensic form in English had been introduced in 1750 and was quite popular. Declamations were arguments written out by students in advance, corrected by the tutor, and then presented by memory as public orations.[32] Both forms allowed creativity and were means to inspire learning.

Inspiration, being an internal quality, is best achieved by the communication of man to man. Yale in 1774, however, did not offer a great leader who could provide that inspiration. The Rev. Naphtali Daggett, who held the position of Professor of Divinity, also served as President Pro Tempore. He had held this dual role since 1766, after the dismissal of the controversial Thomas Clap, whose high-handed and disputatious nature had alienated Connecticut's General Assembly and had weakened the financial base of the entire college. Daggett's personality was different than Clap's. He has been described as a quiet, unprepossessing man who never could have been accused of being either striking or colorful.[33] His demeanor, however, hid a heart full of political conviction. A firm supporter of revolutionary activities, Daggett surprised his contemporaries with a great show of personal courage when the British attacked New Haven in 1779. As the invading army approached the town, Daggett grabbed his fowling piece and turned sniper. Captured, he was physically abused and forced to march barefoot in the hot sun. The treatment he received weakened him considerably and his death in 1780 was traced to the sufferings he endured while a captive.[34]

Despite such personal heroism, Daggett apparently had limited capacity for leading a college. He appeared to have no rapport with the students under his charge, and his boring sermons and other inadequacies led the students to present a petition for his removal in 1776.[35] Fortunately, there were other persons involved with the instruction of the students, individuals who knew how to inspire and to whom the students could look with respect.

Webster's own tutor during most of his tenure at the college was Joseph Buckminster who, when Ezra Stiles assumed the Yale presidency in 1778, filled the pulpit Stiles had vacated in Portsmouth, New Hampshire—a position Buckminster held for the next thirty-three years. As a tutor, he was as concerned with the spiritual development of his students as he was with their intellectual progress. Webster apparently developed an admirable tutorial relationship with Buckminster, as shown by a letter from Buckminster to his ex-charge after they both had departed the college. The letter provides insight into a tutor's view of the achievements of the college in those politically turbulent years, and into the nature of the students. Buckminster comments that his years with Webster's class had been particularly satisfying. He especially was impressed with a number of the young men "possessed of talents capable of extensive usefulness, and of dispositions to improve those talents for the benefit of society." He was not, however, blind to "the independent spirit which was peculiar" to that class and that "made it more difficult to instruct and lead," but saw in that independence, not rebellion, but a willingness to make attempts "to do something for your honor." To some extent, Buckminster alleviated the problems associated with Daggett's leadership.[36]

Another tutor at the college during the same period was Timothy Dwight, who was in charge of the class just ahead of Webster's. Dwight's influence on his students was great. He gathered around him a number of budding scholars and provided them with direction. Under his guidance, Joel Barlow initiated his epic poem, *The Vision of Columbus*. Although he imbibed of the heady optimism of the revolutionary era, Dwight was not an uncritical devotee of Enlightenment philosophy. His belief in human reason and his view of the future greatness of America never were divorced from a Biblical basis and, when he assumed the presidency of Yale in 1795, he further strengthened the preeminence of the Scottish Common Sense philosophy and its supports for Christianity.

Therefore, while Webster's world at Yale introduced him to new concepts, it did not erase the religious instruction of his childhood; rather, it sought to enhance arguments for Christian orthodoxy through rational means. Webster himself, however, emerged from his educational experience more enamored of its rational aspects than the theological. He would not renounce his religious upbringing, but neither would he promote it. He was a man of the Moderate Enlightenment who toyed with a taste of the Skeptical, but who remained comfortable with the blend of rational and spiritual elements.

Webster's class, the class of 1778, boasted many young gentlemen who later became quite active in the formation and development of the new republic. Joel Barlow, already mentioned, became America's leading poet and served as Minister to France. Zephaniah

Swift stayed in Connecticut and was an eminent jurist. Oliver Wolcott, Jr., was one of Webster's main correspondents during the 1790s and early 1800s, and succeeded Alexander Hamilton as Secretary of the Treasury. Others included Uriah Tracy, a future United States Senator; Josiah Meigs, who would be President of the University of Georgia; and Abraham Bishop, who, much to Webster's chagrin, became a leading Jeffersonian politician in Connecticut.[37]

College life was to be anything but ordinary for Webster and his classmates, for at the end of their freshman year, blood already had been spilled at Lexington and Concord. Between the sophomore and junior years, the Declaration of Independence was signed. The Yale students, immediately after the Lexington and Concord engagement, formed their own company and drilled alongside the New Haven militia. Two months after the signing of the Declaration, as Webster himself later recalled,

> In June of that year Gen. Washington passed through New Haven on his way to take command of the army at Charlestown. . . . In the morning he reviewed the military company of the College. Gen. Lee who accompanied him, . . . cried out with astonishment at their promptness . . . . They accompanied him as far out of town as Neckbridge, and he who now addresses you was one of the musicians.[38]

Webster's first two years at Yale passed without extensive disruption. Classes did have to be halted in August 1776, however, when an epidemic of typhoid fever swept through New Haven. Webster returned home to find his brother, Abraham, recuperating from smallpox, contracted while he was serving in the army in Canada. With college in recess, Webster decided to accompany his brother on the journey to Lake Champlain, New York, to rejoin the army. This trip with Abraham marked the first exposure of the younger Webster to the rigors of a soldier's existence. One night in a smoke-filled tent designed to keep out the mosquitoes, another in a boat, a third on the floor of a hospitable farmer's house, and the experience of a dysentery-infested army camp left impressions on Webster that he never forgot. He quickly came to realize that the struggle for independence was not merely a word game for college debates.[39]

Webster's junior year was seriously disrupted. Economic difficulties rendered the purchase of food for the college nearly impossible. Twice the students were sent home, and when they reassembled on 30 April 1777, New Haven was not their destination. Fear of attack and the ability to procure food more easily in other areas forced the classes to split up into different towns. Webster's junior class, still under Buckminster's tutelage, lodged at Glastonbury, a few miles southeast of Hartford.[40]

When he returned home in the autumn, Webster joined his father and brothers in a Connecticut regiment rushing to the scene of battle in New York. The British general, Burgoyne, was attempting to cut off New England from the rest of the colonies. But as the Connecticut volunteers approached Albany, they heard the welcome news that Burgoyne had surrendered, thus ending the threat. In retrospect, this American victory was the turning point in the war because it convinced France to enlist its arms in the colonial cause. For Webster, it signaled the end of his brief stint as a military man.

Webster's senior year at Yale was even worse than the junior year. Most of the class refused the summons to assemble at New Haven, probably because the military threat had not yet abated. In the spring of 1778, however, when the Rev. Ezra Stiles took over the presidency of the college, classes once again started in New Haven.[41]

Stiles was a very learned and respected figure, under whose leadership Yale grew and flourished into the 1790s. He knew better than Daggett how to handle students, a segment of society he branded a "bundle of wild fire." He also realized that although his position as a college President was considered prestigious, it was not unlike wearing a diadem composed of a crown of thorns.[42] Stiles's approach and his own teaching skills made the last few weeks of Webster's education noteworthy. Even though his acquaintance with Stiles was brief, the impressions made upon him were strong. When he sought advice for the titles of the new schoolbooks that he sought to publish in the 1780s, Webster turned to Stiles and adopted his recommendations.

Commencement was held on 9 September 1778, and Webster

pronounced the Cliosophic Oration in English, an honor always given to one of the best students. He was awarded the Bachelor of Arts and had achieved his first real goal. But now he had to wrestle with a new concern: what was he going to do with the rest of his life?

In Search of a Profession

How indeed could a Bachelor of Arts degree from Yale be useful in Revolutionary Connecticut? Certainly it was of no use on the farm. Webster of course had no intention to pursue the agricultural life, yet he returned to his father's home in late 1778, now twenty years old, "without property, without patrons, & in the midst of a war which had disturbed all occupations; had impoverished the country; & the termination of which could not be foreseen."[43] His first inclination was to pursue the legal profession, but he needed a job while he completed the extra study that was essential if he were to become a lawyer.

While he contemplated his future, his father, who certainly had given help beyond his means, concluded that his resources were spread too thin to provide further aid. Webster's account of what happened next was a scene filled with drama, in which the son succinctly recounted the manner in which the senior Webster related his inability to continue his help:

> While there, his father put into his hand an eight dollar bill of continental currency, then worth three or four dollars; saying to him, "Take this; you must now seek your living; I can do no more for you."[44]

Aware now that he was going to have to fend for himself, Webster experienced much anxiety. His response to the challenge was to shut himself up for three days in his room, reading and thinking. There is no indication that he resorted to the typical Puritan solution of seeking guidance through the Bible. As one of his earliest biographers comments,

The period was doubtless an important one in the development of his moral nature and the formation of his character, yet there is no indication that he felt then, as he afterwards felt, the relations of virtue or true manliness to religion or the knowledge and the fear of God.[45]

Instead, he turned to a variety of literary men, one of whom was Samuel Johnson, the English lexicographer. Johnson's *Rambler*, Webster later remembered, "produced no inconsiderable effect" on his mind. One sentence in particular made a lasting impression: "To fear no eye, to suspect no tongue, is the great prerogative of innocence; an exemption granted only to invariable virtue."[46] Webster, after meditation on that passage, "resolved that whatever was to be his fate in life, he would pursue a most exact course of integrity & virtue."[47] Webster's resolve, apparently, was so to order his behavior that he could stand before anyone with the full confidence that he had treated each person justly and, therefore, no charge could be brought against him in regard to his conduct. This philosophy was essentially externally oriented, focusing on proper behavior and just treatment of others. It also looked to the world for approval of that behavior. Furthermore, it exuded youthful confidence that such a life was attainable by human endeavor, without the direct intervention of God, a far cry from the religious orthodoxy in which he had been nurtured.

Clad in his intellectual and moral armor, Webster undertook a profession common to many newly graduated collegians awaiting entrance into the legal community or pastorate—he taught school. Webster taught at Glastonbury until the spring of 1779. He then was invited to teach at a Hartford school, an offer he accepted. While in Hartford, he boarded with Oliver Ellsworth, later the Chief Justice of the United States Supreme Court. Webster's aim was "to pursue his studies to some advantage with that eminent jurist." But the demands of teaching, coupled with an unidentified nervous condition, "frustrated his purpose."[48] The nervous affliction, whatever its nature, probably was caused by his schedule and intense efforts. The daily rigors of school teaching were accompanied by long evenings of reading in languages and the law.[49]

During his stay in Ellsworth's home, Webster took time to write Buckminster. Buckminster's response makes it clear that Webster had elaborated on his future plans and his goals for life. Judging by his former tutor's comments, the young schoolmaster, perhaps as an outgrowth of his experience with Johnson's *Rambler*, had embarked on a strict regimen of discipline in an effort to achieve complete self-mastery. Buckminster, always concerned for the character development of his charges, answered Webster in a fatherly fashion, applauding his zeal but warning against unrealistic expectations. "The resolutions that you form in your Letter are good, to obtain a knowledge of your own Country," Buckminster began, "but you must endeavor not to be forward in applying this knowledge to persons with whom you have but a slight acquaintance." The problem with being "too frank in opening your heart to them," he continued, is "they will be disposed to ridicule you and perhaps set you down among those who have too high an opinion of their own importance." He concluded,

> Your Resolution of making yourself Master of every evil passion and propensity is an exceeding good one, and you will find the benefit of it [in your] future life, but remember that such resolutions are much easier made than kept, and I fear you will often have occasion to reflect that like a Treacherous dealer you have dealt treacherously with yourself.[50]

The tutor's words proved prophetic. Nearly every educational or literary plan Webster formulated underwent criticism from the educated segment of society. And his resolutions for controlling his passions—resolutions firmly grounded in the moral philosophy of Common Sense—would not be as easy to keep as he assumed.

In the winter of 1779-1780, Webster returned to West Hartford and lived in his father's home once again while he taught school. The winter was severe and the snowdrifts high as Webster trudged daily to the schoolhouse to practice his profession. It was a winter of seasoning, allowing him time to think of ways to improve education. These reflections would begin to pay off in just a few short years.

Webster's propensity for the law surfaced once more when, in the summer of 1780, he left the schoolmaster's life to become an assistant to the register of deeds in Litchfield. As he worked, he studied law under the tutelage of Titus Hosmer of Middletown, one of Connecticut's foremost lawyers. Finally, in the spring of 1781, he passed the Hartford bar examination and was admitted to practice.[51] He had achieved another goal. But, as in the case of his college graduation, it offered little consolation. Continuation of the war and the sudden influx of lawyers did not hold out bright prospects. Another career path was necessary until such time as he could afford to begin his practice. Webster once again turned to the only other occupation for which he was qualified—he opened a private school in Sharon, Connecticut, a town situated close to the New York state line.

The young schoolmaster's sojourn in Sharon proved to be a mixed blessing. The school was a success, patronized by some of the leading families in the area. He also made the acquaintance of the Rev. John Peter Tetard, pastor of a church of French Huguenots who had fled persecution. Tetard, after the Revolution, received an appointment as Professor of French at Columbia College, a position he held until his death in 1787.[52] While at Sharon, he became Webster's French tutor and fanned his latent fondness for the study of words.

Also during his tenure in that town, Webster received the Master of Arts degree from Yale. He took time off to attend the commencement exercises and contributed a paper entitled *Dissertation in English on the universal diffusion of literature as introductory to the universal diffusion of Christianity*.[53] This dissertation is the first indication of how the Puritan and Enlightenment traditions influenced Webster's thought. It provides an initial glimpse into Webster's ideas, particularly on the interplay of intellectual and religious/moral questions.

The thesis of the dissertation is the importance of the dissemination of knowledge for the reception and propagation of the Christian faith. Webster begins his discussion with an acknowledgment that man's reasoning is in an imperfect state and liable to err. He then continues with his view that Christianity is the "most rational system of religion ever published to mankind." From that premise, he concludes that it is "impossible for a rational system of religion to exist among a barbarous and illiterate people."[54] He even considers the timing of the appearance of Christianity "a most incontestable proof of its divine origin."[55]

The *Dissertation* continues with a historical commentary on the reception of this most rational of all faiths. Rome, he concludes, came under Christianity's influence because it was a civilized

culture; when the seat of empire moved East, "no sooner had literature vanished, than religion was forgotten, or corrupted with all the
idolatrous ceremonies of pagan superstition." Religion became "an
engine of state" and a system

> fraught with every species of absurdity, calculated to
> astonish the gazing crowd, rather than to enlighten their
> understandings; to fetter the conscience and drain the
> purse, rather than to check the vices and reform the lives
> of its stupid votaries.[56]

The fall of Constantinople, he reasons, brought learned men back
to northern Europe; a revival of learning followed that opened the
way for religious reformation.[57] The work concludes with a defense
of literary improvement and a rejection of the views of those who
feel that the development of the literary spirit brings with it an
increase in vice and immorality. The blame, he insists, has to rest on
the character of men, not on intellectual improvements:

> The objection, therefore, amounts to no more than this:
> that it is impossible to give a perfect religion to imperfect
> creatures; that is, one sufficient, without miraculous inter-
> position, to restrain their vicious inclinations; or to
> express it in other words, that it is impossible to give
> perfection to the moral character of a race of beings, who
> are imperfect in all other respects.[58]

An analysis of Webster's dissertation reveals his debt both to
Biblical and Enlightenment precepts. The imperfection of man, the
exalted place of the Christian religion, and even a hint at the possibility of divine intervention in human affairs reveals a Puritan
impress. Yet the real object of veneration in the piece is not religion, but human intellectual progress, revealing an attachment in
the young author to newer Enlightenment ideas. He does not make
a clean break with his religious roots, but instead transforms
Christianity into primarily a "rational religion," with scarcely a nod
in the direction of personal faith. He is able to approach religion in
this way through his Common Sense training. It bolsters

Christianity through rationality, and Webster clings to the rational element. It allows him to be an Enlightenment philosophe and a respectable Congregationalist simultaneously. Man's intellectual aspirations are fundamentally sound, he affirms; indeed, the only way for Christianity to prosper is if literary improvements are made first. What happened when the influence of literature was removed from Europe? Christianity became corrupted and degenerated into mere superstition, according to Webster. What was Europe's salvation? The return of the literati from the East revived true intellectual and spiritual interests. And the discussion ends with a strong renunciation of those who are suspicious of intellectual achievement, as he utilizes the Calvinist understanding of man's nature to extricate his object of veneration from a chorus of unjust accusations.

It is quite clear from this early work that Webster, three years removed from Yale, was striving mightily to keep the best of both worlds. He could not deny his religious heritage, yet he was deeply impressed with the abilities of the human intellect. Neither could he go the utopian route and expect a secular millennium; the evidence of man's sinful nature was too abundant and his training too clear on this matter. He kept his equilibrium through a philosophy that conceivably could unite Enlightenment and Christian components.

Again, it was Common Sense philosophy that allowed Webster to wed the two strains. Recognition of both the potential heights and depths of human nature was articulated in the faculty psychology of Common Sense. The heights could be equated with the great advances man could make through the gifts God had given him; the depths with the abuse of those gifts by man himself, and could be reconciled with the Biblical view of man as a sinful creature. As Reid comments, "By the proper exercise of this gift of God, human nature, in individuals and in societies, may be exalted to a high degree of dignity and felicity." The opposite, however, also was prevalent: "On the contrary, its perversion and abuse is the cause of most of the evils that afflict human life."[59]

The sojourn in Sharon was not altogether pleasurable. Webster, now twenty-two, was in active pursuit of a wife. His attention was drawn first to nineteen-year-old Juliana Smith, sister to the future Connecticut governor, John Cotton Smith, but she considered his writing "as prosy as those of our horse . . . would be if they were written out," and his conversation even duller than his writing.[60] Her disdain was not lost on Webster, and he turned to a more likely candidate. The new focus of his attentions was Rebecca Pardee, but he lost out to a Continental Army officer with whom she had already developed a relationship. There is no mention of this incident in Webster's "Memoir," and some have doubted its authenticity, but the undeniable fact that immediately thereafter Webster suddenly and without explanation closed his school in midterm and left Sharon lends credence to some type of emotional disturbance at this point in his life.[61]

Webster spent the winter of 1781-1782 seeking "mercantile employment" without success.[62] He also took the opportunity to make his first venture into the public prints. Outraged by what he considered British propaganda in American newspapers, he authored three essays under the title, "Observations on the Revolution of America," which were published in the *New York Packet* in January and February of 1782. In these articles, Webster first emphasizes the reasonableness of the American effort for independence, as opposed to the view that it is nothing more than an emotional frenzy. He then builds the legal case for the separation and emphasizes the ability of America to govern herself without British oversight.[63]

Writing these articles in the midst of such confusion over his direction in life must have been balm for a man who probably was beginning to fear for his future. The winter he had spent seeking employment had accomplished nothing, and in the spring he attempted to start up his school at Sharon once again. This time there was not enough response to justify its reestablishment. He then traveled to Orange County, New York, and took up residence in the small town of Goshen (approximately twenty miles southwest of Newburgh) where he opened a classical school and even experienced the luxury of being paid in silver, rather than depreciated Continental currency. He continued in that position until the spring of 1783.

Although he had employment, Webster was not happy. He did not perceive himself as a perpetual schoolmaster and longed to initiate his law practice, but he was too uninformed with "the forms of proceedings, & could not enter upon the practice with advantage." His "Memoir," written in the third person, reflects upon the state of his mind at that juncture:

> In addition to these circumstances, his health was impaired by close application, & a sedentary life. He was without money & without friends to afford him any particular aid. In this situation of things, his spirits failed, & for some months, he suffered extreme depression & gloomy forebodings.[64]

Nothing had worked out the way he had planned. If he were to return home, he would be admitting defeat and would be forced into the farming routine from which he had deliberately walked away. Continuation in his present state was merely another form of defeat. Seemingly, he had nowhere to turn and no prospects for anything better. For a young man with such high hopes and vision, circumstances certainly did provide an adequate rationale for depression.

[1] Thomas J. Curry, *The First Freedoms: Church and State in America to the Passage of the First Amendment* (New York: Oxford University Press, 1986), 89.

[2] Brooks Mather Kelley, *Yale: A History* (New Haven: Yale University Press, 1974), 52-55.

[3] Nathan Perkins, *A Half-Century Sermon* (Hartford, 1822), quoted in Rollins, 11.

[4] Webster, "Memoir of Noah Webster, L.L.D.," n.d., Webster Family Papers, Manuscripts and Archives, Yale University Library, New Haven, CT, Box 1, Folder 10, 3.

[5] Noah Webster, Sr., to Noah Webster, Jr., 16 December 1782, quoted in Ford, *Notes*, 1:56.

[6] Charles Webster to Webster, 8 August 1796, Noah Webster Papers, Rare Books and Manuscripts Division, New York Public Library, Box 1.

[7] Webster to William Webster, 23 January 1836, Webster Papers, NYPL, Box 1.

[8] J. William Frost, *Connecticut Education in the Revolutionary Era* (Chester, CT: Pequot Press, 1974), 13.

[9] Ibid., 14.

[10] Walter Herbert Small, *Early New England Schools* (Boston: Ginn & Co., 1914; reprint ed., New York: Arno Press and *The New York Times*, 1969), 365.

[11] Ibid., 314. Small adds, p. 316, "After the Revolution private schools became even more numerous. The years from 1790 to 1795 show an especially large number."

[12] Catherine Fennelly, *Town Schooling in Early New England, 1790-1840* (Old Sturbridge Village, Sturbridge, MA: The Meriden Gravure Co., Meriden, CT, 1962), 7.

[13] Kelley, *Yale*, 144, lists the tuition rate in 1795 as $16 per year. He then documents its increase to $24 in 1807 and to $33 in 1815. He gives no figures on earlier years, but the assumption seems to be that Webster probably was charged close to the $16 rate of 1795.

[14] Webster, "Memoir," 3; Warfel, *Noah Webster*, 17.

[15] Webster to Hudson and Goodwin, 28 September 1786, Webster Papers, NYPL, Box 1: "Enclosed is a Letter for my Father, which, with a sum of money, . . . I beg you to forward to him the first opportunity." Webster continued to aid his father in later years, as is shown by a letter from Noah Webster, Sr., to his son, 28 November 1809, quoted in Ford, *Notes*, 2:74: "I received your of E. Belden. I acknowledge with gratitude the Respect you manifest to your aged Parent in sending the 10 dollar Bill which I Received of E. Belden, & your Good wishes for my comfort, & hope the Divine Blessing may rest upon you & your family."

[16] Webster to James Greenleaf, 6 June 1789, Noah Webster Papers, Historical Society of Pennsylvania, Philadelphia.

[17] Webster to James Greenleaf, 4 December 1789, Webster Papers, HSP.

[18] Kelley, *Yale*, 80, 82.

[19] Ibid., 79-80.

[20] Henry F. May, *The Enlightenment in America* (New York: Oxford University Press, 1976), xvi-xvii, describes four categories of Enlightenment thought—moderate, skeptical, revolutionary, and didactic—that influenced America in roughly chronological order. The Moderate Enlightenment sought to balance faith and reason and to assert that they were not contradictory. Common Sense philosophy easily fit into this mold. The Skeptical Enlightenment, however, was characterized by a distrust of revelation-based religion and the promotion of deism. May concludes that the Skeptical stage had far greater success in Europe than in America.

[21] Emory Elliott, *Revolutionary Writers: Literature and Authority in the New Republic, 1725-1810* (New York: Oxford University Press, 1982), 34.

[22] James Beattie, *An Essay on the Nature and Immutability of Truth* (Edinburgh, 1770; reprint ed., New York: Garland, 1983). Reid's *An Inquiry into the Human Mind on the Principles of Common Sense*, published in 1764, provided the basis for Beattie.

[23] For an excellent summary of Reid's Common Sense philosophy, see Sydney E. Ahlstrom, "The Scottish Philosophy and American Theology," *Church History* 24:3 (September 1955): 257-271.

[24] James L. McAllister, Jr., "Francis Alison and John Witherspoon: Political Philosophers and Revolutionaries," *Journal of Presbyterian History* 54:1 (1976): 38.

25 Daniel W. Howe, "The Political Psychology of *The Federalist*," *William and Mary Quarterly* 3d Ser., 44:3 (July 1987): 487.

26 Thomas Reid, "Essays on the Active Powers of Man," in Sir William Hamilton, ed., *The Works of Thomas Reid, D.D.* (Edinburgh: Maclachlan & Stewart, 1872), 2: 543-599.

27 Howe, "Political Psychology," 502.

28 Reid, "An Inquiry into the Human Mind," *Works*, 126-27, quoted in Jane Rendall, *The Origins of The Scottish Enlightenment* (New York: St. Martin's Press, 1978), 112-13.

29 John Witherspoon, *Lectures on Moral Philosophy* (Princeton: Princeton University Library, 1912), 1-2.

30 Lawrence A. Cremin, *American Education: The Colonial Experience, 1607-1783* (New York: Harper & Row, 1970), 460.

31 Webster's reliance on the Common Sense philosophy is inferred from the general tenor of his later writings, most of which, in word usage and principle, are in concert with the basic tenets of Common Sense. Direct references to Reid or other Scottish writers are virtually nonexistent, but Webster rarely quoted his sources. His debt to Common Sense and its faculty psychology will be noted in connection with his later writings.

32 Kelley, *Yale*, 78-82, provides a complete description of the Yale curriculum during Webster's student days.

33 Ibid., 73.

34 Ibid., 74, 94.

35 Rollins, 18, sees the petition as an example of the antiauthoritarian spirit that pervaded the college during the revolutionary era. This fits with Rollins's major premise that Yale was a hotbed of Enlightenment thought and was opposed to Calvinist theology. While it cannot be doubted that Yale partook of both intellectual strains, too much can be made of this petition.
     First, simply by the fact that it was a petition shows that the students were working through the proper channels for a redress of grievances. A petition is not equivalent to outright defiance. Second, Rollins has a thesis to support that is built on the belief that American society in general was antiauthoritarian during this era. Given his psychological presuppositions, it is easy to understand how Rollins can see this petition as an antiauthoritarian manifestation. But the use of psychological models can be critiqued. It is possible that Rollins forces facts to fit into his presuppositions. Forrest McDonald, in *Novus Ordo Seclorum* (Lawrence, KS: University Press of Kansas, 1985), xii, states the concern well when he writes, "Thus, in my judgment, it is a grave mistake to try to understand eighteenth-century Americans through Freudian or other twentieth-century modes of psychiatric analysis. They had their own models of normal and abnormal behavior, and if one is to pry into their psyches, those models alone are relevant."

36 Joseph Buckminster to Webster, 30 October 1779, Webster Papers, NYPL, Box 2.

37 Warfel, *Noah Webster*, 24.

[38] Ford, *Notes*, 1:18. Taken from an address to a Sunday School celebration, 4 July 1840.

[39] Ibid., 1:20-21; Warfel, *Noah Webster*, 29.

[40] Webster, "Memoir," 4.

[41] Ibid.

[42] Warfel, *Noah Webster*, 32-33.

[43] Webster, "Memoir," 5.

[44] Ibid. Rollins reads much more into Webster's account than can be warranted. According to Rollins, this incident was conducted in an atmosphere of "frustration and anger" (p. 19). He comes to this conclusion without the benefit of any apparent corroborating evidence. This conclusion is drawn primarily from the idea that it was the only conversation with his father that Webster ever recorded. Additionally, Rollins asserts that Noah, Sr.'s, words to his son "clearly implied disgust and dismay. In effect, his father and family had bluntly rejected him" (p. 19). Once again, there is no evidence to support this assertion.

[45] Leonard W. Bacon, "Life of Noah Webster," 18, Webster Papers, NYPL, Box 10.

[46] Samuel Johnson, *Essays from the Rambler, Adventurer, and Idler*, ed. Walter Jackson Bate (New Haven & London: Yale University Press, 1968).

[47] Webster, "Memoir," 5.

[48] Ibid.

[49] Warfel, *Noah Webster*, 36, tells of the schedule of Simeon Baldwin, a compatriot of Webster's who was trying to do the same thing. It is reasonable to assume that the two men's schedules were similar.

[50] Joseph Buckminster to Webster, 30 October 1779, Webster Papers, NYPL, Box 2.

[51] Webster, "Memoir," 6.

[52] Ford, *Notes*, 1:44-45.

[53] Webster, in 1790, published this dissertation in a series of articles in the Philadelphia newspaper, the *Gazette of the United States*. The articles ran from 2-16 June under the heading, "The Tablet."

[54] Webster, "The Tablet, No. CXIX," *Gazette of the United States*, 2 June 1790.

[55] Webster, "The Tablet, No. CXX," *Gazette of the United States*, 5 June 1790.

[56] Webster, "The Tablet, No. CXXI," *Gazette of the United States*, 9 June 1790.

[57] Webster, "The Tablet, No. CXXII," *Gazette of the United States*, 12 June 1790.

[58] Webster, "The Tablet, No. CXXIII," *Gazette of the United States*, 16 June 1790.

[59] Reid, "Active Powers," 2:530.

[60] Warfel, *Noah Webster*, 42.

[61] The Rebecca Pardee story is based on an article written by Joel Benton, "An Unwritten Chapter in Noah Webster's Life," *Magazine of American History* 10 (July 1883). Rollins and Moss accept it fully, while Warfel relates it with a certain amount of skepticism and Monaghan passes over it lightly.

[62] Webster "Memoir," 6.

[63] These articles ran from 17 January to 7 February of that year. They also were reprinted in the *Freeman's Chronicle* from 22 September to 6 October 1783.

[64] Webster, "Memoir," 7.

CHAPTER 2

The Schoolmaster as Author: To Instruct a Nation

Webster's feelings of "extreme depression & gloomy forebodings" were another major test of his character. He already had responded to his father's instructions to seek his own way in the world with a rigid determination to live uprightly and to be honored by men. But that positive response had been followed by the abandonment of his labors at Sharon when he suffered rejection as Rebecca Pardee's suitor. Now he found himself at another desperate juncture with the knowledge that his choice could well determine the course of his life.

The inner drive that had led him to start schools and had put his opinions in the public prints found another outlet. "In this state of mind," he later recalled, in the third person, "he formed the design of composing elementary books for the instruction of children."[1] In retrospect, this decision was pivotal and set the stage for his entire career.

Most of early America's school texts continued to be imported from England. Webster felt that this was inappropriate for a nation newly freed from its colonial ties. Since the most basic element of education is the ability to read and spell, Webster concluded that a spelling book with a distinctive American perspective was a pressing need. American educators still were wedded to Thomas Dilworth's *A New Guide to the English Tongue*, a British text first published in America by Benjamin Franklin in 1747; by the time Webster decided to write his alternative speller, Dilworth was approaching its fortieth American edition.[2] Webster considered its British origin unsuitable. In addition, its geographical section focused on the names of English villages and shires and excluded familiar American placenames. Consequently, led by an earnest desire to sever ties with the British past, even while he was suffering under the weight of teaching school and despairing over future prospects, he began his compilation.

Enough of the work was finished by August 1782 to enable Webster to undertake a trip to New Jersey, Pennsylvania, and Connecticut. He embarked on this trip to achieve two objectives: first, he sought advice and counsel from learned individuals to make his work as acceptable as possible; second, he wished to secure copyright legislation in these states to insure that he would receive the full benefit due the author of a seminal work. This effort was essential because no national copyright law existed, and literary piracy was a potential threat to his labors.

Armed with letters of recommendation, Webster first approached James Duane, a Congressman from New York through whose efforts Webster came into contact with James Madison for the first time. In Madison, he found a man sympathetic to the need for copyright legislation. After that initial endorsement, Webster took his manuscript to both the University of Pennsylvania and the College of New Jersey for scholarly critiques. Particularly impressed with the plan at the latter institution was Professor Samuel Stanhope Smith, who subsequently penned a testimonial on Webster's behalf, not only for the merit of the work itself but also for the urgent need for copyright legislation.

Webster was not shy. While in New Jersey he called on Governor William Livingston who, after a meeting with his council, informed the young author that he could offer "little encouragement to expect success in an application to the legislature for the enactment of such a law."[3] Neither the legislatures of New Jersey nor Pennsylvania were in session during Webster's sojourn, and if he felt any discouragement, it would have been understandable. Yet Webster was undaunted. He continued to Hartford where, unlike the previous states, the legislature was meeting. One of his friends from Sharon, John Canfield, Esq., had prepared the way for his presentation of a petition to the General Assembly. The petition described the proposed work, detailed the purposes for which it was to be written, and requested that a committee be appointed to examine its merits and give to Webster exclusive printing, publishing, and vending rights in Connecticut. This *American Instructor* (the intended name) was designed to "promote the interest of literature, & the honor and dignity of the American empire."[4] Webster, however, had arrived too near the end of the legislative session to obtain a hearing. It was to be simply another discouragement for an unknown trying to be known.

From Hartford he turned south, back to the familiar confines of Yale College and the advice of President Ezra Stiles. Stiles liked the work, but not the title. Instead he proposed (since Webster's plan included a grammar and a reader also) a more scholarly appellation, *A Grammatical Institute of the English Language.* Less homey, more ponderous and stately, this title, which Webster adopted, opened the author to charges of vanity. Webster kept faith with Stiles's suggestion until 1787, when he replaced it with the simpler and more patriotic designation, *The American Spelling Book.*[5]

Webster returned to Goshen, to the labors of a schoolmaster, and "to the correction, enlargement & improvement" of his Speller.[6] These endeavors occupied his time throughout the autumn and into the winter. The harder he labored, the more convinced he became of the need for his work. He was not merely giving America another speller; in his vision, he was initiating a system of education that would be uniquely American and also would correct the deficiencies he had found in Dilworth. The first written indication of the depth of Webster's feelings on these issues was expressed to his Sharon friend and legislator, John Canfield, in January 1783. Canfield was continuing his efforts to secure a copyright for Webster in the Connecticut legislature, an endeavor that finally proved successful later that year. The plan, Webster conceded to Canfield, was more work than he had envisioned. "I have been indefatigable this winter; I have sacrificed ease, pleasure, & health to the execution of it." The stress had affected his physical condition so severely that he concluded he must either "relinquish the school or writing grammars."[7] In the same letter, he began to unfold his vision for education:

I must think that, next to the sacred writings, those books which teach us the principles of science & lay the basis on which all our future improvements must be built, best deserve the patronage of the public. An attention to literature must be the principal bulwark against the encroachments of civil & ecclesiastical tyrants.[8]

Still a Puritan at heart, Webster acknowledged the "sacred writings" as the highest source of authority. But reminiscent of his *Dissertation in English on the universal diffusion of literature as introductory to the universal diffusion of Christianity*, he quickly moved on to the importance of the new learning. The principles of science, he enthused, hold the key to all future societal improvements, and the public needs to patronize men such as him who author and promote literary works because only an educated public can withstand tyranny, whether civil or ecclesiastical.

Once he had set the parameters for understanding the magnitude of his labors, he became more specific:

> The more I look into our language & the methods of instruction practiced in this country the more I am convinced of the necessity of improving one & correcting the other. And however some may think, a book of this kind too trifling for public notice, I am fully of the opinion, that the reformation of the language we speak, will some time or other be thought an object of legislative importance.[9]

His Speller, and the Grammar and Reader afterwards, were not to be merely an addition to the schoolbooks already available; they were to begin a reformation of the English language. Webster clearly perceived his work to be a corrective to the way spelling was taught, and he believed that the proper use of language should be considered important enough to capture the attention of legislators. How could he direct people's minds to this worthy matter?

He decided against a treatise from an abstract philosophical approach that "would be read only by a few" and opted for "a little fifteen penny volume, which may convey much useful knowledge to the remote obscure recesses of honest poverty," thus casting "its beams equally upon the peasant & the monarch."[10] His reasoning was shrewd, manifesting an acumen for marketing techniques. He wanted the widest distribution possible, so he was contemplating writing in a form that would ensure a wide appeal. His motive, though, was not purely monetary. He advocated universal education (especially for boys)[11] because of the nature of the American political system; a republic, dependent on the knowledge and virtue of the people, requires an educated electorate.

The task presently at hand, however, was to awaken Americans to their dependence on British educational imports. This would not be simple because people become comfortable with the familiar, whether or not it is best. "Popular prejudice," intoned Webster, "is in favor of Dilworth," and people are "apt to slumber in the opinion that he is incapable of improvement." Not only was Dilworth out of date, Webster felt, but he was "really faulty & defective in every part of his work." The goal for Americans, then, should be a loosening of educational ties with the Mother Country. In ringing words that have been widely quoted ever since, Webster concluded his letter:

> America must be as independent in literature as she is in politics, as famous for arts as for arms, & it is not impossible, but a person of my youth may have some influence in exciting a spirit of literary industry.[12]

This declaration of literary independence became the young author's guiding principle. He would return to the theme repeatedly as he sought to establish an American literary identity. What is probably most surprising is Webster's assertion that he might play a leading role. He had not made any indelible mark on the world as yet; he was a struggling schoolmaster with an idea that still was unpublished. But he remained confident, in spite of external difficulties, that his vision would come to fruition. That confidence soon was subjected to another test.

James Madison, as a result of his meeting with Webster the previous autumn, successfully persuaded the Confederation Congress to pass an act recommending that the states secure to authors a copyright of at least fourteen years. Although the Congress had no enforcement power, the recommendation proved an encouragement to some states. By the end of 1783, five states other than Connecticut had passed legislation protecting newly published works. Yet despite some forward movement on copyright laws, Webster could not benefit from those new laws without a book to be copyrighted. In the spring of 1783, he closed his school in Goshen and removed to Hartford "for the purpose of procuring the publication of his first elementary book."[13] As he went from publisher to publisher, he learned how difficult it could be for a budding author to make his mark.

The first problem, most agreed, was that this young upstart was too visionary. What need was there to uproot education in such a fashion? Hadn't Dilworth been adequate for more than three decades? Who was this twenty-five-year-old self-proclaimed authority? On a more practical level, Webster found himself "destitute of the means of defraying the expenses of publication; & no printer or bookseller was found to undertake the publication at his own risk." If not for the encouragement of his friends and fellow authors John Trumbull and Joel Barlow, he would have received no comfort at all.[14]

Finally, he procured the assent of Barzillai Hudson and George Goodwin, publishers of the Hartford newspaper, *The Connecticut Courant*, to publish the Speller, provided they could have the privilege to be sole publishers of succeeding editions. Although Webster was nearly destitute, he offered to assume the entire risk of the printing cost. He had so much confidence in the success of his book that he believed he could pay the publishers from the sales. The risk was great because if it failed, he surely would be bankrupt.

He waited throughout the summer for the book to be ready. Hudson and Goodwin finished an edition of 5000 copies in October and began advertising its availability in the *Courant*. Webster was rewarded for his confidence; by the spring of 1784, the entire edition was sold out. Apparently, he had calculated correctly on the need for a speller written from an American perspective. His *Grammatical Institute of the English Language, Part I*, even with its pretentious title, was an enormous success.

The Webster Speller

Why should a simple spelling book become so popular? In revolutionary America, spelling books were the primary means for teaching reading and pronunciation as well as spelling. Spelling words properly, in fact, was often considered less important than the abilities to read and speak well. Consequently, the whole basis for producing a literate people rested on the spellers. The appearance of a new speller, with a distinctly American emphasis, naturally would have a broad appeal.[15]

Webster wrote a lengthy introduction to the Speller. It yields insights on his intellectual and moral outlook during this early period. "To attack deep rooted prejudices and oppose the current of opinion," he began, "is a task of great difficulty and hazard." He then acknowledged that new beliefs can be formed only over long periods of time and under the best of circumstances, but that once a belief is established and becomes a general custom, it often has an authority "too firm to be shaken by the efforts of an individual: Even errour becomes too sacred to be violated by the assaults of innovation."[16]

The good news, though, according to the nation's new schoolmaster, was that America was living through an era of wonders in which major shifts in thought had been accomplished "in the minds of men, in the short compass of eight years past, than are commonly effected in a century." America, commented Webster, had broken the bonds of sentiment with Britain and had experienced a political transformation in a very short time. If the political practices of the British were flawed, what of their educational practices? He then offered the opinion that "upon careful examination," Americans might be surprised to find that "their [British] methods of education are equally erroneous and defective."[17]

One great defect in British education, as Webster viewed it, was an emphasis on foreign languages that seriously impaired the further study of English. Neglect of one's own language was inexcusable, and America's imitation of the practice was a grievous mistake. Yet resistance to change was so commonplace "that the whispers of common sense, in favour of our native tongue, have been silenced amidst the clamour of pedantry in favour of Greek and Latin."[18]

Webster then explained that the problem manifests itself primarily in the spelling and pronunciation of words. "We have no guide," he lamented, "or none but such as lead into innumerable errours."

He then focused on the issue most important to him:

> The want of some standard in schools has occasioned a great variety of dialects in Great-Britain and of course, in America. Every county in England, every State in America and almost every town in each State, has some peculiarities in pronunciation which are equally erroneous and disagreeable to its neighbours.[19]

Other spelling-book authors had not attempted to systematize the irregularities of the English language:

> They study the language enough to find the difficulties of it—they tell us that it is impossible to reduce it to order—that it is to be learnt only by the ear—they lament the disorder and dismiss it without a remedy.[20]

The main problem with this dismissal was that instruction in pronunciation was left to "ignorance and caprice—to custom, accident or nothing." Left uncorrected, the language will be "exposed to perpetual fluctuation." This bothered Webster because it made inhabitants of different sections of the Union subject to "reciprocal ridicule."[21]

These comments are an indication of Webster's primary political objective—the forging of a strong, effective union of the States. If citizens of the various States pronounce words too differently, they will look upon one other with less respect, each believing in the propriety of his own dialect. These differences might then become a wedge that will break apart the Union to each State's detriment. For a nation to function efficiently, Webster felt its people must speak the same language. Americans, he argued, need to "unite in destroying provincial and local distinctions . . . and in establishing one uniform standard of elegant pronunciation."[22] His Speller, unlike the others, would meet that challenge, he pledged. It was designed to "introduce uniformity and accuracy of pronunciation into common schools." Conscious that his design might meet with skepticism, Webster sought to meet potential critics head-on:

Those therefore who disdain this attempt to improve our

language and assist the instructors of youth, must be either much more or much less acquainted with the language than I am. The criticisms of those who know more, will be received with gratitude; the censure or ridicule of those who know less, will be inexcusable.[23]

With that statement, he declared his openness to change if shown where he might improve, while at the same time he effectively knocked out the props from under those who were unqualified to offer an appropriate critique.

In form, the Webster Speller looked a lot like Dilworth's, consisting of forty-three tables of lessons, most of which were quite similar to Dilworth's. Like his predecessor, Webster began with the pronunciation of syllables (ba, be, bi, bo, bu, by) and worked his way progressively up to polysyllabic words, stressing the distinctions between words accented on different syllables. He also had tables dealing with spelling and pronunciation irregularities, numbers, homonyms, abbreviations, and geography. He did not include a section on grammar, as Dilworth had, because a separate grammar book was part of Webster's overall plan.

Webster's first noticeable change was in the division of syllables. Dilworth, like all spelling book authors before him, had committed himself to have each syllable begin with a consonant. Words such as habit and cluster were divided ha bit and clu ster. According to pronunciation rules, this would lead children to believe that the "a" and the "u" at the end of the first syllables would have the long sound. Dilworth, in order to offset this violation of pronunciation rules, had to invent markings to indicate that the short sound was to be used. Webster considered Dilworth's scheme to be totally ridiculous and insisted the divisions should be hab it and clus ter.[24]

Another major change in syllabic division was in words ending with -sion and -tion. The usual practice had been to divide such a word—nation, for instance—into three syllables: na ti on. Webster argues for two syllables only:

Mr. Dilworth tells us that ti before a vowel, sound like si or sh; but there are so many exceptions to this rule, that it would better have been omitted. There are several hundred words, in which t̲i̲ before a vowel retain their proper original sound. But they do not sound like s̲i̲, for then nation, motion, must be pronounced na-si-on, mo-si-on. The proper sound of t̲i̲ is that of s̲h̲. Then if we make three syllables of these words, they will stand thus, na-sh-on, mo-sh-on, and we have one syllable without any vowel and consequently without any sound.[25]

This change was not so much an innovation as it was a recognition of an alteration in speaking that had taken place well before Webster's time.

The geographical lists in Dilworth, replete with English place names, Webster transformed into a mini-American gazetteer with particular emphasis on the counties of Connecticut, although all the States were represented. This was the most obvious Americanization of the text, and quite apropos, considering the audience for which he wrote. It was a small beginning in his quest for an America as independent in literature as in political affairs.[26]

His final alteration was more controversial. He was concerned, he said, with the trivialization of the person of God in the other spelling books. "Nothing," Webster contended, "has a greater tendency to lessen the reverence which mankind ought to have for the Supreme Being, than a careless repetition of his name upon every trifling occasion."[27] Such "frequent thoughtless repetition," he continued, "renders the name as familiar to children as the name of their book, and they mention it with the same indifference." His remedy was to select from Scripture certain passages that would inculcate Christian precepts of morality and religion but "in which that sacred name is seldom mentioned." He closed these remarks with the ringing declaration, "Let *sacred things* be appropriated to *sacred purposes.*"[28]

It is difficult to know whether to take Webster's words at face value on this matter. While it may be that he was genuinely concerned for God's reputation, it already has been noted that his own religious views were borderline orthodox, if indeed they could be considered orthodox at all. He still was quite heady with the new intellectual avenues that had opened to him at Yale, and he could have been masking an attempt to move toward a more secular approach in education.

This possibility occurred to the Rev. Elizur Goodrich, to whom Webster had sent some of the early sheets before publication. Generally, Goodrich approved of Webster's plan, calling it ingenious and "a real improvement upon former treatises of this kind." Although he felt the young author was too censorious toward other spelling book authors, he considered Webster's emphasis on pronunciation an element that would "greatly tend to give success to your work." Nevertheless, Goodrich was somewhat concerned over Webster's remarks on the use of God's name. Cautioned Goodrich, "I should be more pleased with your objections, against the frequent repetitions of the name of the Supreme Being, in our spelling-books, did I not fear you carry them too far." He reminded Webster that "the time of childhood and youth is a season, in which reverence for God and religion is best impressed on the mind, and perhaps with due care and prudence, there are no places, in which it may be better impressed than in schools."[29]

Clearly, Goodrich caught a tone of religious laxity in Webster's philosophy that alarmed him. Having cautioned the new author on the danger of extreme views, the minister continued to press home his point. "I would not have the Bible the only book for children of the higher classes in schools," he reasoned, "yet I cannot but desire it should have a daily use in them, as I am so far [from] thinking, that the proper use of it in childhood, and especially in schools, will make them despise it, that I believe it the best way of fixing in them a sacred veneration of it through life." Goodrich believed, "As soon as children can read I would have them read the Bible; for I am convinced from experience and observation, that those young people have the greatest veneration for things sacred, who in their earliest years, have been best acquainted with the book of God." He closed with an expression of confidence: "I am persuaded you do not mean to adopt a contrary scheme: But as some are prejudiced in favour of old things, so others are too much captivated with new; We ought therefore to be on our guard against either extreme."[30]

Goodrich probably came closest to the truth with his final comment. Webster was captivated with a rational approach to religion; in his zeal to write a new spelling book, he probably wanted it to be the best possible model of new Moderate Enlightenment thought. Even so, his modification of the use of God's name did not produce a secular book. The lessons reveal a perspective thoroughly religious in nature. Each lesson was character-oriented with moral admonitions resting securely on a Biblical base. Most of his sentences were as orthodox as anything in Dilworth. Although the name of God is diminished in accordance with Webster's expressed concerns, no pious parent could have objected to the lessons, which largely were quotations from Scripture. Even the portions not taken directly from the Bible could not be confused with secularism:

> This life is not long; but the life to come has no end.
> We must pray for them that hate us.
> We must love them that love not us.
> We must do as we like to be done to.[31]

When Webster gave specific instruction on the type of company a child should keep, he easily could have been mistaken for the stereotypical dour Calvinist preacher when he lectured:

> Play not with bad boys; use no ill words at play; spend your time well; live in peace, and shun all strife. This is the way to make God love you, and to save your soul from the pains of hell.[32]

Webster was a child of the Enlightenment but, again, it was of the Scottish Common Sense variety that integrated well with orthodox Christianity.

The new author concluded the Speller's Introduction with two appeals: the first, for acceptance of his new approach; the second, on behalf of America's future glory. "Mankind are always startled at *new things*; they believe a thing *right* and *best*, because they have never suspected otherwise, or because it is the general opinion." People with good sense, however, demand evidence of the rightness of something, and do not rely on custom or general opinion. People ought to consider, reasoned Webster,

> that every improvement in life was once *new*—the reformation by Luther was once *new*, the Christian religion was once *new*—nay, their favourite Dilworth was once a

new thing. And had *these* and other *new things* never been introduced, we should have all, this moment, been pagans and savages.[33]

The concern for newness neatly discarded, Webster turned rhapsodic about America's future greatness. His expressions clearly depicted America in a superior moral and intellectual role in the world. Europe was old, made old by folly, corruption, and tyranny; it was a continent wherein "laws are perverted, manners are licentious, literature is declining and human nature debased." America cannot adopt European practices, for to do so would be to "stamp the wrinkles of decrepid age upon the bloom of youth and to plant the seeds of decay in a vigourous constitution." America's mission was grand and glorious:

It is the business of *Americans* to select the wisdom of all nations, as the basis of her constitutions,—to avoid their errours,—to prevent the introduction of foreign vices and corruptions and check the career of her own,—to promote virtue and patriotism,—to embellish and improve the sciences,—to diffuse an uniformity and purity of *language*,—to add superiour dignity to this infant Empire and to human nature.[34]

Webster's Speller hardly could accomplish all that, but he considered it a good start for America's future. Apparently, so did most Americans. Although there was some controversy surrounding its publication and the alterations it intended to make, the Speller was successful even beyond the author's hopes.[35] It continued to be printed into the twentieth century. The best estimate is that during the course of its long life, in its various forms, Webster's Speller (commonly known as the *Blue-Back Speller*) sold approximately 70 million copies. It can be said with little fear of overstatement that Webster really did teach America to read.[36]

The publication of the Speller brought remarks from an old friend, the Rev. Joseph Buckminster. Webster's former tutor declared the work to be both instructive and entertaining and one that caused him to reflect with the Psalmist that some students grow wiser than their teachers. He paid Webster a sincere compliment when he said, "It gave me no small pleasure to find, that while so many young Gentlemen soon as they have obtained the honors of College throw off all attention to study and devote themselves to gallantry or dissipation, you had employed your time to better purpose devoting it to correct and improve your own language."[37]

Buckminster had no reason to worry about Webster's continued attention to study. Diligence and industry were to be his most outstanding character traits throughout a long life of scholarly endeavors. The success of the Speller served only to spur him on to other efforts. Now that he was well on his way toward becoming a name familiar in most American homes, he sought not only to solidify his preeminent position in the textbook field, but aimed to make his mark in political thought as well.

---

[1] Webster, "Memoir," 7.

[2] Monaghan, 32.

[3] Webster, "Memoir," 8.

[4] Ibid.

[5] Warfel, *Noah Webster*, 56-7.

[6] Webster, "Memoir," 9.

[7] Webster to John Canfield, 6 January 1783, Webster Papers, NYPL, Box 1.

[8] Ibid.

[9] Ibid.

[10] Ibid.

[11] Webster, "On the Education of Youth in America," in *A Collection of Essays and Fugitiv Writings* (Boston: Thomas and Andrews, 1790; reprint ed., Delmar, New York: Scholars' Facsimiles and Reprints, 1977), 27-30, discusses the education of women. Women, Webster felt, were less likely to be morally corrupted than men and were the primary influence for the preservation of a virtuous society. He concludes that a good education for a woman was one "which renders the ladies correct in their manners, respectable in their families, and agreeable in society." It should concentrate on what is useful—reading and speaking, geography, poetry, and "fine writing," and "some knowledge of arithmetic."

[12] Webster to Canfield, 6 January 1783.

[13] Webster, "Memoir," 9.

[14] Ibid.

[15] For a fuller discussion of the use of spellers and their impact on early America, see Monaghan, 31-33.

[16] Webster, *A Grammatical Institute of the English Language, Part I* (Hartford: Hudson & Goodwin, 1783), 3.

[17] Ibid., 4.

[18] Ibid.

[19] Ibid., 4-5.

[20] Ibid., 5.

[21] Ibid., 5-6.

[22] Ibid., 7.

[23] Ibid., 6.

[24] Ibid., 8-9. Monaghan, 36, notes, "Unknown to Webster, a Scottish spelling book author named William Perry had made the same reform. It would become a permanent feature of the spelling book and dictionary landscape on both sides of the Atlantic Ocean."

[25] Ibid., 9.

[26] Webster's geographical section, Table XXXV, included European countries and their capital cities, islands of the West Indies, Canadian provinces, the states and capitals of the Union, as well as their counties and principal towns. The section was nine pages in length, with Connecticut's portion consisting of two pages.

[27] Webster, *Grammatical Institute, Part I*, 12. An example of that to which Webster refers is found in Thomas Dilworth's *New Guide to the English Tongue* (Philadelphia: T. & W. Bradford, 1793; reprint ed., Delmar, New York: Scholars' Facsimiles and Reprints, 1978), 7. This page has seven lessons, each of which is four lines in length. In twenty-one of those twenty-eight lines, God's name is mentioned. By way of example, lesson 1 states:

> No man may put off the law of God.
> The way of God is no ill Way.
> My Joy is in God all the Day.
> A bad Man is a Foe to God.

> And again, in lesson 3:
> Pay to God his Due.
> Go not in the Way of bad Men.
> No Man can see God.
> Our God is the God of all Men.

28 Ibid., 12. An asterisk after his closing remark leads the reader to a footnote that comments, "The same objection occurs against the frequent use of the Bible as a school book."

29 Rev. Elizur Goodrich to Webster, 29 September 1783, Webster Papers, NYPL, Box 2.

30 Ibid.

31 Webster, *Grammatical Institute, Part I*, 101.

32 Ibid., 102.

33 Ibid., 13.

34 Ibid., 14-15.

35 For a description of the "Dilworth's Ghost" newspaper debate, see Monaghan, 47-49.

36 Monaghan, 219-220.

37 Buckminster to Webster, 17 November 1783, Webster Papers, NYPL, Box 2.

CHAPTER 3

The Author as a Public Man: To Mold a Nation

The success of the Speller was particularly gratifying to a young man who had struggled with his choice of a profession and who had experienced serious doubts about his future calling in life. Webster enjoyed writing, placing his thoughts before the public, and making a name for himself. For the rest of his life, he alternated between production of educational materials and publication of essays and pamphlets that furthered his points of view on a variety of subjects, but always with either an intellectual or moral emphasis. In short order, Noah Webster became a public figure and remained so until death forced him into silence.

Webster chose to stay in Hartford after the Speller's publication and rented lodgings with his friend and supporter, John Trumbull. While there, the new author occupied himself with the completion of his Grammar—the second part of the Grammatical Institute—and with bold new steps into the arena of public policy. He had entered this arena the previous year with his "Observations on the Revolution of America." Now, with the conclusion of the war, a new controversy arose. In 1778, Congress, in an attempt to soothe the hardships of war, had promised Continental Army officers a grant of half pay for life. This promise was altered in 1783 to five years' full pay, a change the officers accepted prior to the Army's disbandment. This promise ruffled some Connecticut citizens who proposed a convention for the purpose of calling on Congress to repeal the law. Opposition to the law appalled Webster, and he began a series of articles in *The Connecticut Courant* against the conventioneers.

The five years' pay, or commutation, as it was called, was not the most important matter in Webster's mind; rather, he was more concerned with the attitude of the complainants, the ingratitude displayed toward those who had fought so valiantly and at such personal risk, and the impact on the operation of government, both at the state and national levels. The commutation controversy helped crystallize his thoughts on government and brought *character* to the forefront of his concerns. And character was the issue upon which he pounced immediately. The motivation of the conventioneers received his scrutiny from the start. "But where is the man," Webster wrote, "that wishes to see them [Army officers] return home victorious, without bettering their circumstances?" Such a stance, he argued, "would be the height of envy and ingratitude." Moreover, it would be "a crime to wish it."[1] He appealed to the people's sense of fair play, reminding them of the risks these officers had taken for their liberty.

An objection had been raised that some of the officers were worthless characters who did not deserve a reward. Possibly true, remarked Webster, but who will stand in judgment on the merits of every officer who has served? "Nothing short of omniscience," he observed, "can do this." He then continued with a theological analogy:

> The Supreme Ruler of the universe suffers the same objection to his moral government of the world; the good and the bad share alike in the benefits of his munificence; the wheat and the chaff grow together 'till harvest: And why should mortals attempt a perfection of civil government which the Deity has not seen fit to introduce into the moral system?[2]

Again, Webster's orthodox heritage influenced his concept of society and placed a limitation on human expectations; civil government is of this world only and perfection is not to be expected.

A subsequent article carried the discussion of character and government a step further. Even as the conventioneers were about to meet in Middletown, Webster spoke out against their jealousies and suspicions toward elected officials. How can they be fearful of elected rulers, he queried, when they can quickly turn them out of office or bring them to trial for any egregious acts of misconduct? "To be jealous of power in such hands, is weakness, folly, and meanness," he lectured. Impeachment was unwise. "You know," he continued, "that they [the elected officials] can vindicate their conduct before God and the world."[3] In other words, these officials had done the right thing for the officers, and any honest man would recognize that. Webster's opinion of the conventioneers' character was unequivocal. In his view they were "a nest of vipers, disturbing the tranquillity of government, to answer selfish purposes."[4]

Selfish, suspicious people could do great harm to the happiness and stability of a government, and Webster saw the beginnings of that instability in calls for an alteration of the Connecticut constitution. In Webster's view, cries for alteration of the governmental structure masked ulterior motives. "People begin to say openly, if they can get rid of the upper house of Assembly, they can do as they please," he warned. "First however, they are attempting to change the members—to drop every man of ability, of liberal and independent sentiments, and in their room, to choose men of intrigue, who are artfully working upon the passions of the multitude to answer their own selfish purposes." Webster clearly was concerned that the people of Connecticut would prove themselves unworthy of the privilege of a republican government. He suggested that even if God should place the angel Gabriel himself in charge of the government, the populace would "find fault with his administration, especially if it were rigourously just—they would wrangle him out of office and choose some ignorant or unprincipled demagogue."[5]

These anti-convention articles, another series of Webster-authored articles entitled "Policy of Connecticut," and the success of the Speller combined to transform the young author into a public figure. His efforts in the commutation controversy brought expressions of gratitude from the governor, and from the legislator (and later Chief Justice of Connecticut), Stephen Mitchell, who informed him directly, "You, Sir, have done more to appease public discontents & produce a favorable change, than any other person."[6] It is not always possible accurately to assess the influence one man's words may have had in the resolution of a conflict, yet

Mitchell's estimation of Webster's effect provides at least one documented contemporary view.

The Grammar

Meanwhile, Webster's labors bore more published fruit. In March 1784, the Grammar—the second part of his proposed *Institute*—appeared, published at his own expense. As with the Speller, the preface offered an explanation of the work's uniqueness, a uniqueness that Webster claimed rested on a divorce from Latin roots. His primary complaint with all other English grammars was that they superimposed Latin constructions upon English. Modeling English grammar upon the Latin, according to Webster, was the wrong approach. English had to be framed upon its *own* principles, not those of a totally different language. Dilworth again was the foe since the grammar portion of his spelling book had the greatest circulation in America. Webster acknowledged that there were points of agreement in all languages, particularly in the definition of terms, but "wherever our language is built upon principles peculiar to itself," the new grammarian exclaimed, Dilworth was "invariably wrong."[7]

Bluntness and directness was as much Webster's forte in this preface as in the Speller's. He aimed at the learned men of Britain, those who had made languages "their principal study" but who never discovered "that the Grammar of one language would not answer for another." Instead, they universally advocated the use of a Latin Grammar to understand English. Webster was outraged. "That such a stupid opinion should ever have prevailed in the English nation—that it should still have advocates—nay that it should still be carried into practice," he exclaimed, "can be resolved into no cause but the amazing influence of habit upon the human mind."[8]

Webster set out to change the grammatical habits of Americans. He refashioned the concept of the neuter gender by pointing out that neuter could more properly be designated as an absence of gender. Verbs should not be divided into active, passive, and neuter, but merely transitive and intransitive. He also championed the use of *you was* to indicate singular, a practice that seemed to be the preference of eighteenth-century literati. In the estimation of one of

Webster's principal biographers, the Grammar was a pioneer in shearing away useless Latin terms and in "describing, not prescribing, actual grammatical usage."[9]

The Grammar shows Webster to be an innovator, someone who was willing to reexamine traditional educational beliefs, uproot where necessary, and build a new edifice. And once again his purpose, though only implicit in the preface, was to establish a system of education appropriate for the new American republic. Part II of the *Institute*, however, did not match the success of the Speller; he was too innovative and lost out in a crowded field of more traditional approaches. Although he continued to revise and publish the work until 1806, its usage declined dramatically before the turn of the century.

The Reader

Just eleven months later, in February 1785, Part III of the *Institute* emerged. The Reader completed Webster's concept of a total elementary education. Together with the Speller and Grammar, the Reader provided children (and illiterate adults) with all he felt was essential to master the rudiments of the English language.

Again, the preface provided the rationale for the work. Webster wished "to furnish schools with a variety of exercises for reading and speaking at a small expense."[10] That was the practical reason, but he went on to detail the philosophical basis. "To refine and establish our language, to facilitate the acquisition of grammatical knowledge, and diffuse the principles of virtue and patriotism, is the task I have labored to perform," he explained, "and whether the success should equal my wishes or not, I shall still have the satisfaction of reflecting that I have made a laudable effort to advance the happiness of my country."[11]

For Webster, the Reader advanced an intellectual pursuit—the continued development of an American language—while it taught moral principles in tandem with patriotic themes. The content of each story was character-intensive and continued to be so in successive editions. Even the "Select Sentences" that followed the rules for reading and speaking were oriented toward that goal. As one biographer notes, the first of these sentences is quite applicable to Webster himself: "To be very active in laudable pursuits, is the distinguishing characteristic of a man of merit."[12]

Short stories and extracts from writings, both published and ·unpublished, formed the main body of the text. Three of the stories were from Webster's own pen. He also included selections from his friends Barlow and Trumbull, as well as an excerpt from Timothy Dwight's manuscript, "The Conquest of Canaan." To round out America's contribution to America's first classroom reading book, he added two addresses of Congress, a portion of Thomas Paine's *Crisis, No. V*, and a letter from an acquaintance on the issue of slavery.

This 186-page volume was greatly enlarged in its 1787 edition. The new offering, doubled to 372 pages, was retitled *An American Selection of Lessons in Reading and Speaking*. It remained devoted to character development and was even more patriotic than the original. On the eve of the adoption of a new national constitution, Webster filled the Reader with Americana: orations on the Boston Massacre; some addresses of Congress; the Declaration of Independence; Washington's Farewell Orders to the Army; speeches by William Livingston, Hugh Henry Brackenridge, Edward Rutledge, and Barlow; and patriotic poems by Philip Freneau. In addition, Webster authored brief histories of the discovery and settlement of America and of the American Revolution. He also incorporated a section on American geography, retained in later editions until Jedidiah Morse's Geography became the standard American text in the mid-1790s.

The emphasis on character was especially pronounced. The table of contents contained short descriptions of each reading selection and they reveal that invariably the development of a certain character trait was the aim of every story. "Honesty Rewarded" was one of the titles, and it described "an industrious and virtuous couple made happy by strict honesty." "Agathocles and Calista" was "an example of the felicity, derived from pure affection between the sexes," and the "Story of La Roche" depicted "genuine sorrow for the death of a near friend, of sincere piety, devotion, and filial obedience." Another offering, the "Story of Sir Edward and Louisa," exhibited "true kindness rewarded by ingratitude—and the injury repaired by a generous act."[13]

Webster's own contributions were similar. His "Emilius, or Domestic Happiness" warned against extreme methods of childrearing and the consequences of being either too strict or too lax.

"Emelia, or the Happiness of Retirement" expounded on "dangers to which young Ladies are exposed in company and the advantages of a domestic education—exemplified in the character of Emelia." Webster stressed the virtue of females, evidenced by another selection he authored, "Juliana, a Real Character." Juliana was a model of "behavior in company—goodness of heart, affability, and unaffected ease"; he praised "her delicacy, firmness, and fidelity."[14]

Clearly, the Reader, by its nature, was more conducive to the development of moral and patriotic themes than either the Speller or Grammar, yet together they formed a three-pronged phalanx to establish a distinctively American educational foundation for the new nation. Webster's conviction that a uniform national language was the key to the promotion of national unity and political happiness continued unabated throughout his life. And his belief in the necessity of moral underpinnings, both in the accumulation of knowledge and in the practice of politics, only heightened as evidence started to mount against his early conception of the ability of education to shape human character.

Thoughts on a National Government

American education, in Webster's view, would help determine the form and effectiveness of American government. Consequently, it seemed quite natural for an educator to turn his pen to the theory and practice of a national government. Just one month after the appearance of the Reader, another product of his ever-active mind was presented to the people. *Sketches of American Policy*, a slim booklet of forty-eight pages, attempted to put the American political experience in a nutshell and to promote a scheme for restructuring the national government that would cement the Union in a way the quite ineffective Articles of Confederation never could. It was an ambitious task for so few pages, but Webster made the attempt.

The first three sections were based heavily on the writings of Jean-Jacques Rousseau and an English preacher of nonconformist persuasion, Dr. Richard Price.[15] The social compact, Webster declared, was the basis of all civil government, and each person should consent to obey the general voice. There could be no concern for tyranny in such a government because the power was in the whole body of the people collectively "and the people will never make laws oppressive to themselves." He concluded section one with the assertion that the best government is that in which "the right of *making* laws, is vested in the greatest number of individuals, and the power of *executing* them, in the smallest number."[16]

Europe, lamented Webster in the second section, was probably a lost cause. Societies usually are preserved by one of three methods (or a combination of the three): a standing army; fear of invaders; and the influence of religion. In Europe, most people were chained by these methods; they were "in vassalage—without knowledge, without freedom and without hope of relief." America, however, had the advantage of being established "in the most enlightened period of the world."[17]

Section three offered hope that Americans could avoid the errors perpetuated in Europe and "lay a broad basis for the perfection of human society." American civil policy could be the result of the collected wisdom of the ages and of the Christian religion that it professed. The annihilation of hereditary ranks in society and the more widespread distribution of land, especially in New England, bode well for the American experiment. Education and religious liberty were the cornerstones for success. "If there are any human means of promoting a millennial state of society," he speculated, "the only means are a general diffusion of knowledge and a free unlimited indulgence given to religious persuasions, without distinction and without preference. When this event takes place, and I believe it certainly will," he hastened to add, "the *best* religion will have the most advocates. Nothing checks the progress of truth like human establishments. Christianity spread with rapidity, before the temporal powers interfered; but," he continued, "when the civil magistrate undertook to guard the truth from error, its progress was obstructed, the simplicity of the gospel was corrupted with human inventions, and the efforts of Christendom have not yet been able to bring it back to its primitive purity."[18]

Webster's reliance on his European Enlightenment sources is most evident in this section. Although he qualified his quest for an earthly millennium with an "if" clause, there seems little doubt that he anticipated an American empire as close to perfection as possible. He continued to insist that Christianity was the basis for this potential achievement, but it had to be a Christianity uncorrupted with human additions, one that was in its original pure state. Webster's view of a pure Christianity was not clearly explained; it is not certain whether he simply meant that it should be free of Catholic traditions or whether it should have a more Deistic flavor, shorn of all belief in the supernatural.[19] The truth probably lay somewhere in between; perhaps Webster himself, at this time in his life, did not have a clear-cut definition of "pure Christianity."

Religion's role was clear in one respect, however. As he began section four, Webster concluded that religion would have "little or no influence in preserving the union of the states." Although Christianity was "calculated to cherish a spirit of peace and harmony in society," it was unable to "balance the influence of jarring interests in different governments."[20] Webster believed that although religion was essential and good for people, it had its practical limitations. It was not the cure for America's ills.

As he unfolded his ideas in the fourth section, the novice governmental theorist walked right into a contradiction with the first three-fourths of his treatise, a contradiction again brought on by his personal intellectual-religious ambiguity. The nation that had every right to expect the millennium was inhabited by people who are patently selfish and self-serving, and who need to be forced to take their responsibilities seriously. He stated it this way:

> If three millions of people, united under thirteen different heads, are to be governed or brought to act in concert by a *Resolve, That it be recommended*, I confess myself a stranger to history and to human nature. The very idea of uniting discordant interests and restraining the selfish and the wicked principles of men by advisory resolutions is too absurd to have advocates even among illiterate peasants. The resolves of Congress are always treated with respect, and during the late war they were efficacious. But their efficacy proceeded from a principle of common safety which united the interests of all the states; but peace has removed that principle, and the states comply with or refuse the requisitions of Congress just as they please.[21]

Corruption and tyranny were possible, even in a nation with as great advantages as America possessed. Such a tragedy, however, could come only from the people's inattention to their power of representation. On the whole, Webster felt America was less liable to corruption than any other nation on earth. He promoted three safeguards: a general diffusion of knowledge; the encouragement of industry, frugality, and virtue; and structural changes in the operation of the national government.

General diffusion of knowledge would come about from a closer attention to the need for education, an education for every social class, not just the high-born. Acquisition of knowledge, Webster declared, "liberalizes men and removes the most inveterate prejudices. . . . Education will gradually eradicate them, and a growing intercourse will harmonize the feelings and the views of all the citizens."[22] One of the chief roadblocks to the cultivation of industry, frugality, and virtue, he felt, was the continued existence of slavery within American borders. Slavery's effects were wholly harmful. Webster considered the institution "the bane of industry and virtue." Slaves might enrich their owners, but they also rendered their owners useless members of society, creating "a haughty, unsocial, aristocratic temper, inconsistent with that equality which is the basis of our governments and the happiness of human society."[23] The primary structural changes Webster advocated were the election of a president to preside over a separate executive branch and a Congress with the power to govern nationally, an arrangement that would not allow one state to overrule the wishes of all the others. Although these changes were not original with Webster, he was one of the first to put into print the outline of a type of national government that eventually emerged from the Constitutional Convention of 1787.[24]

The pamphlet also called for a national consciousness. It appealed to the diverse sections of a large country to start to think *nationally*, rather than strictly provincially. Webster addressed, in particular, each section's self-interest. "Self-interest, both in morals and politics," he explained, "is and ought to be the ruling principle of mankind, but this principle must operate in perfect conformity to social and political obligations." The problem was the definition of self-interest. "Narrow views and illiberal prejudices may for a time produce a selfish system of politics in each state," he predicted, "but a few years' experience will correct our ideas of self-interest and convince us that a selfishness which excludes others from a participation of benefits is, in all cases, self-ruin, and that *provincial interest* is inseparable from *national interest*."[25]

The *Sketches* made the rounds and attracted considerable attention. George Washington received a copy directly from Webster's hand; Washington then showed it to Madison, who acknowledged it in the preface to his notes on the Constitutional Convention. The public man was becoming more public all the time, and he felt the time was right for national promotion of his works.

Webster as Promoter and Lecturer

In May of this year 1785, NW set out on a journey to South Carolina. From Baltimore, he rode to Mount Vernon, where he passed some time, in Gen. Washington's hospitable mansion. . . .

One object of the journey to the south, was, to make application to the legislatures of several states for the enactment of laws to secure to authors the copy right of their writings.[26]

Webster had established himself as an author and a public man, but insecurities remained. He had no legal protection for his writings in many states and, successful as he may have been professionally, he was not yet a financial success. Even though the Speller was a bestseller, he had sold the copyrights to various printers, allowing them to print copies for a certain number of years in exchange for lump sums that were essential for his short-term financial needs. This was not an advantageous settlement for the young author.[27] Financial stability was essential if he had any hope to settle down and become a respectable family man. Although he had no real prospects for marriage in 1785, he had to think ahead.

Webster's personal situation ran parallel with the nation's. Although independence had been achieved, there were insecurities. Economic stability had not returned after the war; threats of revolt were heard from farmers who could not pay their taxes. The national government was perceived as weak and ineffective, a problem

Webster had addressed in his *Sketches*. He longed to help provide unity for his untested nation and, in this quest, national and personal needs could be met simultaneously. His writings would aid in the formation of national union, and copyright laws for his labors would brighten his own financial prospects.

Copyright laws in the southern states would allow Webster to extend the sale of his schoolbooks throughout the nation. He chose Baltimore as his temporary headquarters as he embarked on the life of an itinerant. His first trek was to Mount Vernon, where he spent an evening with the Washingtons. He judiciously presented a copy of his *Sketches* to the most influential man in America and then returned directly to Baltimore, where he took passage to Charleston. Upon arrival at Charleston, he spent a week in the very profitable exercise of handing out gratuitous copies of his Speller and Grammar, a move that helped make his books the standard for the state. He then decided to confine himself to Baltimore for the duration of the summer because legislatures were not in session.

Webster never was able to pass time idly. While he waited for his next assault on the states, he employed his time in writing his thoughts on the nature and purpose of the English language, a pursuit that he soon would turn into a lecture tour and, ultimately, into another publication, which he called *Dissertations on the English Language*.[28] In November, he again attended to the protection of his books; by February 1786, he had registered them in Virginia and Maryland and had petitioned Delaware for a copyright law, a petition that eventually proved effectual.

During his stay in Virginia, Webster visited Washington again and briefly flirted with the idea of securing employment as secretary and schoolmaster to his grandchildren. Webster was shocked to hear that Washington was looking to Scotland for such a man and boasted to the general that "any of the northern colleges could furnish a person who would answer his wishes."[29] He considered himself a person well qualified for the job, and for a month after his conversation with Washington was tempted with the possibility. As he wrote to the general in December:

Faithfulness and industry are all I can promise—The first, I believe proceeds from principle, the last, both from principle and habit. . . . I wish to be settled in life—I wish not for solitude, but to have it in my power to be retired. I wish to enjoy life, but books and business will ever be my principal pleasure. I must write—it is a happiness I cannot sacrifice; and were I upon the throne of the Grand Seignior, I feel as tho' I could pleasure in the education of youth.[30]

This short passage reveals a lot about Webster's perception of himself. He clearly felt that he was a trustworthy and willing worker and that these traits were founded on principle, not merely personal gain. Stability and a settled life were on his mind; his ideal was a gentleman's retirement in which he could devote all of his time to books and writing, activities that he equates with pleasure and happiness. The strength of the sentence, "I must write—it is a happiness I cannot sacrifice," provides insight for his prodigious labors. Although he later would protest quite often that he was done trying to correct the public's views, he never could keep that commitment. Each protest would be followed by one more attempt to educate his countrymen.

Webster's time in Virginia also left him with other indelible impressions, impressions that would affect his view of the southern states for the rest of his life. He noted, for instance, that Virginians seemed "to fix their churches as far as possible from town & their play houses in the center."[31] Although he had attended some plays, Webster held the traditional New England Puritan disdain for the public portrayal of vice that might tempt people into sin. After attendance at a play in early 1786, he recorded in his diary that it contained "some low scenes & indelicate ideas." He further commented, "Every exhibition of vice weakens our aversion for it."[32] One of his newspaper treatises that found its way into his Reader explains,

A theatre under the best regulations is not essential to our public and private happiness. It may afford entertainment to individuals, but it is at the expense of private taste and public morals. The great misfortune of all exhibitions of this kind is this, that they reduce all taste to a level. Not only the vices of all classes of people are brought into view, but of all ages and nations.[33]

The vices of the South seemed to be many. Moral failures and educational defects were intertwined in Webster's mind, and they were linked in his written observations. William and Mary College at Williamsburg he considered well endowed and "pretty respectable," but one academy at Prince Edward and one at Alexandria appeared to be the extent of Virginians' concern with college preparation. "The education," he discerned, "is very indifferent. Plays, horse-races & games are almost the sole objects of pursuit."[34] As his stay lengthened, his perceptions were only confirmed. He concluded, in an almost amusing variety of complaints, that "the Virginians have little money & great pride, contempt of Northern men & great fondness for dissipated life. They do not understand Grammar."[35]

The notes on the English language that Webster had written earlier in the summer provided another occupation while he sought copyrights for his books. Wherever he went, he lectured publicly on the subject and charged admission. He later reflected that lectures on language could not be expected to draw large audiences, but he was gratified to number the most respectable men in the communities as a significant portion of his hearers. Above all, Webster was pleased with the opportunity "of becoming acquainted with many literary gentlemen, in the principal cities & towns, . . . & of extending his knowledge of books treating of the subject of philology."[36] The lecture tour lasted until November 1786 and extended from Richmond, Virginia, to Portsmouth, New Hampshire. His new acquaintances included Timothy Pickering, Benjamin Rush, and Benjamin Franklin. In Franklin, Webster found a mentor in the art of reforming the orthography of the language. Franklin was for introducing a modified alphabet with new characters, a plan that went beyond Webster's desires. Yet he did catch the spirit of reformation that guided the aged philosopher and statesman. In fact, Webster's subsequent attempts to introduce changes into English orthography became a quite controversial aspect of his work.[37]

The language lectures, which were codified in his 1789 *Dissertations*, lay the groundwork for understanding his fascination with words and for comprehending the connection he made between a nation's language and its moral and political well-being. Webster saw words as more than mere expressions of individuals;

he believed they had a profound effect on national unity. And unity was precisely the problem America was facing in the 1780s. English, Webster contended in the *Dissertations*, was being employed "to record almost all the events and discoveries of ancient and modern times." It needed to be cultivated by those who could apprehend "the connection between language and logic, and form an adequate idea of the influence which a uniformity of speech may have on national attachments."[38] Uniformity of language, according to Webster, was essential to political unity. Continuing a theme he had developed in the Speller's preface, he maintained that differences of language, even in local dialects, lead men to ridicule each other, a habit "followed by disrespect—and without respect friendship is a name, and social intercourse a mere ceremony."[39] Political harmony, therefore, depended on linguistic harmony.

Since Webster stridently opposed Americans using Great Britain as the arbiter of language propriety, he called once again for a uniquely American English. It had to be this way, he judged, for a number of reasons: first, Great Britain was a nation of increasingly corrupt language; second, even if its language was not in decline, it was too far away to serve as a model; third, British English was suffering assimilation with other European countries; and fourth, America undoubtedly would chart its own individual course in language development due to its unique circumstances and growth of distinctively American words.[40]

Webster, in the *Dissertations*, urged that two rules be used as guiding lights for the development of an American English standard: universal undisputed practice and the principle of analogy. By the first, he meant simply that no one person or class of people should set themselves up as authorities and dictate the rules of proper language. The very attempt would be arbitrary and might not be accepted because it would go too much against the grain of established practice. "The authority of individuals is always liable to be called in question—but the unanimous consent of a nation, and a fixed principle interwoven with the very construction of a language," he argued, ". . . are like the common laws of a land, or the immutable rules of morality, the propriety of which every man, however refractory, is forced to acknowledge, and to which most men will readily submit. Fashion," he admonished, "is usually the child of caprice and the being of a day; principles of propriety are founded in the very nature of things, and remain unmoved and unchanged, amidst all the fluctuations of human affairs and the revolutions of time."[41]

The principle of analogy was to work in concert with universal practice. Webster contended that the structure of any language, upon examination, would yield a principle of analogy. "We shall find in English that similar combinations of letters have usually the same pronunciation; and that words, having the same terminating syllable, generally have the accent at the same distance from that termination." These principles of analogy, he concluded, "are productive of great convenience, and become an authority superior to the arbitrary decisions of any man or class of men.[42] What, then, should one make of irregularities in language structure? Webster allowed that deviations from analogy could be found, but in such cases they had become the universal undisputed practice and should therefore be accepted as the standard of propriety.

English could not be considered a static language, he argued further, and all languages change from age to age. "Words are like leaves of trees; the old ones are dropping off and new ones growing."[43] Thus, one must look to actual practice rather than certain self-appointed authorities. This penchant for change, though, does not mean the general rules of a language are undergoing constant fluctuation; new words usually conform to old rules. A wordsmith such as Webster could not hope to dictate an entire language, but he hoped to set a standard for pronunciation and orthography that might have a semblance of permanence. And that was his goal.

A national language became Webster's objective, but not a national language for its own sake. Rather, he sought a unity of spirit among Americans that would lead to a strong political union. America, he asserted, again in the *Dissertations*, had the greatest opportunity of establishing a national language that ever had been presented to mankind:

> Now is the time to begin the plan. The minds of the Americans are roused by the events of a revolution; the necessity of organizing the political body and of forming constitutions of government that shall secure freedom and

property, has called all the faculties of the mind into exertion; and the danger of losing the benefits of independence, has disposed every man to embrace any scheme that shall tend . . . to reconcile the people of America to each other, and weaken the prejudices which oppose a cordial union.[44]

Toward a New Constitution

Although Webster spoke glowingly of America's future, he could not help but be aware of the undercurrent of rebellion against state taxes in an enfeebled economy. The unrest erupted in 1786 with its most spectacular manifestation in Shays' Rebellion in Massachusetts. Just a few weeks prior to that uprising, Webster had commented on the situation in a letter to Timothy Pickering and had offered his own solution to the taxation problem. In his letter, Webster considered that "storms of this kind" were both "sudden & transient." The issue was character. Men of good sense and judgment understood the need for some taxes and could live with them, especially when these tax laws were passed by the people's own representatives. The passions unleashed could be tamed by proper application of reason. The problem, Webster deduced, was that many of the complainants were not wise in their expenditures, thus creating a worse situation for themselves. "It is a fact that the common people in this Country drink Rum & Tea sufficient every year to pay the interest of the public debts." Although he acknowledged each person's political right "to make himself sick or drunk when he pleases," Webster clearly considered such actions foolish. "The best way to redress grievances," he continued, was "for every man, when he gets a sixpence, instead of purchasing a pint of Rum or two ounces of tea, to deposit his pence in a desk, till he had accumulated enough to answer the calls of the Collector. Every man who does this sacredly redresses his own Grievances."[45]

In the midst of the Shays' Rebellion controversy, Webster took stock of the state of the nation and suffered a severe, if limited, jolt to his hopes of political utopia. The outbreak of anti-federal sentiment in his home state, paper money legislation enacted in neighboring Rhode Island, and his disgust with Southern electioneering practices combined with the tax rebellion to make him doubt everything he previously had written. In an unsigned letter to *The Connecticut Courant*, he remarked that people in general were "too ignorant to manage affairs which require great reading and an extensive knowledge of foreign nations." This he considered to be "the misfortune of republican governments." Then he made a startling pronouncement:

> For my own part, I confess, I was once as strong a republican as any man in America. Now, a republic is among the last kinds of governments I should choose. I should infinitely prefer a limited monarchy, for I would sooner be subject to the caprice of one man, than to the ignorance and passions of a multitude. I believe men as individuals enjoy more security, more peace and more *real liberty* under a limited monarch . . . than in republics, where people sometimes get furious and make laws destructive of all peace and liberty.[46]

Webster then assured his readers that he was not advocating a change of government. He desired instead that the people be better informed and that men of ability be elected to public positions. Assurances aside, he was, nevertheless, shaken. What possibly disturbed him most was the sight of a New England that he had considered superior in education, morals, and civility becoming the scene of mob action and rebellion. At any rate, shortly after publication of the letter, he left Connecticut. In his diary, he commented that his leaving could be "perhaps for life."[47]

His total despondency over the situation did not last more than a few days, for when he arrived at New Haven, enroute to New York, he had serious discussions with Ezra Stiles, Roger Sherman, and other influential men that succeeded in restoring his damaged faith in government by the people. They convinced Webster that the debtors' errors lay in the methods they chose to redress their grievances and that he should consider their distresses genuine. Perhaps disenchantment could have been expected in someone with as great a vision as Webster. Those who dream much are often hit with harsh realities. Another factor was his relative youth. Although he had made his mark on the national scene, he was only twenty-eight and just beginning to learn how to mesh personal vision with the practicalities of life.

After a few fruitless weeks in New York seeking a new living, Webster headed south to Philadelphia. His time in that city proved valuable personally, as he was able to work more closely with Franklin on language reform and, ultimately, be on the scene while the Constitutional Convention was sitting in closed session. He also found employment. In April 1787, he took the position of Master of the English Language at the Protestant Episcopal Academy. But Webster's focus was not just on his return to the teaching profession, and even before he accepted the position, he already was involved in further discussions on the state of America. Although he had been saved from a permanent lapse into antirepublicanism, the events of the past year had sobered him and his new reflections showed evidence of a more conservative stance toward society as a whole. His modified approach appeared in Philadelphia newspapers in February 1787, in a series of articles titled "Remarks on the Manners, Government, Laws and Domestic Debt of America." "Nothing," wrote Webster in these articles, "can be so fatal to morals and the peace of society as a violent shock given to public opinion or fixed habits." He had seen churches destroyed by the introduction of polemical disputes and wanted none of that spirit to corrupt society. "Public opinion, therefore, in religion and government, the great supports of society, should never be suddenly unhinged," he cautioned.[48] He became particularly attentive to the connection between money and morals. Conforming to his thesis of avoidance of sudden shocks in society, he decried sudden increases in specie and frequent changes of value in money as "more fruitful sources of corruption of morals than any events that take place in a community." He promoted instead "slow and regular" financial gains and deplored the practice of financial speculation.[49]

If it were only the speculators who were corrupted, it would be bad enough, but Webster felt that the corruption naturally would spread to "the honest laborer and the regular merchant" who would be tempted by the speculation. "Every temptation of this kind," he warned, "attacks the moral principles and exposes men to small deviations from the rectitude of commutative justice."[50] Another effect of a flood of money was dissipation, which he later defined as "a dissolute, irregular course of life; a wandering from object to object in pursuit of pleasure; a course of life usually attended with careless and exorbitant expenditures of money, and indulgence in vices, which impair the health or ruin both health and fortune."[51] As evidence of this dissipation he pointed to the doubled expenses for "subsistence, dress, and equipage" experienced by commercial towns during the first two years after the Revolution.[52]

In this series of articles, Webster called for laws to prevent the easy expansion of credit, arguing that such laws actually would be beneficial to the poor. Men in general, he claimed, cannot handle a sudden influx of money. If they do not spend it on gambling, lotteries, or privateering, they at least will be caught off their guard and become "prodigal" in their expenses. "When people can possess themselves of property without previous labor, they consume it with improvident liberality," he believed. Although a prudent man would not give in to this practice, "a large proportion of mankind have not prudence and fortitude enough to resist the demands of pride and appetite. . . . They form habits of indolence and extravagance which ruin their families and impoverish their creditors."[53]

The primary effect of his musings over the previous year's events was to strengthen more than ever his belief in the need for a stronger central government to provide stability for a nation seemingly tottering on the brink of a failed vision. It is no surprise then that he eagerly anticipated the successful conclusion of the convention that began meeting in May to discuss constitutional issues. Webster was personally acquainted with many of the delegates, one of whom, Thomas Fitzsimons of Pennsylvania, wrote Webster a letter just two days prior to the convention's adjournment, requesting the well-known writer to pen an essay in support of the new document that had issued from the deliberations. Webster was more than willing to lend his hand in the making of history.

The fruit of his labor was entitled *An Examination into the Leading Principles of the Federal Constitution proposed by the late Convention held at Philadelphia*. He finished the work quickly and disseminated it in mid-October. It actually was completed a little too quickly for Webster, who considered it "not satisfactory to himself or to the friends of the Constitution."[54] Webster's assessment was written in the 1830s. Contemporary evidence allows a more charitable evaluation, as the essay made the rounds and played a part in the Constitution's ratification.[55] Webster, though, not certain of the response it might receive if his name were appended, signed it simply "A Citizen of America."

The origin of the American republic, Webster contended in the *Examination*, was "distinguished by peculiar circumstances." Whereas other nations had been "driven together by fear and necessity," America's government, in the form of the proposed Constitution, was founded on the accumulated wisdom of the ages: "In short, it is an *empire of reason*."[56] America's arrangement under the Confederation, he argued, was little better than a state of nature, leaving liberty and property in a precarious situation. States taking advantage of one another would lead to tyranny. The state with "the heaviest purse and longest sword" could tyrannize neighbor states who would have no recourse to a superior power that could "oppose the invasion or redress the injury."[57] Americans needed to recognize that the people themselves are the source of power and that a national government, representative of the people, will protect the rights of property, the general and "tolerably equal distribution" of which Webster considered "the whole basis of national freedom." With this declaration, he distances himself from Montesquieu's belief that virtue is the basis for a free government. "*Virtue*, patriotism, or love of country never was and never will be, till men's natures are changed, a fixed, permanent principle and support of government," Webster declared. Instead, "An equality of property, with a necessity of alienation constantly operating to destroy combinations of powerful families, is the very *soul of a republic*. While this continues, the people will inevitably possess both *power* and *freedom*; when this is lost, power departs, liberty expires, and a commonwealth will inevitably assume some other form."[58]

The right of property, combined with the right of choosing one's own representatives, guaranteed, according to Webster, the safety of liberty. The new constitution would be a protection to liberty. He acknowledged that the document was not perfect, but commented, "Perfection is not the lot of humanity. Instead of censuring the small faults of the constitution, I am astonished that so many clashing interests have been reconciled, and so many sacrifices made to the *general* interest."[59] He concluded the treatise with a cataloging of the Constitution's virtues, a reminder that Washington and Franklin were two of its principal supporters, and an exhortation for Americans to put away their fears and unite in a common purpose:

> In short, the privileges of freemen are interwoven into the very feelings and habits of Americans; liberty stands on the immoveable basis of a general distribution of property and diffusion of knowledge, but the Americans must cease to contend, to fear, and to hate before they can realize the benefits of independence and government or enjoy the blessings which heaven has lavished in rich profusion upon this western world.[60]

Ratification of the Constitution placed America on a firmer footing. Washington entered the presidency of a country that needed stability, a need that, despite the tribulations of the 1790s, largely was met. Noah Webster, who had fought long and hard throughout the 1780s for national independence in education and stability in government, could afford to feel a sense of satisfaction as the nation went forward with its new foundations, secure in the knowledge that he had made his contribution. Yet, in his personal life, stability still was lacking; career, finances, and family remained unsettled. It was now time to concentrate on those matters.

---

[1] Webster, "An Address to the Discontented People of America," *Connecticut Courant*, 26 August 1783.

[2] Ibid.

[3] Ibid., 2 September 1783.

[4] Webster diary, 29 March 1784, in Ford, 1:73.

[5] Webster, "An Address," 2 September 1783.

[6] Webster, "Memoir," 11.

[7] Webster, *A Grammatical Institute of the English Language, Part II* (Hartford: Hudson & Goodwin, 1784), 3.

[8] Ibid. The emphasis on habit in this quotation is another indication of Webster's Common Sense philosophical training at Yale.

9 Warfel, *Noah Webster*, 82. In 1807, Webster published *A Philosophical and Practical Grammar* (New Haven: Oliver Steele & Co.), a revamping of his original work. Although it lasted only a few editions, he considered it one of his most valuable efforts, so much so that he prefixed it to his *American Dictionary of the English Language* in 1828.

10 Webster, *A Grammatical Institute of the English Language, Part III* (Hartford: Barlow & Babcock, 1985), preface.

11 Ibid.

12 Ibid., quoted in Warfel, *Noah Webster*, 86-87.

13 Webster, *An American Selection of Reading and Speaking* (Philadelphia: Young & M'Culloch, 1787), table of contents.

14 Ibid.

15 Webster, "Memoir," 12: "In the first sketch, the author treats of the theory of government. This was written soon after reading Rousseau's *Social Contract*, from which he had imbibed many visionary ideas, which subsequent reflection & observation induced him to reject."

16 Webster, *Sketches of American Policy* (Hartford: Hudson & Goodwin, 1785), 4, 10.

17 Ibid., 23.

18 Ibid., 27.

19 Of course, to take the supernatural away from the Christian religion would remove its basic tenet—the intervention of God in the affairs of men through the sacrificial atonement of the Son of God. Logically, this no longer would be Christianity, but a man such as Webster, straining to embrace new philosophical trends while not utterly rejecting traditional forms of belief, often will ignore the inconsistency of such a position. Further evidence of this type of inconsistency can be seen in the attitude of Thomas Jefferson, who, although he edited all the supernatural elements from his version of the Gospels, continued to consider himself a Christian. Jefferson's definition of "Christian"—someone who does his best to live by the moral precepts of Jesus—may have approximated Webster's at the particular point in the young author's life.

20 Webster, *Sketches*, 30.

21 Ibid., 32.

22 Ibid., 44-45.

23 Ibid., 46.

24 Webster always claimed that his *Sketches* was the first written proposal of what later became the American form of government. His work was preceded, however, by a pamphlet authored by Pelatiah Webster (no relation).

[25] Webster, *Sketches*, 48.

[26] Webster, "Memoir," 12-13.

[27] Monaghan, 82, notes, "It was his publishers, not Webster, who were getting rich. By 1791 he reckoned that the rights to his books were worth $2,000 a year to their publishers. 'Could I have kept my copyright in my own hands till this time,' he complained to his brother-in-law, 'I might now have rid in a chariot.'"

[28] Webster, *Dissertations on the English Language* (Boston: Isaiah Thomas & Co., 1789).

[29] Webster, "Memoir," 14.

[30] Webster to George Washington, 18 December 1785 (copy), Webster Papers, NYPL, Box 1.

[31] Webster diary, 27 November 1785, in Ford, 1: 143.

[32] Webster diary, 29 March 1786, in Ford, 1: 153.

[33] Webster, "Remarks on the Manners, Government, Laws and Domestic Debt of America," in *An American Selection*, 215.

[34] Webster diary, 27 November 1785, in Ford, 1: 143.

[35] Webster diary, 7 December 1785, in Ford, 1: 144.

[36] Webster, "Memoir," 13.

[37] Webster's changes are discussed in the next chapter in relation to his publication, *A Collection of Essays and Fugitiv Writings* (1790).

[38] Webster, *Dissertations*, 18.

[39] Ibid., 20.

[40] Ibid., 20-23.

[41] Ibid., 29.

[42] Ibid., 27-28.

[43] Ibid., 29.

[44] Ibid., 36.

[45] Webster to Timothy Pickering, 10 August 1786, in Ford, 1: 118.

[46] *Courant*, 20 November 1786. This letter is acknowledged by Webster and attributed to him by all of his biographers. See Emily Ellsworth Ford Skeel, comp., and Edwin H. Carpenter, Jr., ed., *A Bibliography of the Writings of Noah Webster* (New York: The New York Public Library and Arno Press, 1958; reprint ed., 1971), 440.

[47] Webster diary, 23 November 1786, in Ford, 1: 169.

[48] Webster, "Remarks," in *American Selection*, 223.

[49] Ibid., 224.

[50] Ibid.

[51] Webster, *1828 Dictionary*.

[52] Webster, "Remarks," in *American Selection*, 224.

[53] Ibid., 225-26.

[54] Webster, "Memoir," 18.

[55] David Ramsey to Webster, 10 November 1787, Webster Papers, NYPL, Box 2: "Many thanks to you for your ingenious pamphlet. I have read it with pleasure. . . . I have heard every person who has read it express his high approbation of it contents. It will doubtless be of singular service in recommending the adoption of the new constitution."
    Homer D. Babbidge, Jr., ed., *Noah Webster: On Being American* (New York: Frederick A. Praeger, 1967), 48, considers Webster's *Examination* "the work of an effective eighteenth-century publicist. . . . In it Webster's ability to marshal a variety of arguments, designed to appeal to a wide range of people, in support of his views was clearly demonstrated."

[56] Webster, *An Examination into the Leading Principles of the Federal Constitution proposed by the late Convention held at Philadelphia*, in Babbidge, 50-51.

[57] Ibid., 51-52.

[58] Ibid., 53-54.

[59] Ibid., 57.

[60] Ibid., 58.

CHAPTER 4

Common Sense Philosopher

Rebecca Greenleaf first appears in Webster's diary on 1 March 1787, just one month prior to his taking the teaching position at Philadelphia's Protestant Episcopal Academy. She was visiting the city in company with her brother, James Greenleaf, a wealthy businessman and land speculator with whom Webster had struck an immediate and intimate friendship. His diary entries trace the blossoming relationship with "Becca," and by the time of her departure to her native Boston in late June, it was clear to both the couple and their acquaintances that marriage was a real possibility.

For Webster it would mean moving up in the world not only as a family man, but also as a member of one of the most prestigious families in Massachusetts. Becca's father, William Greenleaf, was a man of means who had served as Sheriff of Suffolk County at the time of the Revolution. Her brother, James, was a successful businessman, as already noted, and brothers-in-law included Dr. Nathaniel Appleton, a member of the Boston school committee, and judges Thomas Dawes and William Cranch. All Webster needed was an income steady enough to provide for a family. His practice of selling his copyright to printers for a lump sum for a certain number of years without receiving a percentage of the profits left him perennially broke. The need for ready cash had severely impaired his hopes for financial success. Webster had to face the reality of his situation. How could he take on a wife and raise a family in his pecuniary condition? What endeavor would allow him to support a family and still make a valuable contribution to American education?

The American Magazine

Encouraged by the success of Philadelphians Mathew Carey and Francis Hopkinson, who had birthed *The Columbian Magazine* in that city, and by the efforts of a former Yale classmate, Josiah Meigs, who had founded *The New Haven Gazette, and the Connecticut Magazine*, Webster resigned his duties at the Academy and left Philadelphia in October 1787. Upon doing so, he "formed the design of publishing a monthly periodical in New York,"[1] a city that he rightly believed would soon become the business center of the nation. With money obtained through the selling of yet another printing copyright for his Speller, he embarked on his new project.

The American Magazine, as Webster envisioned it, was designed to be more than a cut and paste collection of articles and essays reprinted from American newspapers and various European publications. Rather, he was determined "to collect as many original essays as possible," essays that would relate particularly to America, "and contain useful and curious discoveries in the history, or geography of America, or ingenious remarks upon the science of Government, and the peculiar institutions and customs of the people, in the different States."[2] To a large extent he succeeded, even when the original essays had to come from his own hand. Clearly, *The American Magazine* was a cut above other American attempts to provide a platform for learned men to share opinions. Education, government, agriculture, and theology were common topics; poetry and book reviews were regular features. On the whole, according to one of Webster's biographers, the publication had "something of the quality of a modern 'digest,'" and its book review section constituted "the first distinguished department of literary criticism."[3]

The essays closest to the heart of the editor were his contributions on education and government. Both ran in serial formats with the remarks on education beginning in the first issue, December 1787, and ending in May 1788. The essays on government were included in the first four issues. Both provide a clear assessment of Webster's concerns and beliefs during his tenure as a magazine editor. The essays on education particularly reveal the strong connection he made between the quality of education offered to young people and the type of character that would result, not only in the individuals receiving the education but, ultimately, in society at large. The six essays actually constitute a guide for educational philosophy and practical application of that philosophy. They offer an excellent summary of Websterian morality and his vision of American intellectual activity.

It is perhaps in his educational philosophy that Webster mirrors most clearly the influence of Scottish Common Sense faculty psychology on his own thinking. "On the Education of Youth in America" was the title Webster gave to his remarks; in the initial paragraph, he left no doubt as to the importance of the discussion that was to follow:

> The Education of youth is, in all governments, an object of the first consequence. The impressions received in early life, usually form the characters of individuals; a union of which forms the general character of a nation.[4]

Webster contemplated a positive role for government in the educational endeavor. He focused on the importance of educating youth because he believed character was formed early, and the character formed in individuals would determine the character of the nation. These sentiments find expression in Thomas Reid's educational philosophy as well. In fact, as one reads both Webster and Reid, the similarities become striking.

Men, both Webster and Reid agreed, begin life with undeveloped intellectual and moral powers that good education, properly applied, can effectually advance. "The faculties of man unfold themselves in a certain order, appointed by the great Creator," said Reid. "In their gradual progress, they may be greatly assisted or retarded, improved or corrupted, by education, instruction, example, exercise, and by the society and conversation of men, which, like soil and culture in plants, may produce great changes to the better or to the worse."[5]

Webster echoed Reid when he said of children:

> Their minds should be kept untainted, till their reasoning

faculties have acquired strength, and the good principles which may be planted in their minds, have taken deep root. They will then be able to make a firm and probably a successful resistance, against the attacks of secret corruption and brazen libertinism.[6]

Webster then applied the same principle by analogy to different societies. He proceeded to outline how societies develop differently and how education had furthered this process. In so doing, he sounded a warning rooted in a cyclical view of the history of nations: even as nations pass through various stages, so do their educational practices. Education, the new editor wrote, proceeds "by gradual advances, from simplicity to corruption." "Rude" nations are most concerned with safety, while more advanced peoples concentrate on utility. The next stage is convenience, which is then succeeded by "the opulent part of civilized nations," those most enamored by "show and amusement" in their educational undertakings. America, according to Webster's analysis, was a nation not yet firmly established in government and not fully formed in character. Consequently, it was vitally important that Americans adopt educational systems that not only would diffuse the knowledge of sciences, "but may implant . . . the principles of virtue and of liberty; and inspire . . . just and liberal ideas of government, and . . . an inviolable attachment to their own country."[7]

When Webster focuses more narrowly on the character development of the students and the moral attainments of both students and teachers, his debt to faculty psychology is even clearer. Common Sense educational theory held that good examples for youth would help mold the kind of character that would create a better society. As Reid wrote, "Man, uncorrupted by bad habits and bad opinions, is of all animals the most tractable; corrupted by these, he is of all animals the most untractable."[8] The key, therefore, was to get to the children early and place them in an environment free of corrupting influences. Webster was devoted to this theory and elaborated on it in the February and March essays.

A country village, he counseled, is a more suitable locale for a college or university because large cities "are always scenes of dissipation and amusement, which have a tendency to corrupt the hearts of youth and divert their minds from their literary pursuits."[9] Youth, he believed, was "the time to form both the head and the heart." Again repeating Common Sense orthodoxy on the development of the faculties, he remarked, "The understanding is . . . ever enlarging; but the seeds of knowledge should be planted in the mind, while it is young and susceptible; and if the mind is not kept untainted in *youth*, there is little probability that the moral character of the *man* will be unblemished." A final comment summarized his feelings: "But it is to be wished that youth might always be kept under the inspection of age and superior wisdom; that literary institutions might be so situated, that the students might live in decent families, be subject, in some measure, to their discipline, and ever under the control of those whom they respect."[10]

If the moral character of students was a primary consideration, the character of those who taught the students was just as important. The lack of good teachers—men of "unblemished reputation" and competent to teach—was the "principal defect" of American education in his day, Webster commented. It would be better, he reasoned, for youth to have no education at all than be taught by immoral and ignorant men. "It is more difficult," he warned his readers, "to eradicate habits, than to impress new ideas. The tender shrub is easily bent to any figure; but the tree, which has acquired its full growth, resists all impressions."[11]

This role of habit also loomed large in Common Sense. Reid analyzed, "How many awkward habits, by frequenting improper company, are children apt to learn. . . . They acquire such habits commonly from an undesigned and instinctive imitation, before they can judge of what is proper and becoming." Later in life, when they realize that they have unbecoming habits, they may resolve to break them but "such a general resolution is not of itself sufficient; for the habit will operate without intention; and particular attention is necessary, on every occasion, to resist its impulse, until it be undone by the habit of opposing it."[12]

Webster was in full agreement with Reid; thus, the choice of a teacher was of paramount importance. Teachers, Webster counseled, should possess good breeding and agreeable manners; they should cultivate love and respect in their students and be allowed absolute control in the classroom (even the right of corporal punishment). Yet to America's shame, he wrote, the business of education, "an employment of more consequence than making laws and preaching the gospel, because it lays the foundation on which both law and gospel rest for success" was more often than not turned over to "worthless characters."[13] "The practice of employing low and vicious characters to direct the studies of youth, is," he bemoaned, "in a high degree, criminal; it is destructive of the order and peace of society; it is treason against morals, and of course, against government; it ought to be arraigned before the tribunal of reason, and condemned by all intelligent beings. The practice is so exceedingly absurd," he continued, "that it is surprising it could ever have prevailed among rational people. Parents wish their children to be *well bred*, yet place them under the care of *clowns*. They wish to secure their hearts from *vicious principles* and *habits*, yet commit them to the care of men of the most *profligate lives*."[14]

Webster then took to task those who believed children should be exposed to all manner of vice. "Vice," he preached, "always spreads by being published; young people are taught many vices by fiction, books or public exhibitions; vices, which they never would have known, had they never read such books or attended such public places."[15] He advocated instead that the most pernicious crimes be concealed, if possible, from all young people. For Webster, youth were like seedlings that needed time to gain strength. Seedlings left on their own to weather storms would be uprooted and die; children left alone to weather the storms of life and of bad examples also were likely to be uprooted and swept away morally. "The only practicable method to reform mankind, is to begin with children," Webster taught. He wished "to banish, if possible, from their company, every low bred, drunken, immoral character. Virtue and vice will not grow together in a great degree, but they will grow where they are planted, and when one has taken root, it is not easily supplanted by the other."[16] Reid used the same planting analogy when he wrote, "The seeds, as it were, of moral discernment are planted in the mind by him that made us. They grow up in their proper season, and are at first tender and delicate, and easily warped. Their progress depends very much upon their being duly cultivated and properly exercised."[17]

How are habits uprooted? "The great art of correcting mankind therefore," believed Webster, "consists in prepossessing the mind with good principles."[18] His insistence on "principles" at the root of education was another aspect of Common Sense training and would continue throughout his life. He later defined "principle" as "the cause, source or origin of any thing; that from which a thing proceeds; a general truth; a law comprehending many subordinate truths; as the principles of morality, of law, of government."[19] It was necessary then, in Webster's philosophy, to fill young minds with general truths that govern thinking in all aspects of life. Only then would they be well armed to fight off the advances of immorality. Likewise, Reid identified principles as the foundation of man's beliefs and actions. "We may observe," Reid noted, "that men who have exercised their rational powers, are generally governed in their opinions by fixed principles of belief." Further, "men who have made the greatest advance in self-government, are governed, in their practice, by general fixed purposes. Without the former, there would be no steadiness and consistence in our belief; nor without the latter, in our conduct."[20]

Webster's essays on education also identified three crucial flaws in the American education of his time. The primary error, he opined, was "a too general attention to the dead languages, with a neglect of our own."[21] This was nothing new in Webster's American educational philosophy. He already had lectured on the political importance of Americans being united in a common understanding and pronunciation of their language, but in the education essays he fostered an even more practical rationale for the concentration on English. What use have merchants and mechanics for Greek and Latin, he queried? Inattention to English instruction had led to wide diversity in practice and had given the impression that rules and principles for pronunciation and construction were unimportant. Yet Americans needed to understand English well if they ever were to learn other languages with ease. Education must begin with a proper attention to one's own language.

In the January issue, Webster took aim at another old bugaboo—his belief that the Bible was overused in the classroom. Again, his concern was an overfamiliarity that would, in his estimation, "weaken the influence of its precepts upon the heart." It would weaken influence because people would be led to "a careless disrespectful reading of the sacred volume." In other words, Scripture would, in Webster's estimation, lose its divine authority if it were reduced to the level of any common reader. The Bible should be used, not as a basis for all subjects, but for purposes of religious instruction and morality only:

> In some countries, the common people are not permitted to read the Bible at all: In ours, it is as common as a news-paper, and in schools, is read with nearly the same degree of respect. Both these practices appear to be extremes. My wish is not to see the Bible excluded from schools, but to see it used as a system of religion and morality.[22]

Webster had made the same argument in the Speller's preface; five years had not changed his mind. Yet, as in the Speller, he was not calling for the purging of religion from education, but merely assigning a well-defined role for the Bible—the inculcation of religious and moral principles, something he apparently felt could be separated adequately from academic subjects. He remained nominally orthodox and did not dream of toppling one of the firmest pillars of American society, no matter how he might differ on certain doctrinal points.

The third error in education related to the manner in which young boys were taught, and again rested on the faculty psychology of Common Sense. Too much was expected of the very young, whose reasoning powers were not yet prepared for abstract thinking, Webster suggested. Memory is strongest in the young, he declared, so children should be taught reading as soon as they can articulate words. Certain sciences, however, such as mathematics, "should be postponed to a more advanced period of life. In the course of an English Education, mathematics should be perhaps the last study of youth in schools." And neither should children be assumed to be ready for the study of mathematics just because they had reached a certain age. "The proper time," he admonished, "can be best determined by the instructors, who are acquainted with the different capacities of their pupils."[23] In other words, as Common Sense faculty psychology recognized, the development of the different faculties would vary from child to child. Some had a greater intellectual capability than others whose capacities were more limited.[24]

More positively, Webster sounded a call to make American education truly American. This was the same spirit that had animated him in the production of textbooks, and he repeated it in these essays with genuine fervor. Every American child, he believed, should be acquainted with his own country, should rehearse its history, and should "lisp the praise of liberty, and of those illustrious heroes and statesmen, who have wrought a revolution in her favor." More books dedicated to this objective would help; they should treat the history and geography of America, and the principles of its government. They would "call home the minds of youth and fix them upon the interests of their own country, and . . . assist in forming attachments to it, as well as in enlarging the understanding."[25] Although Webster did not specifically mention his own textbooks in this regard, the rhetoric easily led the reader to consider them as an excellent source for appropriate educational use.

Along the same lines, he advised against the obtaining of a foreign education since no European country could possibly provide a proper appreciation for America and her ways. Webster's concluding comment in this education series has been widely quoted as an example of his desire to shake off Americans' dependence on European influences. It also must be viewed as a manifesto for the development of moral character and intellectual advancement. With a flourish, he proclaimed,

> Americans, unshackle your minds, and act like independent beings. You have been children long enough, subject to the control, and subservient to the interest of a haughty parent. You have now an interest of your own to augment and defend: You have an empire to raise and support by your exertions, and a national character to establish and extend by your wisdom and virtues. To effect these great objects, it is necessary to frame a liberal plan of policy, and build it on a broad system of education. Before this system can be formed and embraced, the Americans must *believe*, and *act* from the belief, that it is dishonorable to waste life in mimicking the follies of other nations and basking in the sunshine of foreign glory.[26]

The articles on government reveal the increasing conservatism of Webster's thought. Although he occasionally made a bow to Rousseau,[27] he exhibited a strong adherence to the payment of debts and expressed opposition to the view that elected officials are servants of the people, and to the practice of instructing representatives. In each case, moral issues were paramount.

Too much debt, he believed, was "proof of corruption and degeneracy among the people," and each man should pay his debt "not because there is a law to oblige him, but because it is *just* and *honest*, and because he has PROMISED to pay it."[28] The contraction of debt and its payment were ultimately moral issues involving the giving of one's word; reneging on the promise was an intolerable evil because *duty* had been disregarded. Webster's whole notion of duty and moral obligation resonates with Common Sense philosophy. Reid defined duty as *"what we ought to do—what is fair and honest—what is approvable—what every man professes to be the rule of his conduct—what all men praise—and, what is in itself laudable, though no man should praise it."* Reid elaborated further:

> This principle of honour, which is acknowledged by all men who pretend to character, is only another name for what we call a regard to duty, to rectitude, to propriety of conduct. It is a moral obligation which obliges a man to do certain things because they are right, and not to do other things because they are wrong.[29]

A man's honor and reputation could be judged by his commitment to keep faith with the contracts that he had made. The fate of society itself could be at stake, as Reid perceived:

> It may be observed that fidelity in declarations and promises, and its counterpart, trust and reliance upon them, form a system of social intercourse, the most amiable, the most useful, that can be among men. Without fidelity and trust, there can be no human society.[30]

Webster was in full accord with these thoughts, and although he did allow that states could suspend debt payments in extreme cases if the problem was too extensive to admit of an immediate solution, the weight of his argument fell on each man's responsibility to manage his affairs with a sense of duty to that which was right and proper.

Another problem Webster identified was an attitude on the part of the people that perceived elected officials as servants. "The people," he mused, "ought at least to place their rulers, who are generally men of the first abilities and integrity, on a level with themselves; for that is an odd kind of government indeed, in which, *servants* govern their *masters*."[31] Such an attitude could be danger- ous for the government, he warned, for "We may then expect that the *laws* of those *servants* will be treated with the same contempt, as they are in some other States."[32] And disrespect for law was a sign of a corrupt people, a people deficient in moral character.

Equally outrageous was the claim that the people can instruct their representatives how to vote and bind those representatives to their will. This left no room for individual conscience in regard to what constitutes the public good:

> Suppose a man so instructed should in conscience believe that a bill, if enacted, would be prejudicial to his constituents, yet his orders bind him to vote for it; how would he act between his oath and his instructions? In his oath he has sworn to act according to his judgment, and for the good of the people; his instructions forbid him to use his judgment, and bind him to vote for a law which he is convinced will injure his constituents. He must then either abandon his orders or his oath; perjury or disobedi- ence is his only alternative.[33]

Instructions, according to Webster, called upon a man to violate his conscience, an impulse to which one must never yield. Although a representative was to be concerned with the wishes of his constituents, he owed much more to his own character. As Reid put it:

> But the highest pleasure of all is, when we are conscious of good conduct in ourselves. This, in sacred scripture, is

called the *testimony of a good conscience*; and it is repre-sented, not only in the sacred writings, but in the writings of all moralists, of every age and sect, as the purest, the most noble and valuable of all human enjoyments.[34]

The American Magazine gave Webster an outlet to try a type of writing he never had attempted previously—satire. He concocted letters from the devil urging readers not to believe the writer of the education articles. For example, this "devil" challenged readers:

> Follow my *paradoxical* friend Rousseau's advice as to RELIGION. Let all instruction on this subject come as late as possible. Children who learn with wonderful facil-ity all other branches of knowledge, cannot conceive that they shall be accountable for their actions; that the Deity is witness to all they do, and will reward the good, and punish the bad. Such doctrine checks the propensities of nature. But let the passions open, and let habits be acquired, and you may then preach religion as much as you please; for it will have as little effect as I wish it to have. Your own practice at home will also confirm your son in the belief, that it is all a farce, and that there is nothing so tiresome.[35]

In another "letter," Webster's devil continued his attack. "There is a book called the Bible, and particularly that part called the New-Testament, which I utterly abhor," the "devil" warned. "Pray keep it *carefully* out of your son's hands; for one does not know what passage may strike his mind, and totally ruin the plan of making him a *fine fellow*. As you make little use of it yourself," he added, "except in the way of ridicule and witticism, there is no danger of its doing much harm; and the tutor (if you have made a right choice) will only use it to enable him to get a living, without having any conviction of the truths it contains upon his heart."[36] It is clear in this excerpt that Webster felt the Bible was an essential ingredient in a youth's complete education despite the fact that previously he had cautioned against its "overuse."

Another example of Webster's satire was an essay signed "Peter

Pickpenny" and laboriously entitled "The Art of Pushing into Business and Making Way in the World." In it he jabbed at a number of professions. Of ministers he wrote, "Are you a candidate for the clerical order and wishing to secure a good living? Be careful to embrace no particular creed, till you find a parish; then square your principles to the prejudices, humors and interests of the people. Read such books as favor their general tenets, and place more confidence in them, than in the bible." His instruction continued, "Never be too explicit in reprehending vice—let your censure be so general that no person can ever apply it to himself—Never be so *unpolite* as to name any vice that you know is predominant in the parish, especially among those who have *heavy purses*. Sermons should be wholly free from *personal reflections*."[37]

The jibes also were directed to his own professions as when he says of lawyers, "As to your fees—but no *true Lawyer* needs any advice on this article." Closer to his heart perhaps was this sound counsel to American authors:

> Another thing which is necessary to give reputation to a work, is that it should *cross the ocean*. It is with books as with spirits and ale; they refine and acquire a certain *flavor* and *strength* by long voyages. . . .   It is therefore recommended to all authors to send their manuscripts to London, and on their return, they may be sold for British manufacture, and pass with great reputation. No work, however good, will be esteemed at home.[38]

Not only did satire such as the above bring a little humor to the magazine, but it provided a unique forum for Webster to air his oft-repeated lament on Americans' incredible attachment to anything of European origin.

Webster's hope had been that Americans were ready for the national magazine he was offering. He had written to Benjamin Rush in February 1788, "The best publications in Europe are conducted by societies of literary Gentlemen, & how much more necessary is it in this country? We want a literary intercourse, we want to be acquainted with each other, we want a mutual knowledge of the state of every part of America—in short we want to be *federal.*"[39] *The American Magazine*, though, was not destined to be the avenue of a federal literature. Subscriptions never met his expectations, he lost money on the venture, and publication ended with the November 1788 issue. He was no nearer his goal of financial security. He confided to his diary, with mixed feelings on his birthday, 16 October 1788:

> 30 years of my life gone—a large portion of the ordinary age of man! I have read much, written much, & tried to do much good, but with little advantage to myself. I will now leave writing and do more lucrative business. My moral conduct stands fair with the world, & what is more, with my own Conscience. But I am a bachelor & want the happiness of a friend whose interest & feelings should be mine.[40]

The Moral Prompter

Despite his lack of an assured, steady income, Webster was determined to marry Rebecca Greenleaf. Once it became evident the magazine would not succeed, and that no other arrangements for a new magazine could be worked out, he decided to return once again to Hartford and study law in preparation for opening his own practice. "For several months I have turned my thoughts to your sisters future happiness," he told Becca's brother, James. "I have relinquished all little projects & determined upon my profession as a permanent business. From this resolution nothing but necessity or certain prospects of something better, shall induce me to deviate."[41] His mind now was settled firmly on a legal career and, with that determination, he took Becca as his wife on 26 October 1789. His diary entry notes:

> This day I became a husband. I have lived a long time a bachelor, something more than thirty one years. But I had no person to form a plan for me in early life & direct me to a profession. I had an enterprising turn of mind, was bold, vain, inexperienced. I have made some unsuccessful attempts, but on the whole have done as well as most men of my years. I begin a profession, at a late period of life,

but have some advantages of traveling and observation. I am united to an amiable woman, & if I am not happy, shall be much disappointed.[42]

All later testimony, both from himself and others, indicates that he never was disappointed with his marriage choice.

Webster did not become rich in the law, but with what clients he could attract, "some receipts for the copy-right of his elementary books, a small amount of fees of his business as Notary Public, & the aid of his generous Brother in law James Greenleaf, he was able to sustain his family for a few years."[43] The Websters set up their new home in a rented house and the family began to grow almost immediately with the birth of Emily Scholten on 4 August 1790. Later additions were Frances Juliana (always called Julia), 5 February 1793; Harriet, 6 April 1797; Mary, 7 January 1799; William, 15 September 1801; Eliza, 21 December 1803; Henry, 20 November 1806; and Louisa (apparently retarded), 12 April 1808. Henry died as an infant and Mary died in childbirth at age twenty; the rest all survived their father.

Noah Webster—married man, father, new lawyer establishing his practice. That would have been enough for most men, but as he had shared years earlier with Washington, writing was his life. The "little projects" that he had vowed to avoid became a second occupation. From his pen during his four years in Hartford flowed numerous newspaper articles, an abbreviated grammar entitled *The Little Reader's Assistant*, a published collection of his essays, an edition of John Winthrop's journal, a small book of pithy musings entitled *The Prompter*, and another booklet, *Effects of Slavery, on Morals and Industry*. In addition, to increase his renown as an author and to further literary achievement, he began in 1790 to make a yearly donation to Yale out of the sales of his schoolbooks. The donation amounted to approximately $25 per year and was awarded to the junior or senior who authored the best treatise on ethics, moral philosophy, or belles-lettres. He also made the stipulation that no one could be given this award who had been guilty of a sexual seduction or who had fought in a duel. As always, education and character went in tandem for Webster.[44] In the midst of all this literary activity, he found time to serve as secretary for the Hartford

Anti-Slavery Society (1792) and as a member of the town's Common Council (1792-1793).

In 1790, Webster tried an experiment in orthography. Still enamored of Franklin's design to alter American spelling, he published a collection of his essays in which he attempted, in selected ones, to offer the public a new way of spelling, a way that he considered more consistent with pronunciation. An explanation of the changes and an example of how he changed the spelling occurred in the introduction to his *Collection of Essays and Fugitiv Writings*:

> The reeder wil obzerv that the orthography of the volum iz not uniform. The reezon iz, that many of the essays hav been published before, in the common orthography, and it would hav been a laborious task to copy the whole, for the sake of changing the spelling.
>
> In the essays, ritten within the last yeer, a considerable change of spelling iz introduced by way of experiment. This liberty waz taken by the writers before the age of queen Elizabeth, and to this we are indeted for the preference of modern spelling over that of Gower and Chaucer. The man who admits that the change of *housbonde, mynde, ygone, moneth* into *husband, mind, gone, month*, iz an improovment, must acknowlege also the riting of *helth, breth, rong, tung, munth*, to be an improovment. There is no alternativ. Every possible reezon that could ever be offered for altering the spelling of wurds, stil exists in full force; and if a gradual reform should not be made in our language, it wil proov that we are less under the influence of reezon than our ancestors.[45]

"No alternativ," Webster decreed. Yet the public found an alternative; the book proved to be another financial failure. Ezra Stiles's comment proved prophetic: "You will make a thoro' Experiment upon the public, to what Extent a change in the Orthography of our Language can be carried. I suspect you have put in the pruning Knife too freely for general Acceptance."[46]

After this grand experiment, Webster refrained from the promulgation of drastic changes, but he continued to advocate reform and was successful in making some of his spelling changes permanent: the elimination of "k" from words such as musick and publick, the change from "s" to "c" in words such as practise (practice), and from "s" to "z" in words such as organise (organize) are prime examples of Websterian innovations that have become standard orthography.

After the failures of *The American Magazine, Dissertations on the English Language*, and *A Collection of Essays and Fugitiv Writings*, it might have been easy for Webster to give up his publishing dreams and rest on the laurels heaped upon him for his Speller. Yet he tried again, this time anonymously, with a small book titled *The Prompter*, with the subtitle *A Commentary on Common Sayings and Subjects, which are Full of Common Sense, the Best Sense in the World*. The book (which was a collection of short pieces Webster had sent to various newspapers in 1790 and 1791) consisted of witty homilies designed to poke fun at human foibles, while at the same time providing moral lessons for life. As Webster stated in his "Memoir," "These pieces were anonymous, & for a long period the author was not known to the public, nor even to his family friends. They were written in the familiar style of Dr. Franklin's Poor Richard, & were so popular, that they were republished in many newspapers in the United States, & finally a copy was published in England."[47] Editions of *The Prompter* continued to be published until 1849. It flourished probably because it was so unlike a typical Webster publication—witty rather than sarcastic, light instead of heavy. Yet it achieved the same educational goal Webster sought in his other essays—to provide moral instruction through a literary medium. One example is a selection called "The Fidgets," in which Webster lampooned a certain character trait:

> When a man or woman is very restless, and has many oddities, he or she is said to *fidget*. . . . Simple fidgets, in the first stage, is like a slow fever—it is not violent, but sticks fast to the patient. When the disorder rises to what is vulgarly called the *tantrums*, it then resembles the fever and ague. But in the last stages, when it arises to what is called *blue devils*, it is like an inflammatory or malignant fever. When the violence of

the disorder abates, it often becomes of the putrid kind, and the patient is intolerable. . . .

But of all the fidgets which have fallen under my observation, the most laughable is the *purse fidgets*. . . . The lawyer when he has this disorder cries-adjournment-continuance-false verdict-my client is wronged—I'll have a new trial. . . . The pious parson has the offer of a parish with a salary of one hundred pounds a year—he doubts whether he has a call from heaven—he protracts—he has another offer of one hundred and thirty pounds—his doubts are removed—he sees clearly he has a *call*. Now what is all this but the *purse fidgets*.[48]

Another piece, "He is Sowing His Wild Oats," contained this comment: "It is expected of a young man that he will sow *all* his wild oats, when young; but the mischief is, that a man who begins life with sowing *wild* oats, seldom sows a better kind, in middle life or old age."[49] This was classic Common Sense teaching on the effects of habit. And to those who would say that "reformed rakes make the best husbands," Webster observed, "Upon the honor of the Prompter, it may be so; but such an animal as a *reformed rake*, is as rare as camels or lions in America. . . . The creature is like *patriotism*, much talked about and often praised; but never seen."[50] With *The Prompter*, Webster broke new ground—for him—in that he became a popular writer once his authorship was known.

Webster's period as a Hartford lawyer also saw him actively engaged against the slave trade, for the abolition of slavery itself, and also for improving the condition of free blacks. He was short on money, but he arranged to have a certain percentage of the sales of some of his books donated to the Pennsylvania Society for the Abolition of Slavery.

He also became a spokesman for the extirpation of slavery. "In May 1792," Webster later recalled, "the society for the promotion of freedom appointed NW to deliver the annual oration before the society in May 1793. He took that occasion to write a short treatise on the subject of slavery."[51] This treatise was published under the name *Effects of Slavery, on Morals and Industry*, a title that clearly revealed his concern for the moral condition not only of the black slave, but of the white master as well. Although Webster preferred to take the high moral ground and label slavery as an unconscionable evil that should be abolished on recognition of its vileness, he knew that sermonizing might not have the desired effect. So he took a somewhat different tack and tried to show how slavery actually would hurt the slaveholder's self-interest. The focus on self-interest was another manifestation of faculty psychology's enunciation of the rational faculties of man, in its attempt to fix the mind on long-term interests (regard to good on the whole) rather than on the selfishness of a short-term perspective.

Webster first examined the effects of slavery on the character of the slaves themselves. He concluded that blacks were not naturally inferior to whites, but that the condition in which they were trapped had given rise to the worst side of human nature. "Whenever . . . men are stripped of the power of exerting themselves for their own benefit," he lectured, "the mind, having lost its spring or stimulus, either ceases to act, and men become mere machines, moving only when impelled by some extraneous power; or if the mind acts at all, it is at the impulse of violent passions, struggling to throw off an unnatural restraint, and to revenge the injury." There are certain natural consequences: "Hence it is, that slaves, with few exceptions, may be divided into two classes, the *indolent* and the *villanous*."[52] Furthermore, Webster added, slavery tends to make its subjects "*cruel, deceitful, perfidious*, and *knavish*; in short, to deprive them of all the noble and amiable affections of the human heart."[53]

But slavery also adversely affects the morals of slavemasters. "It is a general truth that the men who, from their infancy *hold*, and those who *feel*, the rod of tyranny, become equally hardened by the exercise of cruelty, and equally insensible to the sufferings of their fellow men," Webster cautioned. "Such is the nature and tendency of despotism, that in its operation, it not only checks the progress of civilization, but actually converts the civilized man into a savage; at least so far as respects the humane affections of the heart."[54]

When individual morals and feelings are so debased and hardened, society at large suffers. This was still another reason why Webster was so opposed to slavery—it would stifle a nation's productivity and creativity:

But in no particular are the deplorable effects of slavery more visible, than in checking, or destroying national industry. Wherever we turn our eyes to view the comparative effects of freedom and slavery on agriculture, arts, commerce and science, the mind is deeply affected at the astonishing contrast. . . .

To labor solely for the benefit of other men, is repugnant to every principle of the human heart. Men will not be industrious, nor is it the will of heaven that they should be, without a well founded expectation of enjoying the fruits of their labor.[55]

The America Webster envisioned, the one he had worked so hard to foster through the publication of textbooks and essays on a multitude of issues, was heading toward an early decline because of its attachment to a system that sapped its character and energy. Slavery had to be checked and somehow ended, but what means would be best? A total sudden abolition, he felt, would leave an impoverished South, hardly a blueprint for prosperity. Colonization, although it might help, was probably impractical. His solution: "raise the slaves, by gradual means, to the condition of free tenants."[56] And, as in many of his treatises, Webster concluded on a ringing note:

Let our efforts then be united to devise the most easy and effectual mode of gradually abolishing slavery in this country. The industry, the commerce and the moral character of the United States will be immensely benefited by the change—Justice and humanity require it—Christianity *commands* it. Let every benevolent heart rejoice at the progress already made in restraining the nefarious business of enslaving men, and pray for the glorious period when the last slave who sighs for freedom shall be restored to the possession of that inestimable right.[57]

Webster needed causes that could involve and absorb his energy and emotions. His crusades in the first years of his married life were an avocation in which he was engaged whenever his obligations as a lawyer did not interfere. Law was not satisfying to him; not only did it not prove as financially rewarding as he had hoped, but it kept him away from the real desires of his heart. A glimpse of Webster's state of mind after nearly two and a half years' residence in Hartford is afforded in a letter from James Greenleaf:

> I am sorry to observe in your last something that borders on a depression of spirits, I hope not a discouragement—if you are not so rich as you wish to be or even as you are conscious of deserving, You have on the other hand such domestic happiness as falls to the lot of but few—look round you & see how many would barter wealth for quiet & contentment; & then reflect, if you can with justice accuse providence of partiality.
>
> Circumstances be assured my dear Brother will not long be wanting for bringing you forward into the walk of life you deem best calculated for you. . . .
>
> Patience, my dear Webster, patience, and believe me all will one day come right.[58]

Greenleaf's prophecy proved accurate. By late 1793, Noah Webster would leave the law behind and once again be engaged in writing and publishing on a full-time basis. This time he would be a newspaper editor. But it took an event on the other side of the Atlantic to bring it to pass.

---

[1] Webster, "Memoir," 19.

[2] "Introduction," *American Magazine*, December 1787, 3.

[3] Warfel, *Noah Webster*, 173.

[4] Webster, "On the Education of Youth in America," *American Magazine*, December 1787, 22.

[5] Reid, "Active Powers," 2: 595.

[6] Webster, "Education of Youth," *American Magazine*, March 1788, 215.

[7] Webster, "Education of Youth," *American Magazine*, December 1787, 23.

[8] Reid, "Active Powers," 2: 577.

[9] Webster, "Education of Youth," *American Magazine*, February 1788, 158.

[10] Ibid., 159.

[11] Webster, "Education of Youth," *American Magazine*, March 1788, 210.

[12] Reid, "Active Powers," 2: 550.

[13] Webster, "Education of Youth," *American Magazine*, March 1788, 212.

[14] Ibid., 213-14.

[15] Ibid., 214.

[16] Ibid., 215.

[17] Reid, "Active Powers," 2: 595.

[18] Webster, "Education of Youth," *American Magazine*, March 1788, 215.

[19] Webster, *1828 Dictionary*.

[20] Reid, "Active Powers," 2: 540.

[21] Webster, "Education of Youth," *American Magazine*, December 1787, 23.

[22] Webster, "Education of Youth, *American Magazine*, January 1788, 80-81.

[23] Ibid., 82.

[24] Reid said, "Active Powers," 2: 527:

> "Every thing laudable and praiseworthy in man, must consist in the proper exercise of that power which is given him by his Maker. This is the talent which he is required to occupy, and of which he must give an account to Him who committed it to his trust.
>
> "To some persons more power is given than to others; and to the same person, more at one time and less at another. Its existence, its extent, and its continuance, depend solely upon the pleasure of the Almighty."

[25] Webster, "Education of Youth," *American Magazine*, March 1788, 216.

[26] Webster, "Education of Youth," *American Magazine*, May 1788, 374.

[27] Webster, "Principles of Government and Commerce," *American Magazine*, December 1787, 10: "But the opinions of the people should, if possible, be collected; for the general sense of a nation is commonly right."

[28] Ibid., 11.

[29] Reid, "Active Powers," 2: 587.

[30] Ibid., 2: 666.

[31] Webster, "On Government," *American Magazine*, January 1788, 75.

[32] Ibid., 78.

[33] Webster, "On Government," March 1788, 207-08.

[34] Ibid., 2: 593.

[35] Webster, "Education Letter II," *American Magazine*, January 1788, 86.

[36] Webster, "Education Letter III," *American Magazine*, February 1788, 161.

[37] Webster, "The Art of Pushing into Business and Making Way in the World," *American Magazine*, January 1788, 103.

[38] Ibid., 105.

[39] Webster to Benjamin Rush, 10 February 1788, in Ford, 1: 176-77.

[40] Webster diary, 16 October 1788, in Ford, 1: 236.

[41] Webster to James Greenleaf, 15 February 1789, Webster Papers, NYPL, Box 1.

[42] Webster diary, 26 October 1789, in Ford, 1: 246.

[43] Webster, "Memoir," 20.

[44] Ford, 1: 281n.

[45] Webster, *A Collection of Essays and Fugitiv Writings, on Moral, Historical, Political and Literary Subjects* (Boston: Thomas and Andrews, 1790), x-xi.

[46] Ezra Stiles to Webster, 27 August 1790, Webster Papers, NYPL, Box 2.

[47] Webster, "Memoir," 22.

[48] Webster, *The Prompter; or A Commentary on Common Sayings and Subjects, which are Full of Common Sense, the Best Sense in the World* (Hartford: Hudson and Goodwin, 1791), 14-15.

[49] Ibid., 75.

[50] Ibid., 76.

[51] Webster, "Memoir," 25.

[52] Webster, *The Effects of Slavery, on Morals and Industry* (Hartford: Hudson and Goodwin, 1793), 6.

[53] Ibid., 8.

[54] Ibid., 18.

[55] Ibid., 22.

[56] Ibid., 37.

[57] Ibid., 48.

[58] James Greenleaf to Webster, 18 January 1792, Webster Papers, NYPL, Box 2.

CHAPTER 5

Defender of the Federal Republic

A merica owed a disproportionate amount of its political and social turmoil during its first decade under the Constitution to a single event in Europe—the French Revolution. It would be reductionist to lay all the blame for problems in the 1790s at the feet of that one cataclysmic episode, but nearly every American political controversy during that period, with many moral and intellectual ramifications, can be traced to the impact of the French upheaval on American politics. Certainly Noah Webster's new career as a journalist and newspaper editor was directly affected.

Although the Revolution began in a reformist impulse, it soon became a powerful movement that attempted to alter every facet of French society by force. There was an impulse and severity to some aspects of it that cannot be explained away as simply the result of an impetuous French national character.[1] According to Robert R. Palmer, noted historian of the Revolution, by October 1789, in the first stirrings of reform, many of the patriots who had signed the Oath of the Tennis Court already were becoming alarmed at the descent of the Revolution into mob rule.[2] French historian Pierre Gaxotte spares no criticism of the Reign of Terror, that period in 1793-1794 when the guillotine worked overtime. He finds it inexcusable to downplay the actions of the Jacobin party as "regrettable excesses" of "legitimate reprisals." He contends the Terror was the "essence" of the Revolution because the revolutionaries were not just changing a system of government, but the entire social fabric of the nation.[3]

Crane Brinton's excellent investigation of the Jacobins reveals that intellectual ideas provided the motivating force behind that party. But they were ideas with a theological base. The Jacobins considered themselves a small band of the elect, and even used terms such as grace, sin, heresy, repentance, and regeneration. Paris was the New Jerusalem and the elect were determined to rule their heaven on earth. Since disagreement is impossible in heaven, those who refused to be converted to the true faith had to be removed. Thus the Terror.[4]

The Jacobin faith, which was an influence on the Revolution from the beginning, could not countenance any rival faith. The Roman Catholic Church had to compromise and submit to the new order. When nearly one-half of the Catholic clergy refused to subscribe to a 1790 oath that they felt contravened their first loyalty to the Pope, the Church no longer was a useful tool in the Jacobin cause and the government embarked upon a policy of dechristianization. At first, Reason became the object of veneration; later, the Jacobin leader, Robespierre, backed away from complete atheism, and instituted the worship of a vague Supreme Being. But both were policies that excluded Christian faith and the attacks upon Christianity combined with the hatred of aristocrats to form the driving force of the Reign of Terror.

It took a few years before Americans could sort all their feelings and thoughts concerning the new Revolution. The United States barely had time to get its new government into operation before the Revolution in France commenced. In the flush of excitement over the prospect of another republican nation, Americans were almost universally enthusiastic over events in France. Only in widely isolated cases could a voice of distrust or criticism be heard. With the overthrow of the monarchy and the proclamation of the French Republic in late 1792, external displays of pro-French sentiment became commonplace. Citywide celebrations took place in Baltimore, Boston, and New York in December. The arrival of the French minister, Edmund Charles Genet, early in 1793, touched off a new round of celebrations in every city he entered on his way to Philadelphia, and 14 July, the anniversary of the overthrow of the Bastille, became an American holiday similar to Independence Day. Americans also adopted French phrases, songs, dances, cockades, and clubs. Americans imitated everything French.

But this unanimity of praise for the Revolution was shaken by the execution of King Louis XVI in early 1793. This execution, in conjunction with the war that erupted between France and other European countries, cooled the ardor of many Americans and raised to respectability those few distant voices that previously had sounded alarms. Two fledgling political parties—the Federalists and the Republicans—developed differences of opinion over the Revolution. Those who eventually lined up as either Federalist or Republican had had their differences over domestic issues before the Revolution became a dominant topic, but the parties' position on France became a primary dividing line between them. It certainly provided the catalyst for a hardening of views that spread from one's attitude toward France to nearly every other policy of the government, foreign or domestic.

The emergent Federalist Party was the main critic of the Revolution. Federalists expressed concern over the apparent excesses of French democracy and the leveling spirit that threatened to destroy established social and cultural institutions such as the local congregational church in New England communities, the hub around which social and cultural activities revolved. Republicans, meanwhile, suspected that Federalist criticisms of the French masked monarchical preferences. Republican fears of a loss of liberty virtually blinded them to the French drive for empire and to the subversion of liberty in the French Republic itself. Jefferson, for example, as leader of the Republicans, rather than admitting France had committed grievous errors, chose instead to believe that a Federalist conspiracy devised by Alexander Hamilton and the British somehow was stirring up anti-French sentiment.[5]

During the 1790s, many of Jefferson's views about France were mirrored in the newly created Democratic-Republican societies. As several of the constitutions of these voluntary societies indicate, their purposes were threefold: 1) to maintain a vigilant watch over the actions of governmental officers; 2) to educate the American public in proper political values; and 3) to build a unified front of opposition to the policies of the Washington administration, both domestic and foreign. The societies were ardently pro-French; the strength or weakness of one's celebration of its Revolution tested the integrity of one's republicanism. Victory for the armies of

France was considered essential for the ultimate victory of republicanism in America and elsewhere.[6]

Forty-two of these societies can be documented, thirty-five of which were initiated in 1793-1794. The anticlericalism of many of their members led to charges of atheism, particularly by the Federalist clergy.[7] Their forthright attacks on ceremonial titles used in official functions, and even such innocuous ones as "sir," "Mr.," and "Rev.," provided sufficient proof to Federalists that their ultimate goal was to level the social rankings of American society.[8] Politically, their criticisms of the Washington administration touched nearly every policy decision. Most of these societies expired in the mid-1790s, after the severe blow of Washington's public disapproval, but their members and many of their ideas found a home in the Republican Party.[9]

The Republicans had preempted the name by which all Americans wished to be known. This aided their cause in the battle for men's party allegiances. Yet the Federalists were just as republican in their commitment. Two different brands of republicanism developed, the one fearing elected officials' abuse of power, the other more concerned with a popular tendency toward extreme democracy, or mobocracy. Rhetoric and tempers flared, and the newspaper became the primary vehicle for rhetorical attack. Men once united in the Revolutionary struggle now called each other traitors. As one scholar of early American affairs notes, "By the middle of the decade, American political life had reached the point where no genuine debate, no real dialogue was possible for there no longer existed the tolerance of differences which debate requires. Instead there had developed an emotional and psychological climate in which stereotypes stood in the place of reality."[10] Each side believed in the rightness of its cause, and each felt that it was the true defender of liberty and republican government. It was this tension-packed, conspiracy-conscious atmosphere that Noah Webster encountered as he once again entered the political fray as defender of the Federalist brand of republicanism.

Thoughts on France

Before attempting to describe Webster's years as a newspaper editor, it is useful to consider a pamphlet he wrote in the first three months of his editorship and published in 1794. *The Revolution in France* offers an excellent snapshot of Webster's views on the French Revolution one year after the execution of Louis XVI and the ascension of the Jacobins to political power.

The Revolution in France probably is the best expression of Webster's devotion to a moderate Common Sense Enlightenment philosophy. Throughout the treatise, he exalts man's rational capacities and man's ability to discipline passions that the Revolution had aroused. "Candid men," he felt, could find much to praise, as well as much to censure in the monumental events taking place across the ocean. He acknowledged that the Revolution's goal was noble, but questioned whether "the spirit of party and faction . . . will not deprive the present generation of the blessings of freedom and good government." He admitted that the onset of the Revolution had filled him with joy and that he had virtually the same hopes for its success as he did for the American Revolution. But the policies of the Jacobins, particularly their "atheistical attacks on christianity," had chilled his initial joy. He was willing to allow that circumstances unknown to him could "serve to palliate the apparent cruelty of the ruling faction," yet he felt that some of these actions could "admit of no excuse but a political insanity; a wild enthusiasm, violent and irregular, which magnifies a mole-hill into a mountain; and mistakes a shadow for a giant." With these concerns clearly enunciated, his preface concluded:

> It is of infinite consequence to this country, to ascertain the point where our admiration of the French measures should end, and our censures begin; the point, beyond which an introduction of their principles and practices to this country, will prove dangerous to government, religion and morals.[11]

Above all, Webster was interested in the effect of the Revolution on America, a nation untried in political controversy under the new Constitution. His concern was threefold: government, religion, and morals. The French people, he believed, were, by and large, ignorant of the principles of government. They were ripe for demagogues who could inflame their passions and enlist them in the cause of "liberty" without a proper explanation of the responsibilities that liberty entails. "As the most of them cannot read," he added, "particular persons were employed in the towns and villages to read to them, the inflammatory writings which flowed from the Parisian presses.[12] The French people first needed a higher degree of literacy to ensure that a truly free government could triumph. Webster was positive that this new literacy would be achieved. Renovated France would enjoy "universal freedom of writing" when the "present storm" subsided. Then the arts would receive "new encouragement, and the sciences new luster" from the genius emanating from that nation.[13]

His analysis then shifted to religion. He censured the French leaders for mandates that established "not deism only, but atheism and materialism." The promotion of death as everlasting sleep he castigated as "an explicit denial of the immortality of the soul." Webster then turned his verbal guns on the "Goddess reason," which he identified with "pride, obstinacy, bigotry, and to use a correct phrase, a blind superstitious enthusiasm."[14] What galled Webster most was that the same persecution of beliefs that characterized the medieval church now was being manifested and fostered in the name of progress and liberality. "The object may change," he commented, "but the imperious spirit of triumphant faction is always the same."[15]

The third problem was moral. A nation could not go through what France was experiencing and not be morally crippled. Even though the Revolution might have been necessary, and even though the goals might have been noble, "such great changes and a long war will have an effect on the moral character of the nation, which is deeply to be deplored." Webster believed all wars have "a demoralizing tendency," but the French Revolution, "in addition to the usual influence of war, is attended with a total change in the minds of the people. They are released, not only from the ordinary restraints of law, but from all their former habits of thinking," Webster warned. "The people are let loose in the wide field of mental licentiousness; and as men naturally run from one extreme to another, the French will probably rush into the wildest vagaries of opinion, both in their political and moral creeds."[16]

Yet no matter how awful Webster painted the picture, he could not abandon hope in the fledgling republic's future. Although "atheism and the most detestable principles" were the "fashion" of revolutionary France, he believed that once the pressure of external foes was removed and the nation could once again take stock of its situation, it would "feel the imbecility of its government" and "embrace a rational religion."[17] Those who were crediting France with the possession of a free government were "egregiously mistaken."[18] Webster ended his discussion of France's prospects with this statement:

> The conclusion of the whole business will be, that civil war and the blood of half a million of citizens, will compel the nation to renounce the idle theories of upstart philosophers, and return to the plain substantial maxims of wisdom and experience. Then, and not before, will France enjoy liberty.[19]

So much for France. What about America? The United States was Webster's main concern, and his pamphlet included a warning for all Americans. "The most important truth suggested by the foregoing remarks is, that party spirit is the source of faction and faction is death to the existing government." The founders had included a constitutional mode for amending the government, and there was no need to resort to "extraordinary expedients."[20] He was thinking of course of the Democratic-Republican Societies as he continued:

> In America therefore there can exist no necessity for private societies to watch over the government. Indeed to pretend that a government that has been in operation but five or six years, and which has hitherto produced nothing but public prosperity and private happiness, has need of associations in all parts of the country to guard its purity, is like a jealous husband who should deem it necessary, the day after his nuptials, to set a centinel over his wife to secure her fidelity.[21]

Besides, he added, France was trying to change from a monarchy to a republic, whereas America already had accomplished the change and had found much greater stability in the process.

Americans were too concerned over trifles such as titles given to those in positions of authority, Webster felt. Incipient aristocracy was not the principal threat in America, certainly not an aristocracy of birth over talent. There was a natural aristocracy, he argued, based upon personal influence, or moral character. "If my ideas of natural aristocracy are just," continued Webster, "the President of the United States is a most influential and most useful aristocrat: and long may America enjoy the blessings of such aristocracy."[22] The real issue, he contended, was how Americans handle themselves; irrational envy toward those in authority might overturn the peace and prosperity that the new government had brought. Webster, at this stage, did not believe that America was yet over the precipice, but he feared it conceivably could reach that point if certain French doctrines and practices were accepted. He embarked, therefore, on a mission to disseminate knowledge; he became a voice of moderation, of Common Sense, seeking to establish reason over violent passion. A newspaper editorship provided that opportunity.

The Crusading Editor

A good Federalist newspaper was sorely needed in New York City, supporters of the Washington administration agreed. Thomas Greenleaf's *New York Journal* gushed a steady stream of Republican criticism. Its doctrines needed to be countered with a knowledgeable, literate source of information that could propagate true Federalist teachings. The man who would shoulder this responsibility had to be an indefatigable worker, totally dedicated to the education of his countrymen. No better person could have been found than Noah Webster. James Watson, a partner of Webster's brother-in-law, James Greenleaf, first suggested to Alexander Hamilton and other Federalist leaders that Webster would be the perfect man for the job. Sometime in the late summer of 1793, Webster accepted an invitation to dine with John Jay, and an arrangement was worked out in which Hamilton, Jay, Rufus King, Greenleaf, and others loaned $150 each for the establishment of the paper. The contract was drawn in Hartford on 2 September. Webster contributed $100, which, combined with the loans, gave him two-thirds' interest in the project. He was to repay the money in five years, without interest, an indication of how seriously the other Federalist leaders took the enterprise.[23]

During his trip to New York to arrange the establishment of the paper, Webster had opportunity to attend a dinner at which the new French minister, Edmund Genet, also attended. Webster and Genet discussed the independence of America. Genet"s comments astounded Webster, as he later attested:

> The deponent representing to Mr. Genet that it would be impossible to subject the independent freemen of America to British or any other foreign power, and that the Executive officers of our national government knew the people too well to harbor a thought of effecting any such purpose, asked Mr. Genet whether he believed our Executive Officers, the President, Mr. Jefferson, Mr. Hamilton, and Gen. Knox to be fools; to which Mr. Genet replied, Mr. Jefferson is no fool![24]

The implication was obvious. For Webster, this episode served only to strengthen his concerns over the irresponsible conduct of the French government.

Although Webster was a strong Federalist, and his paper was underwritten with Federalist money, he still strove mightily to publish a paper that was forthright and honest, impartial toward all foreign countries, espousing primarily the maintenance of a free, independent America. As a supporter of Washington and his official proclamation of neutrality in the European war, Webster naturally received the approbation of fellow Federalists and the opprobrium of Republican politicians and scribes. But, as his main biographer notes, Webster did not promote a blind Federalism; rather, he attempted to offer a fair interpretation of events, translating accounts from French papers as well as from English sources.[25] He sent the paper overseas to prominent individuals such as German geographer Christopher Daniel Ebeling, who penned these words of praise to the editor: "Your instructive Gazette has a great mind by opposing reason to the Clubmen; others I find rather use declamation, which makes bad worse; for declamation is easily mixed with passions and passionate men are likely to go to the other extreme."[26] No more appropriate compliment could have been offered to the man who deemed himself the voice of Common Sense moderation.

Webster's predisposition for innovation soon made itself known in the newspaper business as it had in spelling. By June of 1794, he not only was publishing a daily paper but was taking excerpts from the daily and fashioning a semiweekly digest for the country areas. The semiweekly was known as *The Herald*. The daily began with the grandiose title, *The American Minerva*, "The Patroness of Peace, Commerce, and the Liberal Arts." Later, it became *The Commercial Advertiser*.

The first issue of *The American Minerva* appeared on 9 December 1793, about a month after Webster moved his family to New York. In his introductory remarks, the new editor promised to keep his paper "chaste and impartial" and declared his intention to disseminate knowledge because, as he saw it, "The foundation of all free governments, seems to be, a general diffusion of knowledge." Perfect governments were probably "beyond the powers of man to devise," he admitted, and constitutions, no matter how well crafted, were "not the ultimate security of the rights of men." But when a constitution rests on "the good sense of a well-informed people," he confidently asserted, "the breach" will "always be repaired."[27]

Webster affirmed his faith in the character of the American people when he declared Americans as best in the diffusion of knowledge, as evidenced by "that civility of manners, that love of peace and good order, and that propriety of public conduct, which characterize the substantial body of Citizens in the United States." He also expressed faith that the best-informed people would be the least subject to "faction, intrigue and a corrupt administration." And he appealed to his readers to recognize that government, if it is to be secure, had to rest not on the illusion of public virtue, or the transient effect of popular enthusiasm, but on permanent principles. "Fixed principles only," he admonished, "will maintain government of any kind."[28]

Webster remained active at the helm of the newspaper until mid-1798, approximately four and one-half years of constant attention to publication. He certainly needed all of his famed diligence and industry to keep on top of such an arduous task because he was running virtually a one-man operation. He did most of the writing, all of the translation work from European papers, and even the layout. It was a demanding assignment, to say the least. His brother-in-law, Thomas Dawes, put it aptly when he wrote in a light vein:

> By the way, how do you get thro' the cleaning all the Augaean stables in the manner you do?—translating, transcribing, composing (tho' the last I know you can do when asleep) correcting other peoples' blunders, answering other peoples absurdities, in short finding brains for people who, when theyve got them, dont know what to do with them? Mercy on me (or rather on you) how do you produce so many columns in a week, and so good ones? I dont believe you have kissed Beccy these six months. I am told your eyes begin already to look as if they would be shortly lined with red ferret. Well, drive on. "Youth is the time to serve the Lord."[29]

Drive on he did, day after day, churning out an amazing amount of commentary. The times being what they were, with the French Revolution polarizing American politics and society, Webster's subjects pretty much were provided for him. The major themes of his voluminous writing during this period reveal five major categories: 1) the French Revolution; 2) the aristocracy-equality question; 3) parties and factions; 4) American independence; and 5) American character.

The Revolution . . . Continued

Nearly every issue of the *Minerva* contained some comment on France, but certain essays and comments are representative of the editor's ongoing love/fear relationship with the Revolution. From the start, Webster reaffirmed a hope that the Revolution would succeed and urged his readers to realize that disapproval of Genet's conduct should not be misconstrued as enmity against France itself. "Almost every man who espoused the cause of America, in her struggle for independence," he wrote, "is now friendly to the revolution in France. It is a general wish in America that the revolution might be effected and a free Republican government be established."[30]

In October 1794, he attempted to analyze why the French Revolution was going wrong. He concluded that "most of the violences committed, and miseries suffered . . . have been occasioned by bad management," and that many errors might have been avoided if only the legislators had been "more governed by the maxims of experience, and less by their own passions, or visionary ideas of theoretical forms of government." Certain errors were discernible, the greatest of which was the introduction of a single-house legislature, which lacked the mechanisms to temper discussion and "restrain passions and precipitance."[31] A second mistake was the prohibition on members of the legislature succeeding themselves. This had removed the wisest, most experienced legislators and replaced them with inexperienced enthusiasts who were "intoxicated with the height of their station" and who ran wild in their "projects of Reformation." Had more stable men retained power, Webster surmised, the nation never would have resorted to "that desperate and most fatal expedient, the strength of clubs and irregular collections of people."[32]

Webster also spied an inconsistency in the rhetoric and practice of the French. Although "the rights of man" were on everyone's lips, the "actual exercise of all the powers of government" had been "in the hands of a few men." A distinct minority was running the country. "France," he believed, "has been a prey to a tyrannical few. The nation is not represented."[33] Abolition of a monarchy was not synonymous with the establishment of a Republic that could guarantee liberty. How could a nation as unrepresented as France possibly be free? One form of tyranny had replaced another. Worse still, the French were trying to spread the tyranny elsewhere.

In Webster's view, not only was France a political monster, but its grievous errors were being forced upon other nations. In a 1796 series of articles entitled "Political Fanaticism," he focused on the contradiction of a so-called republic forcing itself and its authority on other peoples. "Now, a new species of fanaticism has seized the French nation," Webster cried, "a zeal to make all the world republics—a zeal as wild and ridiculous as that of Peter the Hermit, to recover Jerusalem from infidels; or as that of the Catholics in France, in past ages, to exterminate Protestants."[34] It was one thing to defend one's nation against aggressors; it was quite another to become an aggressor oneself. "France is now the aggressor with respect to the house of Austria, and is fighting for conquest and dominion, not for defence."[35]

These musings soon brought Webster back to the central problem: the French were not educated, especially in the art of government. "The reason why severe laws are necessary in France, is, that the people have not been *educated* republicans—they do not know how to govern themselves." As a consequence, the French people "must be governed by severe laws and penalties, and a most rigid administration."[36] Men who cannot rule themselves require a ruler. The French demonstrate that maxim. Their lack of knowledge had produced a fanatical abuse of governmental power, as the case of Robespierre manifested: "He [Robespierre] really thought it was right to put to death all those who did not join heart and hand in his measures. . . . This was his crime or error, a fanaticism in the cause of republicanism."[37]

Again and again Webster returned to the thesis that the goal of the Revolution was right but its methods were wrong. In late 1796, he reiterated, "The principle of the revolution was a glorious one; and afforded to all good men substantial joy and satisfaction." But he continued,

> But when the work of reformation was usurped by faction; by irregular associations of men; and desperate bands of lawless ruffians, no apology can be made for their proceedings. In such hands, the revolution itself becomes an evil, and produces tenfold more abuses than the ancient despotism.[38]

The deplorable French scheme dedicated to "unhinging all settled principles, annihilating all ancient habits and customs, subverting all old institutions, and introducing all universal revolt and insubordination" was its downfall.[39] And the most galling aspect of this disintegration was that it desecrated republicanism. Thus, it was Webster's commitment to republicanism that animated his principal objection to the turn of events in France. "We have been free in censuring some of the proceedings of the French, in the progress of their conquests, not from any particular enmity to that nation, but because it is our sincere belief that the French abandon their own principles—Not because we are enemies to republicanism, but because we are persuaded the French are taking direct steps to render republicanism odious, and retard its progress in the world."[40]

Far from condemning the Revolution wholesale, Webster went to great lengths, even as late as 1797, to applaud all hopeful signs of change. He reported in June that France "has been curing herself of the folly, the baseness and the iniquity of the revolutionizing projects of her first Jacobinical Government, and of the danger of putting arms and power into the hands of unprincipled and unautho-rized men." He believed the nation "has learnt the wickedness of her resolution to carry sedition into neighboring countries, under pretext of giving them freedom, and the dreadful effects of commit-ting peace, property and personal safety to the wild fanaticism of popular societies."[41] He even accepted that France had assaulted American maritime commerce more out of hostility to Great Britain than to America. "Of the truth of this sentiment," he judged, "we believe little doubt can be entertained."[42]

Why did he give so much space and attention to the French Revolution in his newspaper, Webster was asked in late 1797? His answer was simple and direct. "The revolution," he responded,

> is so novel in principle and pregnant with so many impor-tant changes in the political aspect of nations, and in the moral habits of mankind, that all the ordinary occurrences in the world are absorbed and lost in the magnitude of events produced . . . by that revolution.[43]

Ultimately, Webster's concern was the possible adverse effect of the Revolution on American society and government. The ideas it spawned raised questions of profound significance for Americans. Was America to be ruled by a monarchical-leaning aristocracy? Did the proliferation of voluntary political societies pose a threat to the continuance of government? Could too close a relationship with another nation undermine American independence? Did Americans possess the moral character to maintain their republican institu-tions? Webster touched on all these issues.

Aristocracy and Equality

What is an aristocrat? The future lexicographer offered a satirical definition—one that he felt had become too much accepted during the furor over the Revolution. "One man," he suggested, "thinks the government of the United States vests too much power in particular officers; this man of course is a *republican*. Another," he continued, "thinks it has scarcely energy enough to preserve the union and secure the rights of a nation; this man of course is dubbed an *aristocrat*."[44] Another satire brought unexpected results. In February 1794, a letter to the editor written by Webster himself and signed "Democrat," pretended horror at the danger posed to liberty and equality because New York still had streets named "King, Queen, Princess, and Duke." Much to Webster's amazement and chagrin, this satire produced a change of those street names in the city. From the vantage point of nearly two centuries later, it seems incredible that Webster's fabricated letter could have been taken as sincere. Yet it does add credence to his contention that America was becoming obsessed with trifles such as official titles of distinction, and it reveals much about the political atmosphere of the era.[45]

Webster sought to lay the charge of aristocracy where he felt it actually belonged, not on New England (where most Republican critics placed it), but on the South, where a true aristocracy based on slavery, class distinctions, and Sunday amusements existed.[46] This Southern slaveowner aristocracy, Webster held, was aristocracy at its worst because it was based on artificial distinctions and accidents of birth. There were natural distinctions among men that should be recognized and that were quite different from the unnatural distinctions in the South. In Connecticut, contended Webster, the system of government controlled by a few families might be called aristocratic by Jacobin-minded critics but, he argued, "I care not what it is called—for it is the influence of God and nature, cherished by education, preserved by the laws, and a main pillar of public tranquility and happiness."[47] In other words, it was a *natural* aristocracy of ability and good upbringing that was undeniably beneficial for everyone. For Webster, this "aristocracy" was not incompatible with republican government, since men of ability and education naturally would be chosen to serve as the people's representatives.

Yet Webster knew that terminology carries emotional impact. "The term aristocracy," he acknowledged, "is a name that incurs odium; it answers its purpose, of exposing any man that the demagogue of the day wishes to get rid of, to popular resentment and fury." History, he said, "will hereafter recount numberless instances of men, who have fallen a sacrifice to that single word, fixed upon them by a jealous rival, without committing the least crime against their country."[48] In any war of terminology and definitions, Webster could more than hold his own. Every effort of the *Minerva* was aimed at the education of its readers and proceeded on the belief that reason would, in the end, triumph.

Parties and Factions

Webster's view of political parties, or "factions," was a view shared by most public men of his day, Federalist and Republican alike. A man of "party spirit" was unprincipled, unconcerned with truth, and primarily attentive to his own interests at the expense of others. For Webster, the Republicans and their allies, in particular the Democratic-Republican Societies, were dangerous sources of party spirit because they refused to support a duly elected administration. For them, the party was all-important. On the evil effect of party spirit, Webster affirmed that "dissatisfaction arising from *things*, is afterwards transferred to *persons*; and when a new question arises, men do not examine it impartially, and espouse or reject it according to its merits; but they enquire on which side the leaders of *their party* have enlisted, and take the same side."[49]

The real problem is that a party stifles impartial reasoning and makes personal attachments more important. Truth and good policy suffer. And if anyone opposes a party position, even from good principles, he is ostracized because he does not go along with the group. Popular opinion thus intimidates anyone who thinks differently from the crowd. This was why Webster feared the influence of Democratic-Republican Societies: they decried the actions of the Washington administration as if they lived "under the dominions of a pope, a Spanish inquisition, or the dey of Algiers" rather than a freely elected constitutional government. Then they exerted their own brand of tyranny in an attempt "to frighten their opposers, and control their opinions." Every threat of this kind, warned Webster, was "an act of tyranny; an attempt to abridge the rights of a fellow citizen."[50] In another essay, he continued the thought by remarking that whenever freedom of opinion is opposed—whether from a

French king or a mob in America—it has to be considered "an outrage on the liberties of others. It is an attempt to subdue opinions, the right of which is sacred and inviolable."[51]

American Independence

Another issue just as sacred to Webster was the maintenance of an independent America. As a young textbook writer, he had sought to help establish American independence in literature; now as a newspaper editor, he disseminated information designed to keep America politically independent. The Federalists of the 1790s, although distressed by the events in France, did not display abject servility to Great Britain. Emotional ties still existed, but a politically strong and independent America was their goal. Webster himself would have been one of the last Federalists to subordinate the United States government to British policies. American independence remained his fixed objective.

In one of his first *Minerva* essays, addressed to the French minister Genet, Webster sounded an American independence theme that was to be repeated countless times in the next four and a half years. Genet had served America well, Webster wrote, if only because his "rash intemperate measures" had "taught us the danger of *all* foreign influence and the necessity of guarding against its mischievous effects. . . . Never will the brave freemen of our Republic permit the secret influence or open forces of a foreign nation to dictate to them what measures to pursue, or what men to employ in public stations."[52] Nearly three years later, while defending his editorship, Webster reminded his reading public that the goal of his instruction always had been the permanent independence of the American nation. He wrote, "I have cautioned my fellow-citizens against all foreign intrigues because I was aware of the fatal dissensions they would introduce into our councils, and because I hold it proper for us to attach ourselves to no foreign nation whatever, but to respect ourselves, and be in spirit and truth, Americans."[53]

On other occasions, Webster spelled out even more clearly that American independence meant neither Britain nor France were to be given special status. "We are not to be governed by prejudice," he counseled *Minerva* readers in late 1796. This meant Americans were not to "reject any thing good, because it is British, nor are we to copy any thing, merely because it is French. Thank God, our Constitution is neither English or French, and neither aristocrat or Jacobin."[54] Even more forcefully, just over a week later, Webster announced to the new French minister, "I'll tell you citizen, there is still living a great number of revolutionary whigs, who spurned the insolence of British power, even when immense fleets and armies were in our harbors to back their menaces." He gave notice that these men would "again spurn the shackles prepared for them, by a smiling, fawning, cringing, race of hypocritical foreigners. Nor will their sons disgrace the manly heroism of their fathers. Be assured citizen, neither British force nor French cunning, will subdue the Americans to the views of either nation."[55]

And for William Cobbett, the English immigrant and editor-publisher of [Peter] *Porcupine's Gazette*, Webster had similar words: "The success of Peter's pen, in attacking the democratic factions of our country, has perfectly intoxicated him; and he mistakes the sense of America extremely, when he supposes the danger we have escaped of being prostrated at the feet of France, will urge us to lay our Country at the feet of Great Britain."[56] So Cobbett would not misunderstand, Webster instructed him further:

> Such, Peter, is my political creed—I know no party, but that of MY COUNTRY. My country is INDEPENDENT; it is for *our* interest, the interest of Great Britain, and of all Europe, that it should be so; and the man who seeks to tack it on to any foreign country, to involve it in European broils or make its independence the sport of European policy, is conceived to be an ENEMY.[57]

It would be difficult to imagine a stronger statement of political independence. Webster's 1797 declaration of independence was just as vehement as any he pronounced in 1793. More than three years of warning against the philosophy and practices of the French Revolution did not make him any more desirous of closer relations with Great Britain. American independence remained his watchword.

American Character
The key to maintaining American independence was the charac-

ter of the American people. Would they be duped by foreign stratagems and cleverness? Would they surrender American interest on the altar of selfishness and corruption? How far could the common people be trusted? Did Webster's perception of American character darken during his tenure as *Minerva* editor?

Webster pursued the issue of American character in the address to Genet mentioned previously. He was hard pressed to find words glowing enough to describe the vast majority of Americans, especially those removed from the intrigues of large towns and cities. Genet, said Webster, was a stranger to nine-tenths of intelligent American citizens. If he had spent time informing himself of their true nature, he would have discovered a people "enlightened, informed, acquainted with books, and all the current political maxims of the present age." In addition, he would have found Americans "judicious, cautious, discerning . . . a people who know their rights, and will neither suffer you or any other man to invade them."[58] Yet a scant five months later, the scene of American citizens rushing to view a guillotine puzzled Webster. He questioned "why civilized man delights to hear of blood and slaughter, and to see even the instrument of the horrid business?" Waxing philosophical, he inquired further, "what is man, this noblest work of God, when honest; but inflamed by passion, what is he but a beast of prey? . . .   One part of men are forging instruments to flay another part," he sighed, "and a third, more fortunate people, amuse themselves with staring at the horrid spectacle."[59]

The publication of Thomas Paine's *Age of Reason* provided another point of concern for Webster. Paine's bold assertion of deism and his attack on revealed religion did not mesh with Webster's Common Sense philosophy. Paine's "reason" seemed to be of an entirely different nature. If anything could have awakened the Puritanism in Webster's personality, the *Age of Reason* was it. "Mr. Paine is not an old man," mused the editor, "but his faculties are evidently impaired, or he could never have called his book the "Age of Reason."

> Such is the last production of a writer who began his literary career with common sense. Whether this book is destined to overthrow the system of christianity in

America, . . . we shall not predict. Certain it is, that the tendency of such books, which are industriously circulated by certain democrats, is to level Jesus Christ, as well as the monarchies of the earth. We trust that the body of people in America have too much good sense to be deceived, and that they will not exchange good laws, freedom and a pure religion, for the principles of anarchy, and infidelity.[60]

Although he said he would not predict whether the book would overthrow Christianity in America, in fact, Webster relied on the basic "good sense" of the American people and their distaste for anarchic, society-destroying principles. This confidence in the people's good sense remained throughout 1794.

Cracks appeared, however, in 1795. In a letter to his regular correspondent, Oliver Wolcott, Jr., Webster prophesied an inevitable separation between the Northern and Southern states. He lamented, "Sorry I am that our predictions relative to the instable nature of republican governments are in too fair a way to fulfilment."[61] He also witnessed what he considered to be a temporary lapse of wisdom in the American people in their criticism of the Anglo-American Jay Treaty (1795). He lectured them: "Your passions have been taken by surprise; you have been precipitated into rash opinions, and violent measures, by a set of men who are the foes of our present free and happy government and its administration."[62] The opposition, Webster felt, was led by scoundrels and demagogues; their true nature had to be explained to the people, who still could be rallied to Common Sense-ical, self-evident truths. As he explained to Wolcott,

Depend on it, faction is busy, & the friends of government must be active and vigilant—they must lay aside that delicacy about characters which men of honor observe in ordinary cases—they must expose the *real characters, public & private,* of the leaders of opposition . . . . It is necessary to expose the private views of the leaders, by disclosing facts & anecdotes of their past lives which will clearly illustrate their selfish views. A great portion of the substantial people of the country stand neuter, as to the parties now prevailing. If their opinion is tested, it will ultimately decide for *truth*; but *facts* must be known & so must *characters*.[63]

Probably the most revealing letter about Webster's views on a variety of subjects during this time was written to the French author and scientist, C. F. Volney. Volney had sent a circular letter to *The Herald* asking for facts to help with a scientific study he was undertaking at that time.[64] Webster responded with information on Volney's questions, but also commented on matters that most occupied the editor's mind in 1796:

> I congratulate you, Sir, on the late important revolution in France; an event that will result in immense advantages to the French people; & which seems to be but a prelude to a general regeneration in Europe.
>
> My enthusiasm in favor of republicanism was as warm & animated, during the revolution in America, as that which has distinguished the French people. The *mad work* which factions make with free governments, both in Europe and America, much of which has fallen under my own observation, has somewhat abated the ardor of my enthusiasm. But I cannot withdraw my confidence from a republican form of gov't. I must believe this form, even with all its present evils, to be the only legitimate form of government; & I cannot but hope, that proper systems of education will diffuse so much light among the mass of people, as to place them more beyond the influence of ambitious men, who never cease to impose on their credulity. It is a Herculean task, even in the United States, to keep the *People* from committing *suicide*; that is, enlisting under bold factious men, & destroying their own government, under pretence of establishing liberty. Republican government has ever been, & I fear, always will be, a prey to faction. I still hope that the progress of reason will, from age to age, lessen the danger arising from their source.[65]

The letter contains almost every Websterian concern this study has undertaken to elucidate: anxiety over the French Revolution; promotion of republican government; the importance of education; and the necessity for moral character. Even in mid-1796, Webster was committed to the diffusion of knowledge as the best means for maintenance of the republic. The American people could be trusted *if* they had the correct information on which to base their decisions. But the growing problem was the rise of "factious men" who were attempting to lead the people astray. The ignorance of the masses, combined with the corruptness of power seekers, could ruin America's promising beginning.

Webster's message was not well received by Republican editors, and he soon became a prime target for their abuse. Even before he took on the editorship, he had not been totally naïve respecting possible attacks. In a response to one reader, he said, "I undertook the direction of it [*The Minerva*], with diffidence and reluctance; knowing the difficulty of gratifying readers of various tastes, and apprehensive that too much would be expected from the compilation. I find my apprehensions not ill founded."[66] He did not have to wait long for the opposition press to act. In 1794, he was accused by *The New York Journal* of concealing news favorable to France. Indignantly, Webster shot back, "The insinuation that I have concealed something from the public . . . is as base as the writer's heart. . . . I gave the public a literal translation of every sentence . . . contained in the two Paris papers I received." He then took the offensive with a pledge to honesty: "The printer of that paper and his partizans may call me by what names they please—nothing they can say will affect my reputation, for I stand on the high ground of integrity and the purest intentions. In my present employment," he continued, "I adhere strictly to this maxim, neither to conceal, nor misrepresent a single fact. When I am guilty of this, I expect to meet with the censure of all good men."[67]

Clearly, Webster did not consider himself guilty of the charge; neither did he consider his accusers "good men." But the *Journal* was not finished. A few months later, it implied that "some papers" (it did not take much imagination to guess which it meant) were trying to stir up anti-French feeling by forging atrocity stories. This accusation angered the *Minerva* editor even more than the previous charge and he responded, "We only declare that every syllable published in the Minerva respecting the bloody work of the Jacobins or others in France, is taken from Paris publications, many of them official—and not a fourth of the bloody stories there related, are transcribed into this paper. The charge against the Minerva is therefore FALSE."[68]

Another Republican paper that attacked all things Federalist was the Philadelphia *Aurora*, published and edited by Benjamin Franklin Bache, grandson of the recently deceased Benjamin Franklin, who had been Webster's friend. The *Aurora* charged Webster with heading the Federalist "faction" in the country, to which Webster almost good-humoredly replied,

> The Editor waves the honor here intended him. The President of the United States is the head of the faction, composed of the old whigs of the country, the friends of the present Republican constitution, and determined foes of Jacobin clubs. Under the President there are the Vice-President, the twenty senators, the heads of departments, and several hundred thousand individuals, who are firm supporters of the federal government. Among the number of private citizens of this faction is the Editor of the Minerva.[69]

And to a later *Aurora* charge that Webster was under British influence, the schoolmaster instructed Mr. Bache, "If there is a paper in the United States conducted independent of all influence of men, nations or parties, it is the Minerva."[70] Thus, in defense of his own integrity, Webster also was able to make what he hoped would be a telling point about his accuser.

Generally, Webster fielded all comers without losing his decorum. But the continual battle to educate the American people and fend off attacks from opposing papers did take its toll. It was difficult always to remain self-governed in the face of what were tantamount to deliberate lies. An exasperated Webster in mid-1797, for instance, vented his frustration in an editorial lambasting the character of the American people. "From the days of Adam, to this moment," he overstated, "no country was ever so infested with corrupt and wicked men, as the United States. . . . We see in our new Republic, the decrepitude of Vice; and a free government hastening to ruin, with a rapidity without example."[71] Less than a year before Webster stepped down as daily overseer of the paper, he tendered half an apology for allowing himself to give in to some of the pressures to act like his opposers. It was half an apology because he remained convinced that he gave the reading public the truth as best he could express it. He wrote:

> If the fault of personality has, in a few instances, been justly laid to our charge, it will be ascribed to its true motive: an honest wish to expose corruption. We shall however in future be more sparing of remarks on characters; it being sufficient for public purposes, and more honorable, to state facts fairly, and leave an intelligent people to make their own comments.
>
> But if *characters* are spared, *measures* will not escape severe animadversion. The honor, the interest, the prosperity of the American Empire will be defended and maintained, against the intrigues of designing men, as well as the assaults of hostile nations.[72]

Webster, in spite of attacks from other papers, a poor selection of partners to help print the paper, and the drain on his health (twice he suffered from illnesses that appeared life-threatening), had put together a publication that was read from Georgia to Montreal—respected by Federalists, panned by Republicans. Yet he was tired of carrying on the fight. Four and a half years of unremitting effort, and faith in the virtues and reason of the American public had seemingly brought little fruit. His relationships with Hamiltonian Federalists were strained because of his solid defense of the President in the party split between John Adams and Hamilton. He was disgusted with Republican and Federalist alike, and on 1 April 1798, he withdrew from active direction of both papers and took up residence in New Haven. He wrote to Timothy Pickering in July 1798, "When *aliens* (a reference to William Cobbett and his *Porcupine's Gazette*), assume such a tone and abuse honest faithful men, it is time for native citizens to retire and seek peace and quietness in more private occupations. I could raise a flame even now about the heads of the English," he asserted, "but it would be against the public interest. I therefore choose to retire, and be the victim of party rancor."[73]

In his place of retirement in New Haven, Connecticut, where he had once long ago started his quest for knowledge, Webster was asked to give the Fourth of July oration in 1798. He complied, and had the oration printed in full in the *Commercial Advertiser* (the *Minerva*, now renamed). As all July Fourth orations tend to be, it is flowery in spots and a little overextended, both in length and claims. Yet it reveals where Webster stood at the end of nearly five arduous years of journalistic enterprise. Although he wryly commented that "the noblest efforts of wisdom and genius, are liable continually to be defeated by blockheads," he nevertheless reaffirmed his confidence in the American experiment. Americans, he warned, have to withstand the pull of wrong political principles and moral vices. Despite the storms of the 1790s, Americans still were the best-informed people on the face of the earth. "In the general information of the body of citizens, and in mechanical ingenuity," he exulted, "the American character stands probably unrivalled—in every branch of science, it is highly respectable. No nation can boast of more industrious and enterprizing citizens."[74]

America remained a country "reserved by Heaven" where "religion, virtue and the arts may find a peaceful retirement from the tempests which agitate Europe." Economically, America was prospering and, Webster counseled, "the less the mind is restrained by the authority of laws, in regard to its exertions for personal benefit, the more vigor will be displayed." This is not the advice one might expect from a Federalist who felt his world was collapsing around him. Indeed, he basked in the "blessings of freedom" that America enjoys and fervently believed America still was destined to show Europe how to govern. Republican government remained his ideal. He only warned his hearers not to exchange "our civil and religious institutions for the wild theories of crazy projectors; or the sober, industrious and moral habits of our country, for experiments in atheism and lawless democracy. Experience is a safe pilot; but experiment is a dangerous ocean, full of rocks and shoals."[75]

Among those who read the Oration was Benjamin Rush. Rush

focused on what he deemed to be a flaw in Webster's proposed solutions for the maintenance of American prosperity:

> I have read your oration with great pleasure. But Alas! my friend, I fear all our attempts to produce political happiness by the solitary influence of human reason, will be as fruitless as the search for the philosopher's stone. It seems to be reserved to Christianity alone to produce universal, moral, political & physical happiness. Reason produces it is true, great & popular truths, but it affords *motives* too feeble to induce mankind to act agreeably to them. Christianity unfolds the same truths & accompanies them with *motives*, agreeable powerful & irresistible. I anticipate nothing but suffering to the human race while the present systems of paganism, deism & atheism prevail in the world. New England may escape the storm which impends our globe, but if she does, it will only be by adhering to the religious principles & moral habits of the first settlers of that country.[76]

A decade later, Webster would agree with Rush. Until then, he had to rediscover purpose and direction. This time he would find a vocation to last his entire life.

---

[1] James Thompson, "A French Tradition," in Frank A. Kafker & James A. Laux, eds., *The French Revolution: Conflicting Interpretations* (New York: Random House, 1968), 225-228, attempts to explain away the excesses of the Revolution in this manner.

[2] Robert R. Palmer, *The World of the French Revolution* (New York: Harper and Row, 1971), 67.

[3] Pierre Gaxotte, "The Desire to Communise," in Kafker & Laux, 263.

[4] Crane Brinton, *The Jacobins: An Essay in the New History* (1930; reprint ed., New York: Russell & Russell, 1961), 203-39.

[5] Lawrence S. Kaplan, *Jefferson and France* (New Haven: Yale University Press, 1967), 77.

[6] Eugene Perry Link, *Democratic-Republican Societies, 1790-1800* (New York: Columbia University Press, 1942), 8, 45, 125-29.

[7] Ibid., 114-21.

[8] Charles D. Hazen, *Contemporary American Opinion of the French Revolution* (Johns Hopkins Press, 1897; reprint ed., Gloucester, MA: Peter Smith, 1964), 213-17.

[9] Link, 206.

[10] John R. Howe, Jr., "Republican Thought and the Political Violence of the 1790s," *American Quarterly* 19:2, Pt. 1 (1967): 150.

[11] Webster, *The Revolution in France, Considered in Respect to its Progress and Effects* (New York: George Bunce & Co., 1794), preface.

[12] Ibid., 8.

[13] Ibid., 17.

[14] Ibid., 20-23.

[15] Ibid., 31.

[16] Ibid., 32-33.

[17] Ibid., 34-35.

[18] Ibid., 69.

[19] Ibid., 71.

[20] Ibid., 41-42.

[21] Ibid., 42.

[22] Ibid., 61.

[23] Warfel, *Noah Webster*, 223; Webster, "Memoir," 28; Gary R. Coll, "Noah Webster, Journalist, 1783-1803," (Ph.D. dissertation, University of Southern Illinois, 1971), 175-76.

[24] Ford, 1: 370; also found in Webster to Oliver Wolcott, Jr., 26 September 1793, in the Oliver Wolcott, Jr., Papers, Connecticut Historical Society (CHS), Hartford, CT.

[25] Warfel, *Noah Webster*, 224-25, states, "No other newspaper of the time recorded so fully America's striving toward complete independence nor suggested so many means of attaining it."

[26] Christopher Daniel Ebeling to Webster, 7 August 1795, Webster Papers, NYPL, Box 2.

[27] Webster, "The Editor's Address to the Public," *The American Minerva* (New York), 9 December 1793.

[28] Ibid.

[29] Thomas Dawes to Webster, 9 February 1795, Webster Papers, NYPL, Box 2.

[30] Webster, "A Candid Address to the Minister of the French Republic," *Minerva*, 26 December 1793.

[31] Webster, "Revolution in France," *Minerva*, 20 October 1794.

[32] Ibid., 28 October 1794.

[33] Ibid., 3 November 1794.

[34] Webster, "Political Fanaticism, No. I," *Minerva*, 10 September 1796.

[35] Webster, "Political Fanaticism, No. II," *Minerva*, 14 September 1796.

[36] Webster, "Political Fanaticism, No. III," *Minerva*, 21 September 1796.

[37] Webster, "Political Fanaticism, No. IV," *Minerva*, 28 September 1796.

[38] Editorial note in response to a letter questioning Webster's "inconsistencies" toward the French Revolution, *Minerva*, 31 October 1796.

[39] Webster, "To the People of the United States, No. XI," *Minerva*, 1 March 1797.

[40] Webster, editorial, *Minerva*, 24 October 1796.

[41] Webster, editorial, *Minerva*, 13 June 1797.

[42] Webster, editorial, *Minerva*, 27 June 1797.

[43] Webster, editorial, *Advertiser*, 6 December 1797.

[44] Webster, "A Freeman," *Minerva*, 11 December 1793.

[45] Webster, "Alarm! Alarm!" *Minerva*, 11 February 1794.

[46] Webster, "The Times, No. VI," *Minerva*, 16 April 1794.

[47] Webster, "Revolution in France," *Minerva*, 31 October 1794.

[48] Ibid., 4 November 1794.

[49] Webster, "A Freeman," *Minerva*, 11 December 1793.

[50] Webster, "The Times, No. X," *Minerva*, 30 April 1794.

[51] Webster, "The Times, No. XI," *Minerva*, 2 May 1794.

[52] Webster, "Candid Address," *Minerva*, 26 December 1793.
[53] Webster, "To the Public," *Minerva*, 2 May 1796.

[54] Webster, "The Times, No. XV," *Minerva*, 31 October 1796.

55 Webster, "The Times, No. XVI," *Minerva*, 8 November 1796.

56 Webster, editorial, *Minerva*, 21 March 1797.

57 Ibid.

58 Webster, "Candid Address," *Minerva*, 26 December 1793.

59 Webster, "The Times, No. III," *Minerva*, 10 April 1794.

60 Webster, editorial, *Minerva*, 4 August 1794.

61 Webster to Oliver Wolcott, Jr., 30 July 1795, Wolcott Papers, CHS.

62 Webster, "Vindication of the Treaty, No. XII," *Minerva*, 5 August 1795.

63 Webster to Oliver Wolcott, Jr., 1 November 1795, Wolcott Papers, CHS.

64 Ford, 1: 406.

65 Webster to C.F. Volney, 10 July 1796, Webster Papers, NYPL, Box 1. Rollins, 79, says, "After 1794, he [Webster] would never again agitate for an extension of man's freedom or for his right to make decisions for himself." Judging by Webster's letter to Volney, Rollins seems to have made a rather hyperbolic statement. While it is true that Webster was debating the merits of the people's decisionmaking capabilities, he still was, two years after Rollins's fixed date, a true believer in republicanism. In fact, as the rest of this study will demonstrate, Webster remained a republican all his life.

66 Webster, "The Editor of the *Minerva* to Justitius," *Minerva*, 26 February 1794.

67 Webster, "To the Public," *Minerva*, 29 November 1794.

68 Webster, editorial, *Minerva*, 18 February 1795.

69 Ibid., 6 August 1795.

70 Ibid., 13 June 1796.

71 Ibid., 12 July 1797.

72 Ibid., 2 August 1797.

73 Webster to Timothy Pickering, 17 July 1798, in Ford, 1: 464-65.

74 Webster, "Fourth of July Oration," *Advertiser*, 24 July 1798.

75 Ibid. A thorough reading of Webster's *Advertiser* in his final year as active editor, along with a careful study of his Oration, do not reveal a man who has given up on republicanism. Rollins, 86-87, says that the Oration shows that the idealistic democrat of the 1780s and the true republican of 1793 had "vanished," and that the Oration itself ended with "a frenzied call for order and authority." The definition of frenzy is "a violent mental agitation resembling temporary madness; wild excitement of enthusiasm; delirium." That seems quite foreign to the reasoned approach of the Oration.

Here again, Rollins stretches his already-thin thesis far beyond validity.

76 Benjamin Rush to Webster, 20 July 1798, in Ford, 1: 466.

CHAPTER 6

Transition

Noah Webster's life, from his first post-Yale days to his editorship of the *Minerva*, had been a Common Sense crusade to provide intellectual and moral uplift to his fellow citizens. The elevation of their characters and the glory of the new American nation were his goals, whether he served as schoolmaster, writer, lawyer, or editor. When he retired from active oversight of the newspaper in 1798 and returned to New Haven, the life of a Common Sense crusader was beginning to fade. From 1808 on, his life and direction would be changed completely. But in 1798, Webster did not know this. He could not foresee that he was entering a period of transition from the old to the new.

For the Webster of 1798, life seemed simply to have taken another short turn. Once again it seemed time to determine how to pass the years usefully and constructively—for himself, his family, and his country. Until 1803, he maintained the editorship of *The Advertiser* and *The Spectator* (formerly *The Herald*), although from New Haven he served as absentee editor with an ever-decreasing role in the actual operation of the papers. He also became active in local and state politics, serving as New Haven councilman (1799-1804), alderman (1806-1809), justice of the peace (1801-1810), judge of the county court (1806-1810), and New Haven representative to the Connecticut General Assembly (1800-1807). These years offered practical experience as a legislator. Even more important, they led him to reconsider his sanguine views about America's future.

The disappointment Webster felt over the failure of his newspapers to turn the political trends and attitudes of the American public in the right direction was profound. His plans for political education through the dissemination of knowledge seemed negated by the deceptions of the Jeffersonian political opposition. And the extent of personal abuse he had taken as editor of the papers had been the deciding factor in his relocation. As he wrote to an irate subscriber who had sharply criticized one of his articles, "I found myself exposed to so many personal indignities from different parties that retirement was essential to my happiness, if not to my life. . . . It wounded me to the soul," he added, "that the purest motives were often misinterpreted into the basest designs; the worst possible construction was put on paragraphs; articles and opinions laid to my charge which were easily known to come from other quarters; and any little mistake was laid hold of to injure my feel-ings, and as an excuse for exercising revenge, by discontinuing papers." He clearly was fed up with the agony of it all. "A property of this kind is hardly worth the purchase, and in the collision of hostile passions in our country few men of honour and feeling can consent to take charge of public papers—they must generally be superintended by men who are callous."[1]

Webster found it difficult to be indifferent to criticism. He was sensitive to attacks on his reputation. In particular, he was hurt by the hostility of Federalists with whom he had been on good terms but who, in the split between President Adams and Alexander Hamilton, castigated him for defending Adams's actions in de-esca-lating the Quasi-War with France (1798-1800). Webster firmly supported Adams, while trying to maintain his ties with the disaf-fected Federalists who sought full-scale war. But when these same Federalists established another newspaper in New York, the *New York Evening Post*, to compete with the *Commercial Advertiser*, the insult to his abilities and the threat to his income prompted a forthright and spirited counterattack. In a letter to Wolcott, he offered a threat of his own. "I shall turn my pen against the men who thus treat my former services with contempt, & rob me of bread; & I will exhaust the remaining powers of body & mind, to defeat the views of the party," he warned. "In doing this I shall oppose none of my principles—but I shall be compelled to call into view many facts & transactions of particular federal men, which will do infinite mischief to *them*." He had no desire to do this, so he wrote to Wolcott "that you may use your influence to prevent it.— But such gross & cruel ingratitude to a man who has spent the largest part of 18 years in opposing Democracy, & one half of that time without reward or the hope of it, cannot be overlooked or forgiven."[2]

Webster even found himself criticized in a Federalist newspaper, the *New England Palladium*, which blasted his plans for writing a dictionary. In response to the *Palladium* critique, Webster decried the manner in which Federalists were attacking each other. "How much the essential interests of morality, religion, and good government will ultimately suffer," he wrote to the editor, "by dissensions among their defenders, incautiously provoked and wantonly inflamed, is left for your own good sense to determine." But just in case the editor could not figure it out on his own, Webster continued, "When the citadel of all we hold dear as men, as citizens, and as Christians is assaulted on every side, it is folly and madness for the garrison to weaken their strength by wrangling among themselves about the loss of the outworks or about trifling points unconnected with the defence."[3]

Fighting against unprincipled Jacobins was one thing; to be forced to contend with those who were supposed to be allies was another. If the constant newspaper battles of the 1790s had drained him, striving against his erstwhile Federalist allies and friends doubly depleted him. Depressed and withdrawn, Webster grew sullen and somewhat testy. When asked to furnish information "on some subject relative to the town of New Haven" for the Connecticut Academy of Arts and Sciences, he responded sulkily that he could not oblige. He has been engaged in the service of his country for nineteen years, he said, yet he had been treated badly. "The efforts which have been made and are now making to deprive me of the confidence of my fellow citizens, and of course of my influence, and reputation, efforts not limited to this town," he added, "render it necessary for me to withdraw myself from every public concern, and confine my attention to private affairs and the education of my children."[4] The letter is an indication of the depth to which Webster could plummet emotionally when circumstances seemed bleak. He chose, on that occasion, to withdraw into family and self-pity. More than a year later, in another letter to Wolcott, he made an even more sweeping comment when he penned, "For myself, I regret now that I have devoted my time & the vigor of life to a business so precarious, but regret is useless."[5]

The despondency that Webster felt during the three years from 1800 to 1803 gradually lifted. Time healed much of his bitterness, and one of the chief causes of depression—an ever-present financial insecurity—also eased. When his copyright on the Speller expired in 1804, he not only undertook a major revision of the work, but also altered arrangements for the book's sale. This time all licensees were required to provide him with an account of the number of copies printed and to pay him one cent for each copy sold. This 1804 arrangement represented a great improvement for Webster financially. Now he would be able to profit according to the quantity of books sold.

Morality and Politics

Webster was far more comfortable attacking Jeffersonian Republicans than fellow Federalists. Jefferson and his adherents, according to Webster, not only had exceeded propriety by opposing the Adams administration after it had been duly elected, but had resorted to deceptive, even demagogic, distortion in their attacks on Adams's policies. The newspaper war into which Webster had been drawn left him with an image of Jeffersonians as scurrilous slanderers whose pernicious influence had to be countered. He found this distasteful, but for the sake of the country, it had to be done. To Wolcott he again confided, "It certainly is degrading for the govt to carry on Newspaper Controversy with its opposers, but our govt stands on *popular opinion*, & if that should fail to support it, it must fail to be supported." Falsehoods could not be tolerated; they served as "principal instruments of extending the opposition to an alarming degree." No government could expect to survive "the licentiousness of the press that now disgraces our country. Jacobinism must prevail, unless more pains are taken to *keep public opinion correct.* This *can* be done, & I think it *ought* to be done."[6]

Webster looked for ways to coax American public opinion to his point of view. In 1800, he published two pamphlets, both in response to printed Republican works. *Ten Letters to Dr. Joseph Priestley* was an answer to Priestley's 1799 publication entitled *Letters to the*

Inhabitants of Northumberland and its Neighborhood. Priestley, a personal friend of Jefferson's, a recent immigrant from Britain, and a firm supporter of American Independence during the Revolutionary War, had taken it upon himself to comment on American politics. His version of Jeffersonian Republicanism, Webster felt, required a strong rebuttal. The tenor of Webster's letters to Priestley vacillates from calm, reasoned analysis to personal vindictiveness. One biographer calls the letters "a caustic, rude, insulting diatribe."[7] Webster himself recalled years later, "Some of the author's friends, who generally accorded with him in opinion, thought that in these letters, he had treated the Doctor with too much severity."[8] Webster did not offer his own opinion on his friends' comments, but the inclusion of them in his Memoir tends to suggest that he realized they had merit. Overall, though, when one examines the letters to Priestley carefully, it is impossible not to see that Webster is committed primarily to expounding perceived truth in opposition to what he considers erroneous Republican principles.

The French Revolution continued to be a source of concern in 1800. Although the Revolution had spawned a reaction within France, Webster still felt the French were dominated by Jacobin philosophy. He took Priestley to task for claiming that Americans had changed their opinions of the Revolution because American principles had changed. The real reason for the change in Americans' attitudes toward the French, Webster informed him, was the revelation of French contradictions to the spirit of true republicanism. "The people of America, Sir, abandoned the French cause, when the French themselves abandoned the principles of their own Constitution." Webster explained further:

> By French principles are now meant, principles of Atheism, irreligion, ambition, and Jacobinism. The citizens of this part of America are firmly persuaded that French conquests, or attempts to reform Europe by the sword, are inconsistent, not only with their own professions, but with the peace of the world. They believe the opinion, that man can be governed by his *reason improved*, without the usual aids of religion and law, to be not merely a chimera, but a dangerous doctrine, calculated

to undermine the foundation of morals and all social confidence and security.[9]

This passage reveals that Webster was developing a greater interest in religion as an essential force for good in American life. Religion, he had declared in his 1785 *Sketches*, did not offer a sufficient basis for political security. Now, in 1800, he was committed to the proposition that religion is essential to morals and societal stability. Reason was no longer the prime ingredient for societal improvement. This signals a modification of some of the more utopian aspects of the Common Sense philosophy in respect to the dissemination of knowledge. Reason has need of religion and law to guide it into proper avenues. He never had believed that reason could function alone, but now a new emphasis on religion and lawful constraints appeared.

Webster also critiqued Priestley's idea of America's government. America was not a democracy, because a democracy implied a system of government "where the legislative powers are exercised directly by all the citizens." Rather, America was a republic, where governmental power resided in the hands of elected representatives and the powers of the people were "principally restricted to the direct exercise of the rights of suffrage."[10]

Character also was a major concern. Priestley erred, Webster believed, in holding that the character of those in public office was of no greater consequence than the character of private citizens. On the contrary, the character of elected officials was paramount to the integrity of a society "because they represent the laws." He explained: "A portion of the respect which men have for the laws, is inseparably attached to the personal character of the man; and a degradation of the man is always followed, in a greater or less degree, with contempt for the laws."[11] It was wrong, therefore, to treat elected officials as "servants," because the appellation demeans them and leads to disrespect for the laws they represent.

The letters against Priestley also manifest a decidedly more pessimistic outlook about the nature of man than Webster had held previously. In a discussion of the importance of a strong national defense, Webster warned that the threat of war "will be durable as the human race. What man has been, I believe he always will be—

until the millennium; and I am not skilled enough in prophecy to discern, at present, the approaches of that happy period."[12]

Further insight on Webster's view of man is found in his comments against Priestley's suggestion that America withdraw all marine defense of merchants. Being isolated from world commerce, Webster maintained, would not lead to national happiness, primarily because of the way man is fashioned. "The happiness of man seems not to depend so much on *property*," he advised, "as on the *pursuit* of it." Webster resumed, "Virtue, health, the vigor of the mind, intellectual improvements, every thing that goes into the composition of happiness and greatness, seem to depend on active industry and employment." This could not be achieved by hampering commercial activities; honest industry should not be restrained. "The better way is to leave the mind of man as free from fetters as possible—and the nation that does this, will be great, and I believe, in general, will be more virtuous and happy, than a nation whose genius is limited to one spot on the globe."[13] Virtue and intellectual progress, through an active commercial citizenry, was a theme that Webster began to propound more regularly. And the emphasis on lack of governmental constraints reveals the impress of yet another Scottish philosopher, Adam Smith.

The second pamphlet published in 1800, *A Rod for the Fool's Back*, was a scathing denunciation of Abraham Bishop's *Connecticut Republicanism, An Oration*. Bishop had been a classmate of Webster's at Yale but, Webster believed, had degraded himself by his espousal of Jeffersonian Republicanism. Bishop's treatise argued that the Federalist naval program to protect commerce was too expensive, and that American shipping would have to fend for itself. In the last resort, foreign ships could purchase and carry American goods if they wanted them. Webster's critique of Bishop's ideas, which went beyond his personal dislike of the man, centered on the economic and, ultimately, moral dangers of such a policy. "If we cease to carry our produce abroad," cautioned Webster, "nations of wiser policy will immediately supplant us by supplying those markets, and *most of our produce would perish on our hands*." Disastrous moral consequences would then follow:

The farmer would cease to raise what he could not sell;

no man would plant more than for his own consumption, industry would flag and idleness succeed, with want of money, poverty and all species of vice. Public virtue depends greatly on steady attention to business, and business at home depends on a constant market for surplus produce, which must inevitably fail if we cease to be our own carriers.[14]

Morality could not be separated even from commercial activities. The suspension of those exertions would produce a degenerate people—indolent, lazy, and disinclined to engage in honest labor. To promote such policies was madness, but Webster comforted himself with the assurance that such views could not succeed. "One thing is certain," he said with relief, "that when men of your stamp creep into offices of consequence, by flattering the people, the *delusion cannot be durable. . . .* As certain as the sun shines, the reign of weak and wicked men in this country must be short."[15]

As optimistic as Webster sounded in the public prints, his writings masked a deep concern, one that he shared with Benjamin Rush near the close of 1800 after the presidential election that put Jefferson into office:

As to mankind, I believe the mass of them to be "copax rationis." They are ignorant, or what is worse, governed by prejudices & authority—& the authority of men who flatter them instead of boldly telling them the truth. . . . It would be better for the people; they would be more free & more happy, if all were deprived of the right of suffrage until they were 45 years of age, & if no man was eligible to an important office until he is 50, that is, if all the powers of govt were vested in our old men, who have lost their ambition chiefly, & have learnt wisdom by experience, but to tell the people this would be treason.[16]

Webster probably was wise *not* to tell the people his views. He knew he had to live with reality and his musings to a friend were just that—musings only, with no expectation of fulfillment. What is most evident in the letter is Webster's loss of confidence in the common people's ability to tell the difference between truth and falsehood. This is an extension of the problem he began to notice while active editor of the *Minerva*. Although their hearts were pure, their minds could be twisted through cunning deception. No small part of being deceived is the susceptibility of men to appeals of ambition or personal gain, a susceptibility that all too often outweighs their rational faculties. He could only hope that perhaps men who are further along in life, and have been made wiser by accumulated experience, might have stronger reasoning faculties and a more steadfast adherence to conscience.

When Jefferson won the election of 1800, Webster naturally was concerned for his country's future. He resolved, however, to be silent for a while and counseled obedience to the new administration until it was possible to see how Jefferson carried out his responsibilities. Six months into Jefferson's term, Webster could hold back no longer. He perceived hypocrisy and a relaxation of moral standards in the new administration that demanded an end to his self-imposed silence. In a series of letters printed in his New York papers, Webster took Jefferson to the verbal woodshed on several matters, not the least of which were religion and morality. Seizing on Jefferson's inaugural address, Webster chided the new president for concealing his unorthodox religious beliefs and for cloaking himself in phrases such as "enlightened by a benign religion" and "an overruling providence," while omitting any specific mention of a supreme intelligent Being or Christianity. "Whether this omission was accidental or intentional, I will not venture to pronounce; but your predecessors did not leave us room to question their opinions on this interesting subject."[17] That such matters were taking on new importance for Webster is an indication that his religious views were changing.

Jefferson's political appointments also received a share of Webster's criticism. The new president was failing to select men of integrity and virtue. The bestowal of offices in New England always had required men of good moral character. Webster warned that such disregard of character always accompanies "the progress of national decline," and had been "the prelude to great public calamities, or total destruction."[18] He then queried, "Is it possible that you have adopted the opinion avowed by one of your adherents, that '*integrity* in private life has no manner of connection with *political* character?'"[19] Webster considered this view an immoral proposition. Private morality could not be separated from public morality. He concluded that Jefferson, in choosing men to serve in his administration, had given little thought "to their moral characters, nor to the estimation in which they are held, by the moral and respectable part of their fellow-citizens." Furthermore, he had taken as advisers "men, who openly revile and hold in contempt the religious institutions of their country—men, who openly blaspheme the name and attributes of God and Jesus Christ—men, who live in the habitual indulgence of the most detestable vices." By so doing, Jefferson had "opened a wide door for the entrance of every species of corruption and disorder in the executive departments."[20] A man's moral character, Webster continued, is an indivisible thing, and vice entering into one part will soon infect the rest. In classic Common Sense faculty psychology, he explained:

> A man may indeed be addicted, for a time, to one vice and not to another; but it is a solemn truth, that any considerable breach in the moral sense, facilitates the admission of every species of vice. The love of virtue first yields to the *strongest* temptation, but when a part of the rampart is broken down, it is rendered more accessible to every successive assailant. Hence no man whose character is stained with habitual vices, can possibly deserve and enjoy a full portion of confidence, in a public office.[21]

Another ramification of placing such men in positions of authority was the encouragement it offered the propagation of vice. Webster's analysis of human nature shifted to an examination of the effect of public opinion on moral character. "Nothing," he observed, "tends more to restrain men from open licentiousness, than for public opinion to frown on immorality; and it is no objection to this mode of checking vice, that it makes men hypocritical; for they may and often do become attached to what they are at first compelled to practice. Besides," he argued, "even hypocrisy may have no small effect on public manners, by preventing the influence of example."[22] Hypocrisy was a false issue; the real problem was the actual practice of vice by Jefferson's appointees:

> But when the most impious and scandalous vices are no objection against a candidate for office; what a flood of immoralities may we not expect from the removal of this powerful restraint on the vicious propensities of man! Surely, Sir, your respect for public opinion, if not for virtue, ought to make you more cautious in conferring governmental favor. Corruption of morals is rapid enough in any country, without a bounty from government. And if great depravity marks the last stages of a free government, and is the certain prelude to the destruction of liberty, (which is universally agreed to be the fact,) the Chief Magistrate of the United States, should be the last man to accelerate its progress. For the sake of humanity, Sir, let not our republic be planted with grey hairs in its infancy, and pass at once from the vigor of youth, to the decrepitude of old age.[23]

His appeal to Jefferson went unanswered.

In 1802, as in 1798, Webster was asked to give the July Fourth oration in New Haven. He took the opportunity to describe clearly his vision of America and its government. The two most significant modifications in Webster's thought discernible in the oration are the admission that Americans are not a superior people after all, and a closer identification of American government with Christianity.

The first proposition Webster addressed almost immediately. Nations, he cautioned, sometimes begin their political existence in the same way some young men enter the world—"with more courage than foresight, and more enthusiasm than correct judgment."[24] Perhaps he was thinking back to his own entrance into the world after his father had urged him to go out on his own. He certainly had been courageous and enthusiastic, ready to conquer the world for the rising genius of America. "Such are the mistakes of reformers," he continued, "and such have been the illusions of the enthusiastic friends of the revolution."[25]

What were the illusions? First, the sheltered position of America had bred the belief that the troubles of Europe would not affect American citizens. That had been roundly disproved by the French Revolution. A second illusion was that the general diffusion of knowledge would enable America to produce constitutions of government "less defective than any which have preceded them." Webster, who himself had placed most of his faith in knowledge and education, felt that the crises of the 1790s—the Democratic-Republican Societies, the influence of Jacobinism, the threat to America's independence—had displayed weaknesses in the republican systems, both national and state. The final illusion was that public virtue would secure a faithful, incorrupt, and impartial administration. He hardly needed to inform his audience that, in his estimation, the Jefferson administration did not meet those standards. The lesson was that the existence of these illusions betrayed Americans' pride and lack of wisdom. "If Moses," Webster affirmed, "with an uncommon portion of talents, seconded by divine aid, could not secure his institutions from neglect and corruption, what right have we to expect, that the labors of our lawgivers will be more successful?"[26]

Later in the speech, Webster gave attention to his second modified proposition, that Christianity must be the basis for America's republican government. A perfectly free and permanent government, he asserted, must rest upon a religion that was "perfectly republican"; a religion that could "humble the pride," "restrain the magistrate from oppression and the subject from revolt," secure "a perfect equality of rights," and bring "a strict subordination to law." Such a religion was Christianity, but not the Christianity of ecclesiastical domination. The abuses of Christian faith were to be distinguished from the faith itself. It was absurd, Webster charged, for "a set of fanatical reformers, called philosophers," to ignore the sacred origins of Christianity, narrowly focus on the abuses, and call for the extirpation of its doctrines and institutions. "Strange, indeed," he puzzled, "that the zealous advocates of a republican government, should wage an inveterate war against the only system of religious principles, compatible with rational freedom, and calculated to maintain a republican constitution!"[27] Clearly, the Christian religion was becoming more important to him. His disappointment with the American electorate and American leadership were nudging him back to a reexamination of the teachings he received as a child. This reexamination, by 1802, led to an application in the political realm; in just a few years, a more personal application would be made.

For the rest of his life, Webster wavered between a disgusted withdrawal from the arena of politics and a bold frontal attack on political heresies. His optimism would ebb, then surge just when it seemed that he harbored no further hope for change. Already, in the first years of the new century, this mercurial disposition was evident. In 1803, he wrote to Joel Barlow that he had little concern with politics, "having seen the ostracism of most of the illustrious men of my country, . . . & the govt entrusted to their calumniators—having seen the most important offices gained by direct bribery—& the possession of eminent talents the ground of proscription from public favor." He was "more & more confirmed" in the opinion "that men are neither wiser nor better than they were two thousand years ago. And I grow indifferent to the conduct of public men—satisfied that even in govts nominally republican, *corruption & base arts* are to perform the part which is executed by force in other forms of govt." Indeed, "The electors—the men who have the disposal of public favor—are corrupted—deeply corrupted already & the evil is growing beyond calculation."[28]

This melancholic spirit surfaced again in an 1805 letter, in which Webster bemoaned the beginning of Jefferson's second term. "I know," he told Connecticut Congressman and future Supreme Court Justice Simeon Baldwin, "how much you & our friends in Congress must feel the degraded state of our national character—But I know of no consolation but to eat & drink & forget."[29] This was Webster at his lowest ebb. Yet when Rufus King wrote him in 1807 and expressed his despondence over the political state of America, Webster replied, "I hope our condition is not remediless, and perhaps the crisis is hastening which will lead, through many evils, to a remedy." He was speaking of the possibility of war, which, he continued, "must necessarily tend to unite men who have been divided; and men of talents, whom demagogues have influenced the people to proscribe, will be solicited to lend their aid to defend their country." He even gave advice to Federalists that sounds a note of moderation and practicality:

There is one particular in which, I think, the leading gentlemen of the Washington School have uniformly erred. They have attempted to resist the force of current popular opinion instead of falling into the current with a view to direct it. . . . But in this, I think, they err, either from scrupulous regard to *principle* or from mistaking the means by which all popular governments are to be managed. Between the unbending firmness of an Hamilton and the obsequiousness of a Jefferson, there is a way to preserve the confidence of the populace without a sacrifice of integrity. . . . And it is vastly important that such men should not lose their weight of character; for if *they* do not lead the people, fools and knaves will.[30]

Webster was willing to compromise on nonessential issues for the sake of national unity, and his counsel that political flexibility and commitment to principle were not incompatible manifests a desire to find a common ground between the parties. Perhaps he, more than most Federalists, could see the problems of both, simply because he had felt the force of criticism from each side. He already had commented in the introduction to his 1802 publication, *Miscellaneous Papers*, "Both parties have committed errors—the true policy of our country unquestionably lies between the extremes of their measures."[31] He also had written James Madison, commenting on the same publication, "You will see by that work how much I differ in opinion, from the leading men of the two parties. I wish for more harmony of councils; but I have little hope of seeing that event." Although he often suffered from a sense of despair and withdrawal, at his best Noah Webster maintained an independence of mind and a sincere desire for reconciliation. As he also wrote to Madison, "A more temperate policy on the part of the present administration would have reconciled all sober, impartial federalists to the change, & this without any considerable sacrifice of principles on the part of the present ruling men."[32]

Educational Endeavors
"I once intended to devote my life to literary pursuits," Webster confided to writer Joseph Dennie in 1796:

The cold hand of poverty *chilled* my hopes but has not wholly *blasted* them. The necessity of attending to business to procure a living for my little family *retards* my projects, but they are not *abandoned*. My plan of education is but barely *begun*. When I shall complete it is uncertain.[33]

Retirement from his newspapers brought Webster free time, which he filled with the literary pursuits he craved. During the first decade of the new century, he published a treatise called *A Brief History of Epidemic and Pestilential Diseases*, the first volumes of *Elements of Useful Knowledge*, *A Philosophical and Practical Grammar*, and the *Compendious Dictionary*.

Educational developments had not been extensive during Webster's absence from direct involvement in schools. The Latin Grammar Schools had been largely superseded by private academies that emphasized a broader and more practical curriculum, the type of curriculum that Webster himself often had urged. Founded mainly by churches stirred to action by the Second Great Awakening (ca. 1797-1810), or by philanthropic individuals and groups, the academies reigned supreme from immediately after the American Revolution until the Civil War.[34] The push for government-controlled schools was in its infancy at the beginning of the nineteenth century, and did not command undue attention until the days of Horace Mann in Massachusetts and Henry Barnard in Connecticut in the 1830s. The recitation method still held sway in all types of schools. The Lancastrian method, which utilized older children as tutors for the younger, first appeared in New York City in 1806, but never became very popular in American schooling.[35]

College education became even more firmly entrenched in Common Sense philosophy in the last few years of the old century, and it remained the dominant intellectual force until the ascendance of evolutionary thought after the Civil War. This philosophy fit in well with the prevailing Protestant orthodoxy that was reinvigorated by the Second Great Awakening and the advent of revival meetings. Although it is difficult to distinguish between good academies and small colleges, it is estimated that five hundred new colleges started in the period between the American Revolution and the Civil War.[36]

Webster's interest in education had not diminished during his editorship. In his letters to Priestley, he commented on the state of American education in 1800, particularly that of colleges. One of his few agreements with Priestley was that American colleges "are disgracefully destitute of Books and Philosophical apparatus." Webster was "ashamed to own, that scarcely a branch of science can be fully investigated in America, for want of books." Learning in the "higher branches of literature," he felt, was "superficial, to a shameful degree." Although law, ethics, and politics as academic subjects were in a healthy state, he lamented that in such subjects as history, mathematics, and the physical sciences "we may be said to have no learning at all, or a mere smattering."[37] Webster's assertion of inferiority in these areas was probably correct. America had lagged behind in the development of a distinct class of professional scientists. Colonial America had featured naturalists who were primarily "collectors," not systematizers. But new professorships in the sciences and other fields were being introduced.[38] Timothy Dwight, president of Yale, established a medical school and professorships in chemistry, languages and ecclesiastical history, and law.[39] Webster asserted that Americans were capable of producing educational and literary efforts equal to Europe, but "opportunity, means, patronage alone" were lacking; if provided, it would raise "the character of this country to an eminent rank among nations."[40]

Webster's first attempt to offer the world an American literary effort second to none was a scientific treatise, *A Brief History of Epidemic and Pestilential Diseases*, published in 1799, with a British edition in 1800.[41] Interest in the subject was occasioned by a visitation of yellow fever in 1798, from which Webster himself had suffered. A prodigious amount of effort went into the research and compilation; eighteen months after commencing the project, Webster had completed the "brief" 712-page, two-volume work. Although now recognized as advanced for its time, Webster admitted that the work brought no profit, "was little read, & excited little notice."[42]

His next effort, which met with greater success, was the multivolumed *Elements of Useful Knowledge*. When completed, the four volumes covered the history and geography of the United States (volumes I and II), the history and geography of Europe, Asia, and

Africa (volume III), and a history of animals (volume IV). The first volume was published in 1802 and the others appeared in 1804, 1806, and 1812, respectively. Together, they were intended to fill an important gap in the literature on these subjects. Webster's informative preface, as in all his works, furnished the rationale for undertaking the endeavor.

First, Webster was not impressed with the order followed and methods used in most elementary books on history, geography, and science. He also was concerned that they were "destitute of the moral, philosophical and practical remarks, which are necessary to enliven a narrative of facts." He would remedy these defects by following the pattern of the external world, a pattern that offered order and leads man to ponder the being of God:

> Nature, in all her works, proceeds according to established laws, and it is by following her order, distribution and arrangement, that the human mind is led to understand her laws, with their principles and connections. It is also by carefully observing the uses of the productions of nature, and the adaptation of every thing in creation to its particular purpose, that the mind is led to just views of final causes, and to such conceptions of the attributes of the divine author, as to confirm a belief in his being and perfections.[43]

Webster felt the order in his first two volumes exemplified the pattern he saw in nature. He began with a discussion of the solar system and gradually devolved into more particular aspects of that system—the earth in its entirety, the geography of the United States as one portion of the earth, then into particulars about the United States. He was careful to point out the evidences of the hand of God in the natural world. "In every part of this work," he enthused, "occasions frequently occur of deducing moral and pious reflections from the subjects treated." On these occasions, he would take special care "to lead the mind of the reader, from a consideration of the order, beauty and fitness of all parts of nature, to contemplate the necessity and certainty of the existence of a Creator, of infinite power, wisdom and goodness." This was a tried and true technique, "practiced by the ablest authors and best men in all ages" and furnishes "powerful aids to that firm belief in the being and providence of God, and that pious veneration for his character and attributes, which are the prime ornaments of a wise man and a good citizen."[44]

The objectives of the work were intellectual and moral. He wanted to help in "enlarging the minds of our citizens, and directing their hands to useful employments." "Most of the books now used in schools for reading," he continued, "are composed of solemn didactic discourses, general lessons of morality, or detached passages of history. These are indeed useful; but why may not children read for common lessons, the known and established principles in philosophy, natural history, botany, rhetoric, mechanics, and other sciences?" There also was the ever-present moral consideration, advanced along Common Sense lines, which included Reid's nurtured seedling analogy:

> By reading frequently and repeatedly, passages containing just rules and principles, even above the comprehension of young minds, the pupils will learn many of them by heart, and bear the impressions into future life; by which means, when their understandings are more matured, they will be enabled to direct, to useful purposes, the principles with which they had stored their minds in school. In this manner, useful rules and facts, acquired in youth, like seed sown in a good soil, will produce their fruit in riper years, and increase the harvest of knowledge and improvement, to enrich the community.[45]

Webster might have lost his utopian educational concepts, but he retained a strong belief in the lifelong effects of impressions made on young minds. This work was an effort to train those young minds into certain habits of thinking that would stay with them all their lives, surfacing at the appropriate moment when the community would need their abilities.

A Philosophical and Practical Grammar of the English Language was published in 1807. It was, basically, a major revision of the Grammar he had first published in 1784. He had been convinced by the reading of British grammarian John Horne Tooke's *Diversions of Purley*—which he had digested in 1787—that he had been guided by false principles in the writing of the first Grammar. Tooke had been a guiding light in his *Dissertations on the English Language*, and now Webster was prepared to put Tooke's insights into his new Grammar. The new Grammar rested wholly on the belief that Anglo-Saxon, rather than Latin, provided both the principles and usages for modern English. He also experimented with standard grammatical terms, substituting *attribute* for *adjective*, *connective* for *conjunction*, and *substitute* for *pronoun*. The book did not sell well because of its innovations. But Webster was so satisfied with his conclusions, and so convinced of their import, that he tried a republication in 1822, the insertion of the Grammar into his large dictionary in 1828, and a revision of it in 1831. None of the attempts proved profitable; neither did Webster's ideas catch on with academics. However great his influence in spelling and lexicography, he never made an impact in the grammar field.

The Lexicographer Begins His Work

Webster spelled out his educational plan for Joel Barlow in 1807. His objective, as in 1783, was to assert and implement America's linguistic and literary independence from Great Britain:

> For more than twenty years, since I have looked into philology and considered the connection between language and knowledge and the influence of a national language on national opinions, I have had it in view to detach this country as much as possible from its dependence on the parent country.[46]

The plan consisted of four steps: first, perfection of the Speller; second, the four volumes of *Elements of Useful Knowledge*; third, the *Philosophical and Practical Grammar*; and fourth, dictionaries.[47] A speller, texts on specified subjects, a grammar, and dictionaries—these four together comprehended the Webster plan for a basic American elementary education designed to supplant British imports. Most of the rest of his life he devoted to the last stage, the first fruits of which was *A Compendious Dictionary of the English Language*, published in 1806.

Dictionary-making was a new endeavor for Americans. Most people relied on Samuel Johnson's British production, the standard work since its publication in 1755. The first American to offer even an abridgement for the use of schoolchildren was Samuel Johnson, Jr. [no relation], a schoolteacher in Guilford, Connecticut who, in 1798, compiled *A School Dictionary*. Johnson had been a Yale student the same time as Webster, and Webster's name was appended to an endorsement of the dictionary in the *Connecticut Journal* on 8 November 1798. The American Johnson's dictionary was in no way a rival to the other Johnson's. It was a 198-page, 4,100-word compendium intended for the exclusive use of young children. After the printing of one edition, Johnson collaborated with the Rev. John Elliott of East Guilford on a new and larger work. The first edition, published in 1800 and entitled *A Selected, Pronouncing, and Accented Dictionary*, was expanded to 223 pages and approximately 9,000 words.[48]

In that same year, Caleb Alexander, a Presbyterian minister and schoolteacher in Massachusetts, published *The Columbian Dictionary of the English Language*. More ambitious than Johnson's attempts, Alexander extended the work to 514 pages and 25,700 words, although much of the increase was accountable to the same word being repeated for different definitions of the word. One year later, William Woodbridge, also a former fellow student of Webster's at Yale, and first preceptor of Phillips Exeter Academy in New Hampshire, published *A Key to the English Language, or a Spelling, Parsing, Derivative, and Defining Dictionary*. Its 348 pages held approximately 20,000 definitions.[49] Thus, when Webster determined to proceed with his educational plan, no one had yet made a noteworthy entrance into dictionary-making; the field was his to shape.

But it would not be easy because opposition to his approach was quick and often severe. The *Compendious*, comprised of 408 pages and 40,600 words, and offered to the public as an improvement on the widely-used *Entick's Spelling Dictionary*, drew fire almost immediately simply because the author was Webster, that brash innovator who had tried to alter the orthography of the language with his *Collection of Essays and Fugitiv Writings*. That previous effort had failed miserably; now it seemed he was taking up the cause once more. In fact, Webster was, but in a more restrained manner. Since it was obvious that radical changes in American vocabulary never would be accepted, he chose a cautiously innovative path somewhere between Franklin's new alphabet and those who felt the language should be written in stone. Most of his changes were moderate enough and had been seen before in the Speller, although some, like the attempt to drop the final "e" in words like *determine* and *examine*, ultimately were rejected. The addition of nearly 5,000 words to Entick included certain Americanisms, words of localized use (properly designated as such), and new scientific terminology.

Criticism came from both Republican and Federalist camps. Webster's definition of Federalist as "A friend to the Constitution of the U. States" had Republicans up in arms. Many Federalists, meanwhile, were distressed over Webster's willingness to tinker with the language. *The Monthly Anthology*, a Boston literary magazine operated by Federalists and established in 1803, ravaged Webster's lexicographical pronouncements as heresies. Webster himself was considered "the wildest innovator of an age of revolutions."[50] Undaunted by these criticisms, Webster actively collected an impressive array of endorsements from the faculties of Yale, Princeton, and other colleges.[51] He had his detractors, but his adherents were many.

In the final paragraphs of the preface to the *Compendious*, the new lexicographer unfolded the ultimate dream and direction for his lexicographical investigations:

> I have entered upon the plan of compiling, for my fellow citizens, a dictionary, which shall exhibit a far more correct state of the language than any work of this kind. . . .
>
> However arduous the task, and however feeble my powers of body and mind, a thorough conviction of the necessity and importance of the undertaking, has overcome my fears and objections, and determined me to make one effort to dissolve the charm of veneration for foreign authorities which fascinates the mind of men in

this country, and holds them in the chains of illusion. In the investigation of this subject, great labor is to be sustained, and numerous difficulties encountered; but with a humble dependence on Divine favor, for the preservation of my life and health, I shall prosecute the work with diligence, and execute it with a fidelity suited to its importance.[52]

That was written in 1806. Webster had no idea just how much labor was going to be required and that publication of the proposed dictionary was still more than twenty years in the future. Neither did he realize that the phrase "humble dependence on Divine favor" was going to take on a greater significance.

---

[1] Webster to E. Waddington, 6 July 1798, in Harry R. Warfel, *Letters of Noah Webster* (New York: Library Publishers, 1953), 181-82.

[2] Webster to Oliver Wolcott, Jr., 1 October 1801, Wolcott Papers, CHS.

[3] Webster to the *New England Palladium*, 10 November 1801, in Warfel, *Letters*, 245-46.

[4] Webster to Stephen Twining, Secretary of the Connecticut Academy of Arts and Sciences, 22 January 1802, in Ford, 1: 524-25.

[5] Webster to Oliver Wolcott, Jr., 13 April 1803, Wolcott Papers, CHS.

[6] Webster to Oliver Wolcott, Jr., 23 June 1800, Wolcott Papers, CHS.

[7] Warfel, *Noah Webster*, 264.

[8] Webster, "Memoir," 34.

[9] Webster, *Ten Letters to Dr. Joseph Priestley* (New Haven: Read & Morse, 1800), 8.

[10] Ibid., 9.

[11] Ibid., 16.

[12] Ibid., 18-19.

[13] Ibid., 20.

[14] Webster, *A Rod for the Fool's Back* (New Haven: Read & Morse, 1800), 4.

[15] Ibid., 9.

[16] Webster to Benjamin Rush, 15 December 1800, in Ford, 1: 479.

[17] Webster, "An Address to the President of the United States," in *Miscellaneous Papers, on Political and Commercial Subjects* (New York: E. Belden & Co., 1802), 13-14.

[18] Ibid., 54.

[19] Ibid., 56.

[20] Ibid., 56-57. Webster repeated his attack on Jefferson's disregard for moral character in *An Address to the Citizens of Connecticut* (New Haven: J. Walter, 1803), 14, when he denounced Jefferson's contempt of the Christian religion by his reception of Thomas Paine. He continued, "That he [Jefferson] has not disturbed our religion, is also true—for he has nothing to do with it—*except to bring disgrace by encouraging its inveterate enemies.*"

[21] Ibid., 57.

[22] Ibid., 57-58.

[23] Ibid., 58.

[24] Webster, *An Oration, Pronounced before the Citizens of New Haven, on the Anniversary of the Declaration of Independence; July, 1802* (New Haven: William W. Morse, 1802), 6.

[25] Ibid., 7.

[26] Ibid., 7-8.

[27] Ibid., 13-14.

[28] Webster to Joel Barlow, 20 March 1803, David Humphreys Papers, Yale.

[29] Webster to Simeon Baldwin, 2 February 1805, Baldwin Family Papers, Yale.

[30] Webster to Rufus King, 6 July 1807, in Warfel, *Letters*, 277-78.

[31] Webster, *Miscellaneous Papers*, vi.

[32] Webster to James Madison, 9 April 1802, James Madison Papers, Series 2, Library of Congress.

[33] Webster to Joseph Dennie, 30 September 1796, in Warfel, *Letters*, 141-42.

[34] Otto F. Kraushaar, *Private Schools: From the Puritans to the Present* (Bloomington, IN: Phi Delta Kappa Educational Foundation, 1976), 16-18.

[35] David L. Madsen, *Early National Education, 1776-1830* (Wiley, 1974), 101-104.

[36] Ibid., 110.

[37] Webster, *Ten Letters*, 22.

38 Brook Hindle, *The Pursuit of Science in Revolutionary America, 1735-1789* (University of North Carolina Press, 1956), 308.

39 Charles E. Cunningham, *Timothy Dwight, 1752-1817: A Biography* (New York: Macmillan, 1942), 169-233.

40 Webster, *Ten Letters*, 23.

41 Webster, *A Brief History of Epidemic and Pestilential Diseases*, 2 vols. (Hartford: Hudson & Goodwin, 1799); British edition published in London by G. Woodfall, Paternoster-Row, 1800.

42 Webster, "Memoir," 33. Warfel, *Noah Webster*, notes, 250-51, "The *History* is not only the best general summary of epidemiological opinion at the end of the Eighteenth Century, but it is surpassed by few works as a compendium of earlier speculations on this subject."

43 Webster, *Elements of Useful Knowledge*, 2 vols. (Hartford: Hudson & Goodwin, 1806), preface.

44 Ibid.

45 Ibid.

46 Webster to Joel Barlow, 12 November 1807, in Warfel, *Letters*, 294.

47 Ibid., 296-97.

48 Eva Mae Burkett, *American Dictionaries of the English Language Before 1861* (Metuchen, NJ: The Scarecrow Press, 1979), 8-16.

49 Ibid., 24-34.

50 *The Monthly Anthology and Boston Review*, VII (1809): 247-64, in ibid, 131.

51 Webster to Joel Barlow, 12 November 1807, in Warfel, *Letters*, 299, states, "The *Gazette of the United States* and *Portfolio* in Philadelphia, the *Evening Post* in New York, the *Anthology* in Boston are all arrayed against *me* and my *designs*. Perhaps an apology may be found for the publishers in their utter ignorance of the subject or of my views. The gentlemen are among those who repose implicit confidence in Johnson's opinions, never having examined the subject enough to question their justness. This opposition may be weakened immediately and ultimately overthrown; but it requires some address, for I believe they are supported by the weight of public opinion—all founded on that confidence in English authorities before mentioned. In my favor is President Smith, of Princeton, and the faculties of most of the northern colleges—Dr. Mitchill, Dr. Morse, and so forth. Indeed, the men of education generally in the country towns, if not favorable, are at least unprejudiced. The large towns are more thoroughly English in this respect than the country."

52 Webster, *A Compendious Dictionary of the English Language* (Hartford: Hudson & Goodwin, 1806), preface, xxiii.
Joseph H. Friend, *The Development of American Lexicography, 1798-1864* (The Hague & Paris: Mouton, 1967), 14-15, affirms, "Webster knew better than anyone else

that he had made no more than a creditable start in the right direction and that he had a long way to go. He also knew his destination and had been mapping his course. It was intended to lead to a dictionary that should not merely rival the great Dr. Johnson but outdo him—extend the word list far beyond both the *Compendious* and the fullest revisions of Johnson's *Dictionary*, correct Johnson's many errors, reveal the true etymologies as no one had yet done, provide properly discriminated definitions, guide the user to valid *American* usage in all departments. . . . The *Compendious* was a way station; the grand terminal had yet to be built, and the architect had little doubt of his ability to do the whole job single-handed."

CHAPTER 7

Conversion

In 1808, Noah Webster experienced that regeneration of the heart that theologians term "conversion." In the process, Webster finally made peace with the faith that had existed in an uneasy tension with his early optimistic views of man, education, and government. Webster's conversion was the intellectual and moral watershed of his life. As such, it provided him with a spiritual and intellectual framework that extended into every sphere of life, including perceptions of and judgments about man, morality, government, education, and the very purpose of being. It was a watershed also because it came at the opening stages of his lexicographical studies. These studies would bear the impress of Webster's newly revitalized Christian convictions.

There are two types of conversions—internal and external. Whenever a person changes his official membership in a religious body, whether from Jew to Christian, Catholic to Protestant, or even Lutheran to Baptist (and all of these examples could be reversed), he can be said to have converted. Yet, in this context, the focus is on the external move from one institution to another. Such moves can be made for a number of reasons, only one of which may be a sincere alteration in belief. Conversion, in Webster's case, was the second, or internal, type. Internal conversion results in a profound alteration of an individual's conception of the nature of God, man, and sin, and brings a transformation in both thought and action.

Conversion is a phenomenon described in both the Old and New Testaments. Hebrew words (Old Testament) and Greek words (New Testament) relating to the conversion experience all express

167

essentially the same idea—that conversion is a return to God, a restoration of the relationship God originally had intended to have with man, through a turning *away from* sin (i.e., rebellion against God's commands) and a turning *to* the mercies of a forgiving Father. Whether in Old Testament or New, the passages in which conversion is described indicate that change is essential, and that a recognition of sin is the starting point for that change.

Webster's religious views developed gradually. In his early years, he was at best a nominal Christian. His disdain for certain religious rites and rituals shows in his diary from time to time. In 1785, for example, he notes, "Fast day. We must fast regularly every year, whether we are plunged in calamities or overwhelmed with the blessings of heaven! Strange superstition! the effect of custom."[1] In 1786, when he prepared a new edition of *The New England Primer*, he substituted certain innocuous rhymes for some of the traditional Calvinist maxims. For instance, "A. In Adam's Fall, We sinned all" was amended to read "A. Was an Apple-pie made by the cook." And in his *American Magazine* in 1788, Webster reviewed Timothy Dwight's *Triumph of Infidelity* in the following words:

> Does this abuse proceed from the pen of a christian? . . .
> In short the author appears to be a theological dogmatist, who has found the right way to heaven, by creeds and systems; and with more imperiousness than would become infinite wisdom and power, damns all who cannot swallow his articles of faith.[2]

Later that same year, a letter from his future brother-in-law, Nathaniel Appleton, shed more light on the young Webster's beliefs. "Am very happy to find," wrote Appleton, "that my opinions of certain supposed Doctrines of the Christian Religion accord so well with yours. When Revelation was made manifest, our benevolent Parent never designed that we should extinguish Reason, that noblest gift of Heaven to Man."[3]

Yet even in the midst of his skepticism, Webster never actually broke with his Congregational roots. The same man who criticized fast days was miffed when people used bad weather as an excuse not to attend church.[4] The same man who had excised portions of the *Primer* still designed it to include religious instruction, incorporating a catechism, Watts's Cradle Hymns, and prayers.[5] And the same man who urged that reason determine proper doctrine could not abide where reason led the French.[6]

The horrors of French political developments and their prefigurements in America, the ascension of Jefferson to the presidency, the personal abuse Webster sustained from both Republicans and Federalists, and the financial distress he suffered, surely helped prepare him for his subsequent conversion. It already has been noted that the public pronouncements he made after 1800 had a more Christian emphasis. His earlier optimism shaken, he needed a cohesive worldview to make sense of his many disappointments and setbacks, to know that he, as an individual, did have value. Webster, though, did not consciously seek a cohesive worldview, at least not until the Second Great Awakening.

The Second Awakening began as a backwoods revival in Kentucky and soon spread to all parts of the nation, New England included. In the East, its manifestations were different—less emotional, more tied to traditional forms—but the effect in many towns was observable. In 1807, a revival began in New Haven, stirred by the Rev. Moses Stuart, pastor of Webster's church, the First Congregational Church of New Haven (commonly referred to as Center Church). Stuart, twenty-two years Webster's junior, was a Yale graduate. He had tutored for a few years at the college, and then settled in at Center Church in 1806. He became a Hebrew scholar, wrote a Hebrew grammar in 1813, and spent most of his life after 1810 as professor of sacred literature at Andover Theological Seminary in Massachusetts. After Webster's conversion, Webster and Stuart became close friends, with Stuart present at Webster's deathbed.

The best way to analyze Webster's conversion experience is to let him tell it, a method followed by none of his biographers.[7] As Webster stated in his "Memoir":

> In the year 1808, the religious views of NW were materially changed. Information of this fact coming to the knowledge of his brother in law, Judge Dawes of Boston, the judge sent him a letter with a pamphlet containing sentiments not in accordance with those which NW had

embraced. This called forth a reply from NW, in which he gave a succinct relation of the manner in which his views had been changed.[8]

Webster's lengthy reply described his upbringing, his college years, the doubts he had entertained about certain doctrinal stands of the church, the immediate events leading up to his conversion, the experience itself, and ruminations on what the Christian life really entails. Having once read it, one can have no doubt that Webster's conversion was authentic and produced a basic reorganization of his entire life. In Webster's world, God moved from the periphery to the center, providing him a new purpose and focus.

"Errors are always mischievous," he informed Dawes as his letter began, "but never so much so as in the concerns of our immortal souls and in the relations which exist between God and ourselves."[9] Errors concerning the God-man relationship then, in Webster's view, were the worst kinds that could be made. Already this was an indication of the new priorities his conversion had wrought. A brief background then followed:

> Being educated in a religious family, under pious parents, I had, in early life some religious impressions, but being too young to understand fully the doctrines of the Christian religion and falling into vicious company at college, I lost those impressions and contracted a habit of using profane language. This habit however was not of many years duration—profaneness appeared to me then as it now does, a vice without the apology which some other vices find in human propensities, and as unworthy of a gentleman as it is improper for a christian.

In retrospect, Webster believes his parents had been faithful to teach him God's plan for men. But obstacles had blocked the way: a lack of understanding and the company into which he fell while at college. Webster had renounced profane talk, not as a Christian would, as an affront to God, but simply the way in which any well-bred gentleman might—as a practice "unworthy" of his position in life.

The long-ago episode in which he shut himself in his room to determine what to do with his life after college now was a cause for regret, and not a reason for bravado:

> Being set afloat in the world at the inexperienced age of 20, without a father's aid which had before supported me, my mind was embarrassed with solicitude, and over-whelmed with gloomy apprehensions. In this situation I read Johnson's Rambler, with unusual interest and with a visible effect upon my moral opinions, for when I closed the volume, I formed a firm resolution to pursue a course of virtue through life, and to perform all moral and social duties with scrupulous exactness; a resolution which I have endeavored to maintain, though doubtless not without many failures. I now perceive that I ought to have read my Bible first, but I followed the common mode of reading, and fell into the common mistake of attending to the duties which man owes to man, before I had learned the duties which we all owe to our Creator and Redeemer.

The Bible should have been his first recourse, Webster reflected. Duties to man, as necessary as they are, cannot be placed before duties to God. The strong sense of duty Webster iterated in this letter was not new: it was present in the Common Sense faculty psychology he so often relied on for his worldview. Although Common Sense identified man's principal duties to God, and although the philosophy was much employed to buttress orthodox arguments, the focus of the philosophers' many treatises had been on the social duties of man. Webster now saw a distinction that he had not acknowledged previously: God had to come first; He had the primary claim on a man's duties.

From this brief recollection of his early manhood, Webster jumped forward to the immediate past:

> For a number of years just past, I have been more and more impressed with the importance of regulating my conduct by the precepts of Christianity. Of the being and attributes of God I have never entertained a doubt, and

my studies as well as frequent contemplations on the works of nature have led my mind to most sublime views of his character and perfections. These views produced their natural effect of inspiring my mind with the highest admiration and reverence, mingled with gratitude; and for some years past, I have rarely cast my eyes to heaven or plucked the fruit of my garden without feeling emotions of gratitude and adoration.

The more obvious references to God and the Christian religion in Webster's writings after 1800 are indications of the impressions made on his mind during this period. In particular, as he stated in the preface to *Elements of Useful Knowledge*, the evidences of God in nature were, for him, a constant source of contemplation. It was a "natural effect" for nature to make a man think of God and for the contemplation of God to produce admiration, reverence, and gratitude. But these feelings were not enough for a true knowledge of the God that nature has manifested:

> Still I had doubts respecting some of the doctrines of the Christian faith, such as regeneration, election, salvation by free grace, the atonement and the divinity of Christ; these doubts served as an apology for my forbearing to make a profession of religion; for though I could never read or hear that solemn declaration of our Savior, "whosoever shall confess me before men, him will I confess before my Father who is in heaven," without some compunction and alarm; yet I endeavored to justify my neglect by a persuasion that I could not conscientiously assent to the usual confession of faith required in Calvinistic churches as the condition of admission to their communion. That is in plain terms, I sheltered myself as well as I could from the attacks of conscience for neglect of duty, under a species of scepticism and endeavored to satisfy my mind, that a profession of religion is not absolutely necessary to salvation. In this state of mind I placed great reliance on good works, or the performance of moral duties, as the means of salvation,

although I cannot affirm that I wholly abandoned all dependance on the merits of a Redeemer. You may easily suppose that in this state of distraction, and indecision of opinions, I neglected many duties of piety.

Total reliance on the merits of Christ as Savior bothered Webster. The orthodox plan of salvation did not mesh with his reason. After his conversion, he honestly could declare that he had suffered from pangs of conscience all those years, but had set his conscience aside as best he could. He had placed his hopes for salvation on his outward actions—the propriety with which he handled himself toward others. But this quasi-confidence was shaken:

> About a year ago an unusual revival of religion took place in New Haven, and frequent conferences or private meetings for religious purposes, were held by pious and well disposed persons in the Congregational societies. I felt some opposition to these meetings, being apprehensive that they would by affecting the passions too strongly, introduce an enthusiasm or fanaticism which might be considered as real religion. I expressed these fears to some friends and particularly to my family, inculcating on them the importance of a *rational religion*, and the danger of being misled by the passions.

Enlightened men educated in the eighteenth century deplored anything approaching "enthusiasm," their word for an inappropriate display of emotion. This was in particularly bad taste in the religious realm. Religion was reasonable, as Common Sense abundantly had shown. A man could subscribe to certain formulations and be assured he had a right relationship to God. Passions had to be controlled because they embodied the lower faculties of man; reason, the highest faculty man possessed, a faculty he did not share with the lower animals, but with God only, must rule. Webster was especially concerned for the effect these "fanatical" meetings might have on his own inner circle:

> My wife, however, was friendly to these meetings and she

was joined by my two eldest daughters who were among the first subjects of serious impressions. I did not forbid but rather discouraged their attendance on conferences. Finding their feelings rather wounded by this opposition, and believing that I could not conscientiously unite with them in a profession of the Calvinistic faith, I made some attempts to persuade them to join me in attending the Episcopal service and ordinances. To this they were opposed. At some times I almost determined to separate from my family, leaving them with the Congregational Society and joining myself to the Episcopal. I went so far as to apply to a friend for a seat in the Episcopal Church but never availed myself of his kindness in offering me one. In this situation my mind was extremely uneasy. A real desire of uniting myself to some church by a profession of faith, a determination not to subscribe to all the articles of the Calvinistic Creed, and an extreme reluctance against a separation from my dear family in public worship, filled my mind with unusual solicitude.

This religious rift in his own family constituted a crisis of sorts for Webster. He already was experiencing disenchantment with his Enlightenment optimism and the direction of American government and society; his literary endeavors, though keeping him active, were, apart from the Speller, not overwhelming financial successes. His family had become the bedrock of his existence, an anchor of solace in a disappointing world. Now the unity and safety of this retreat was threatened. Another potential disappointment loomed.

Webster began to compare Congregational and Episcopal beliefs in earnest and then engaged Stuart in a one-on-one dialogue concerning the doctrinal points with which he was having trouble. In the process, some of his objections were removed. Yet a mere intellectual assent did not bring total release:

During this time, my mind continued to be more and more agitated, and in a manner wholly unusual and to me unaccountable. I had indeed short composure, but at all times of the day and in the midst of other occupations, I was suddenly seized with impressions, which called my mind irresistibly to religious concerns and to the awakening. These impressions induced a degree of remorse for my conduct, not of that distressing kind which often attends convictions, but something which appeared to be reproof.

These "impressions" are open to different interpretations. A secular interpretation would portray Webster's struggles and the strong impressions on his mind as the natural effect of a man in torment, an agitation caused by stress and inner psychological turmoil. The orthodox theological position would consider them as the working of God through the Holy Spirit, bringing conviction of sin—a kind of reproof, as Webster saw it. The latter interpretation is what Webster acknowledged. In any case, as Webster described it, repentance and peace of mind finally came:

These impressions I attempted to remove by reasoning with myself, and endeavoring to quiet my mind, by a persuasion, that my opposition to my family, and the awakening was not a real opposition to a *rational religion*, but to enthusiasm or *false religion*. I continued some weeks in this situation, utterly unable to quiet my own mind, and without resorting to the only source of peace and consolation. The impressions however grew stronger till at length I could not pursue my studies without frequent interruptions. My mind was suddenly arrested, without any previous circumstance of the time to draw it to this subject and as it were fastened to the awakening and upon my own conduct. I closed my books, yielded to the influence, which could not be resisted or mistaken and was led by a spontaneous impulse to repentance, prayer and entire submission and surrender of myself to my maker and redeemer. My submission appeared to be cheerful and was soon followed by that peace of mind which the world can neither give nor take away.

Self-surrender is the way Webster characterized it. It was both gradual and sudden, a long time in the offing, with weeks of agony, then, in a brief, but memorable, moment, it was done. The conversion account to Dawes complete, Webster continued with an analysis of its supernatural origin:

> That these impressions were not the effect of any of my own passions, nor of enthusiasm is to me evident, for I was in complete control of all my rational powers, and that the influence was supernatural, is evident from this circumstance; it was not only independent of all volition but opposed to it. You will readily suppose that after such evidence of the direct operation of the divine spirit upon the human heart, I could no longer question or have a doubt respecting the Calvinistic and Christian doctrines of regeneration, of free grace and of the sovereignty of God. I now began to understand and relish many parts of the scriptures, which before appeared mysterious and unintelligible, or repugnant to my natural pride. . . . In short my view of the scriptures, of religion, of the whole christian scheme of salvation, and of God's moral government, are very much changed, and my heart yields with delight and confidence to whatever appears to be the divine will.

Webster was convinced he had experienced a direct operation of God on his own heart *while still in possession of his rational faculties*. It wiped away all remaining doubts and intellectual obstacles. And, more importantly for this study, the conversion altered profoundly his view of God's purposes in the world. This alteration would have an immediate impact on his views of education, morality, and government, and, within a short time, of language, too.

Webster continued the letter with observations on the process of learning and his own tendency toward error:

> Permit me here to remark in allusion to a passage in your letter, that I had for almost fifty years, exercised my talents such as they are, to obtain knowledge and to abide by its dictates, but without arriving at the truth, or what now appears to me to be the truth of the gospel. I am taught now the utter insufficiency of our own powers to

effect a change of the heart and am persuaded that a reliance on our own talents or powers, is a fatal error, springing from natural pride and opposition to God, by which multitudes of men, especially of the more intelligent and moral part of society are deluded into ruin. I now look, my dear friend, with regret on the largest portion of the ordinary life of man, spent "without hope, and without God in the world." I am particularly affected by a sense of my ingratitude to that Being who made me, and without whose constant agency, I cannot draw a breath, who has showered upon me a profusion of temporal blessings and provided a Savior for my immortal soul. To have so long neglected the duties of piety to that Being on whom I am entirely dependent, to love whom supremely is the first duty, as well as the highest happiness of rational souls, proves a degree of baseness in my heart on which I cannot reflect without the deepest contrition and remorse. And I cannot think without trembling on what my condition would have been had God withdrawn the blessed influences of his spirit, the moment I manifested opposition to it, as he justly might have done, and given me over to hardness of heart and blindness of mind. I now see in full evidence, the enormous crime, the greatest, man can commit against his God, of resisting the influence of his holy *Spirit*. Every sting of conscience must be considered as a direct call from God to obey his commands; how much more then ought man to yield to those pungent and powerful convictions of sin which are unequivocally sent to chastise his disobedience and compel him to return to his Heavenly Father.

Feeling spiritually transformed—internally changed—Webster was at last ready to make an external confession of his faith.

In the month of April last I made a profession of faith; in this most solemn and affecting of all transactions of my life, I was accompanied with my two eldest daughters; while I felt a degree of compunction that I had not sooner

> dedicated myself to God, it was with heartfelt delight, I could present myself before my Maker, and say, "Here am I, with the children which thou hast given me."
>
> Mrs. W. was confined at the time and could not be a witness of this scene, so interesting to her, as well as to us who were personally concerned, but you may easily conceive how much she was affected, the first time she met her husband and children at the Communion.

For the Webster family to be united in its confession of faith was a primary, if not *the* primary, joy of Webster's later years. He often commented on the comfort provided by that unity.[10]

As Webster concluded his "conversion letter" to Dawes, he added a personal note of respect and friendship, an indication that his conversion would not cause a separation from those he most loved who might not share his convictions:

> Of your benevolence, sincerity and affection for me, I have had sufficient proof and my heart reciprocates all your kind wishes for my welfare. I have long been accustomed to consider you as the best of men, and if we have not corresponding views of Christian principles, my friendship for you will remain undiminished.[11]

Dawes responded to Webster in February 1809. The liberal religious views he expressed led Webster to write another letter, this time more theological in content. The letter then appeared in the *Panoplist*, an evangelical magazine edited by the Rev. Jedidiah Morse, under the title "Peculiar Doctrines of the Gospel." The word "peculiar," to a twenty-first-century audience, connotes "strange," but in the context of Webster's day, the word meant "appropriate." To understand how thoroughly Webster's views were reoriented to orthodox Christianity, one need only study this particular treatise.

"I was opposed to every thing, that looked like *enthusiasm* in religion," Webster remarked toward the beginning of *Peculiar Doctrines*, "and talked much about the propriety of being a *rational Christian*. I am still opposed to enthusiasm," he continued, "but I am now convinced that my former opinions were erroneous, and that I formerly included under that term, a belief in some of the fundamental, and *most rational* principles of the gospel."[12] For Webster, no longer was it absurd to consider Biblical doctrines reasonable; they made complete sense to him, and he wished to extricate those same doctrines from the false accusation of irrationality. It certainly made no sense to him to separate duties owed God from those owed men. Advocates of a moral religion who ignored man's principal duties were undermining the gospel message. It was not even reasonable to assume that a man "destitute of a principle of holiness, or a supreme love and regard to his Maker, can perform the moral duties, in the manner which the laws of God require." The problem, Webster asserted, was that his motives could not be pure; they could not "spring from the right source." Neither would any man, he maintained, "without a higher principle, than a mere regard to social happiness, ever be able to perform all the moral duties with steadiness and uniformity."[13]

Man's first class of duties, those owed to God, were, Webster affirmed, "dictated by reason and natural religion, as well as commanded in the Scriptures. They result necessarily from our relation to the Supreme Being, as the head of the Universe."[14] Man's knowledge of these first duties comes not from revelation only, but through right reason. Divine revelation is God's means of confirming what the heart of man already comprehends, albeit incompletely. These duties to God Webster classified as "piety." The second class, termed "morality," were duties to one's fellow men. Both classes together were found in the Ten Commandments, the first four directed toward God, the last six specifying obligations toward men. Webster then challenged men who focus on the last six at the expense of the first four to think rationally:

> Now let me ask the advocates of a *moral* religion, with what propriety or by what authority, can we dispense with the *first* tablet of the law, or even postpone it to the *second*? Are not the duties of *piety* as necessary and as positively commanded as the duties of *morality*? And more, are they not placed at the head of the list? The command, "thou shalt have no other God before me," which enjoins supreme love, reverence, and adoration, as

duties to the creator of the universe, *precedes* all the other commands, not only in the order of arrangement, but in the order of *propriety*, resulting from God's character and supremacy.[15]

Webster continued to stress the *intelligence* and the *wisdom* of following the commands of God. God was the "first great cause" and the "last end of all things," according to Webster, and, therefore, "the *foundation* of all true religion in the heart." This being acknowledged,

> It results that intelligent creatures must give to him the first place in their hearts, or they do not conform to the standard of moral rectitude, which God has established; and if they do not conform to that standard, they cannot be entitled to the happiness which results from such conformity. Hence we are repeatedly informed in the Scriptures, that "the fear of God is the beginning of wisdom": the foundation—on which the whole system stands.[16]

God gave man an excellent head start. He furnished man with "intellectual powers to learn the character of God" as well as the duties he must perform. Also given to man were "the word of God to direct us, and a free will to accept or reject the offers of salvation." A holy life, Webster continued, could never come from man's own attempts to be moral because it is impossible for moral duties to be acceptable to God "unless they proceed from faith and holiness." This would be possible only through regeneration, or a conversion such as Webster had experienced, "a doctrine which many men, called christians, deny, and which the morality system utterly excludes."[17]

Conversion was necessary because man is "naturally destitute of holiness, or true love to God," a fact Webster considered "equally proveable from the Scriptures and from observation." Indeed, "That the natural heart is at enmity with God, one would think any person must admit, who reads history, or observes the state of society within his own view."[18] A few decades earlier, Webster had wrestled with the lessons of history and had hoped for better in man; now he no longer harbored illusions. Man could not save himself; a savior was necessary. Webster no longer had the slightest doubt about the divinity of Christ:

> I once had doubts on this subject; but my mind is now satisfied with the divinity of our Saviour. . . . The prophecies respecting Christ, and the astonishing train of events, recorded in the Jewish history, as preparatory to his appearance, have had no small effect in satisfying my mind on this subject.[19]

His conversion might have been, in his mind, a direct operation of God upon the heart, but his intellect still required proof. He may have yielded to the Holy Spirit on that day in early 1808, but he still demanded that Biblical doctrines be rationally explicable and be in accord with history. Webster's belief that the gospel he had received *was* in agreement with observable facts and scholarship confirmed the reality of what he had experienced. God had not created man simply to exist and then to perish like the beasts of the field. The existence of man's capacity to think and reason, to use his powers creatively, attested to a greater plan. "Surely then man was endowed with superior powers and faculties for some important purpose," Webster speculated. "The soul bears some resemblance to divinity, and is evidently designed for enjoyments of a superior rank." Consequently, it was essential for man "to direct the intellectual powers . . . to their proper objects," objects that could only be known, because of man's inherent sinfulness, through a divine revelation of God's will through the Scripture. This was why man had to depend on the Bible; only through the Bible, God's communication to man, could man understand the proper use of his powers and faculties.[20]

Webster's new understanding of God and His purposes also prompted him to confess how he had followed what he now sees as false philosophy. While he always had believed in a general providence that works through the laws of the universe, he had not believed in a special providence that works through the personal involvement of God with individuals. He was baffled how he ever could have doubted such a matter, "for it as unphilosophical as unscriptural, to admit a general providence without a special one: as a general providence implies particular providences." He concluded he probably was led into this error "by the false philosophy which prevails in the world, by propagating which men strive to exclude the agency of God from all direct concern with the affairs of this world, and of the universe." It was a philosophy that "substitutes for the mighty hand of Deity, the operations of *second causes*, and *laws of nature*." Youth are taught "that nature or created things, are subject to certain *laws*," through which "we pretend to account for all the phenomena of the universe, without the direct agency of a superior, intelligent Cause." But all laws of nature are "immediately dependent on the Almighty Author," Webster declared, and he was "compelled to resolve all the *laws of nature* into the direct agency of the *Almighty First Cause*."[21] Webster's objection to a mechanical, Deistic universe rested on both scriptural and philosophical grounds. Such a universe did not coincide with Biblical tenets and, on the whole, did not seem to be a truly intelligent, rational proposition. His newfound Biblical approach to life initiated the questioning; a satisfactory conclusion was reached through the powers and faculties supplied by God.

But it was not simply on philosophical grounds that Webster embraced Biblical doctrines. In the struggles of everyday life, as man seeks to conquer his passions, Webster saw that man needs an agency higher than himself to succeed. "Nothing seems effectually to restrain such passions but divine grace," he deduced. "The fear of man, and a regard to decorum will not produce the effect, in minds of a particular structure. But the humbling doctrines of the gospel change the tiger to a lamb."[22] Fear of man (retribution for wrongdoing), a desire for decorum, and devotion to the rules of civility had been Webster's guideposts for nearly five decades; apparently, he was here acknowledging a personal failure, as well as a general observation.

Near the conclusion of his little treatise, Webster commiserated on the insensitivity, ingratitude, and outright stupidity of the majority of men:

> It is with heart felt regret, that I see a large portion of the world so inattentive to religion. Men often live for many

years gazing upon the stupendous fabric of the universe, apparently without a sentiment of piety; and wander among the charming beauties of the earth, where the power, the wisdom, and the beneficence of the Creator, are displayed on every flower, and every leaf, with as little admiration and gratitude as the beasts that graze on the field. Equally insensible are they to the beauties of the divine character, unfolded in the works of providence and grace; forgetting that the same God who arrays the lillies of the field, with more splendor than Solomon's glory, is ready to clothe his children with the splendid robes of the Redeemer's righteousness. And what is astonishing, but often true, the more temporal blessings men enjoy, the less disposed they are to love and obey their heavenly Benefactor. . . . Indeed it is extremely painful to a reflecting mind, to observe men in affluence, who live amidst a profusion of every thing the bounty of heaven bestows, indulging in sensual gratifications and rolling in splendor; but forgetting, or insulting the Benefactor, while they riot on the benefit.[23]

Webster's *Peculiar Doctrines* made quite a ripple in the religious community. Unitarians vilified it, and their feelings helped color their evaluation of Webster's philological labors. As Moses Stuart told Webster a year later, "The Anthology [a Boston literary magazine dominated by Unitarian thought, even though Federalist in politics] is outrageous against you. I believe it will do good, & promote the very cause, which it means to destroy. . . . Be assured, the object of their vengeance is more against your religion than against you; & be also assured, that your friends will view things, in their just light."[24] The orthodox, meanwhile, were so pleased with Webster's effort that they tried to convince him to turn his whole attention to apologetics. But Webster's direction was fixed; he knew his life was dedicated to philological undertakings. As an endorsement at the end of one letter notes, "I have not time nor talents, nor reading to qualify me for theological discussions."[25]

Yet despite Webster's reluctance to become a career apologist, his conversion affected every aspect of his life. Joel Barlow, his old friend, wanted Webster to provide a good review of his poem, *The Columbiad*. Webster could only reply, "Of the poem, as a poem, I can conscientiously say all, perhaps, which you can expect or desire, but I cannot, in a review, omit to pass a severe censure on the atheistical principles it contains." He acknowledged the long-term friendship he and Barlow had enjoyed, claiming, "No man on earth not allied to me by nature or by marriage had so large a share in my affections as Joel Barlow until you renounced the religion which you once preached, & which I believe. But," he continued, "with my views of the principles you have introduced into the 'Columbiad' I apprehend my silence will be most agreeable to you, & most expedient for your old friend and obedient servant."[26]

Again, ten years later, in a letter to another old Yale classmate, Abraham Bishop, whom he had ripped in *A Rod for the Fool's Back*, Webster sighed,

> Notwithstanding my old attachments to the members of the class, I cannot but deeply regret that so few of them, appear to be religious characters. How much should I rejoice if to all the bonds by which we are attached to each other, there were added that strongest of all ties that can bind men to each other on Earth, a union of hearts in Christian love. However I may respect the talents & acquirements of the friends of my youth, you can hardly imagine how much I feel the want of that close alliance, which springs from a cordial union of souls in undissembled piety.[27]

Noah Webster, from 1808 onward, was a Christian in the deepest sense. His faith permeated all of his life, leaving no corner untouched. The profound spiritual experience he underwent had ramifications for every sphere of his thought and endeavors. Morality, government, education, and linguistic study—all now had to pass the inspection of a deep Christian faith informed by Biblical standards. In some ways, the Biblical standard confirmed what Webster had believed all along. In others, a thorough reorientation was necessary.

[1] Webster diary, 20 April 1785, in Ford, 1: 128.

[2] *American Magazine*, July 1788, 589-90.

[3] Nathaniel Appleton to Webster, 30 November 1788, Webster Papers, NYPL, Box 2.

[4] Webster diary, 4 April 1784, in Ford, 1: 73-74: "At church, a small congregation. Bad weather is a common and often a very trifling excuse for neglect of public worship."

[5] Warfel, *Noah Webster*, 91.

[6] Webster, "Revolution in France," *Minerva*, 30 October 1794, states, "Robespierre was as much of an Atheist as Hebert; but he found his system would not go down with the multitude; he then tacked about and formed a scheme to establish Atheism under the name of One Supreme or Eternal. With this sort of God and a dozen inferior deities, and each a festival annually, a kind of pompous frolick, the stratagem succeeded, and all Paris sings the praises of this unknown something."

[7] Ford, in her *Notes*, does reprint most of Webster's own comments on the experience, but without any serious analysis. Other biographers either give the entire episode a passing mention (Warfel, Monaghan, and Unger) or spend more time on their own theories than in a discussion of Webster's account (Rollins and Moss). Moss, 18, follows in Rollins's wake in asserting that religion in Webster's life became merely a "device to control the passions of the people."

[8] Webster, "Memoir," 43. Dawes's letter, 25 October 1808, Webster Papers, NYPL, Box 4, had said in part: ". . . that I may know whether it be true that N.W. has lately recieved [sic] some impressions from above, not in the ordinary way of ratiocination. What I now write is as sincere as you can possibly wish your friend to be. I am no *dis*believer. I have had many doubts, but never was sure, as many dogmatists are. . . . I have thought that we must exercise our *reason*, and that Faith is not knowledge. I have read everything I could obtain, pro and con, about the Xtian revelation—*and I believe it*—but I never could believe, *satisfactorily*, in the conversion by a ray of light. I have thot' that to exercise our talents, such as we have, to obtain knowledge, and honestly to abide by the dictates thereof, was all that could be expected by our maker."

[9] All quotations in Webster's description of his conversion experience are in his letter to Thomas Dawes, 20 December 1808, Webster Papers, NYPL, Box 1. No further citations of this letter will be made.

[10] Webster to Emily Webster Ellsworth, 3 April 1838, Webster Papers, CHS: "You have many things to console you; & not the least of these, the circumstance that your children are embracing the offers of salvation. If there is one thing on earth that preeminently adds to parents' happiness, it is to have their children embracing the gospel. I have a great deal of this happiness in the course of my children and grandchildren. Give my kindest love to your children, & assure them I rejoice at their determination to lead a life of Christian integrity. They will find religion their best support in the multiplied trials & adversities which must necessarily be encountered in the changeable world."

The one member of the Webster clan who brought some grief to his parents was William, the sole surviving son, who became Episcopalian. Webster wrote to him, 27 June 1835, Webster Papers, Yale, as follows: "The separation [from William's family in Cincinnati] was as severe to me as any that I have ever experienced, except that of your leaving the church to which you belonged & all your family connections have belonged from the first settlement of the colony. This is the heaviest stroke to me. But separated as we are, I trust our affection will remain undiminished, and may the good providence of God render the separation beneficial to you & your family."

[11] An interesting footnote to Webster's conversion is appended to his account of the letter to Dawes in the "Memoir," 50. Webster relates:

"The following fact is remarkable. Not long after I had become reconciled to the doctrines of scripture, I was for some time afflicted with a local pain. I used various remedies for it without success. After being disappointed repeatedly, I resolved to supplicate ease from the only Being who is able to deliver us from troubles. I rose in the morning, retired to my study, & falling on my knees, I earnestly prayed to God for relief. No sooner were my words uttered, than the pain ceased, & never returned. That this was a supernatural interposition of divine power, I do not know; but the fact I know; respecting this there can have been no deception, & the frequent recollection of this fact has had no small influence in confirming my faith through life. And it deserves to be considered, whether modern Christians, on the ground that miracles have ceased, do not go too far in denying or disbelieving the special interposition of divine power, in the ordinary course of God's moral government; & whether this is not a material difference between Old Testament saints & modern Christians."

As a result of this experience, Webster questioned the prevailing theological conception that miracles stopped when the canon of Scripture had been completed. Apparently, he was willing to go against the grain of belief of the majority of his Christian colleagues, an indication that he did not take an uncritical, unreasoning, lockstep approach to his faith.

[12] Webster, *Peculiar Doctrines of the Gospel* (Poughkeepsie: Joseph Nelson, for Chester Parsons & Co., 1809), 3.

[13] Ibid.

[14] Ibid.

[15] Ibid., 4.

[16] Ibid., 5.

[17] Ibid., 6.

[18] Ibid.

[19] Ibid., 9.

[20] Ibid., 11.

[21] Ibid., 12.

[22] Ibid., 14.

[23] Ibid., 15.

[24] Rev. Moses Stuart to Webster, 16 March 1810, Webster Papers, NYPL, Box 4.

25 Endorsement to letter from Dr. Spring, 16 August 1809, in Ford, 2: 50.

26 Webster to Joel Barlow, 13 October 1808, in Ford, 2: 39.

27 Webster to Abraham Bishop, 16 October 1818, Webster Papers, Yale.

CHAPTER 8

Christian Foundations: Morality and Government

More than twenty-eight years after his conversion and only seven years before his death, Webster analyzed the foundations of good government in these words:

> An attempt to conduct the affairs of a free government with wisdom and impartiality, and to preserve the just rights of all classes of citizens, without the guidance of Divine precepts, will certainly end in disappointment. God is the supreme moral Governor of the world He has made, and as He Himself governs with perfect rectitude, He requires His rational creatures to govern themselves in like manner. If men will not submit to be controlled by *His* laws, He will punish them by the evils resulting from their own disobedience.[1]

These words indicate that his 1808 conversion had been permanent. From 1808 on, Noah Webster saw the world through the eyes of a man convinced of a new truth, a truth that, of necessity, inspired every sphere of his activity, intellectual and practical. Virtually every important belief Webster held prior to the conversion was reexamined and tested against the standards of his newfound faith. In the process, Webster's beliefs were profoundly altered.

An analysis of three of Webster's most enduring and active interests—government, education, and language—demonstrates this generalization. In each of these subject areas, Webster formulated a new Christian foundation for his thinking. The degree of change varied. In government and politics, Webster's former ideas were deepened, fortified, and given divine sanction. His educational theories underwent substantial revision. Most dramatic of all, his ideas about language experienced a near-revolution.

Good morals in government, both in elected officials and the electorate, always had been a concern for Webster, as indeed it was for most of his contemporaries. But whereas, previous to his conversion, his foundation for morality was philosophical, based in large measure on the rationalistic tendency of the Common Sense school, afterward it became Bible-centered. Indicative of this shift is a letter written shortly after his conversion to an uncle, Elijah Steele, who recently had attacked certain Federalists in the Connecticut government. Webster chided his uncle: "I am very much hurt that you should think the *morals* of this country can be safe under the government of men who openly disclaim all belief in revealed religion, & whose morals are, beyond measure, dissolute and corrupt." Steele had labeled certain members of the Governor's Council as villains; Webster proceeded to lecture his Quaker uncle that such branding was unchristian:

> Is this, my friend, the language of men who have a regard to religion or morals? Is this consistent with the humility of a Christian—the meekness recommended by Christ? I know the Governor & Council well & from long acquaintance I can affirm that they are men of integrity & pure motives. All men are liable to err but error, if they have erred, ought not to subject them to such harsh language.
>
> Indeed, in this letter, I see many things which I cannot reconcile to any principles of religion or to the spirit of the *Friends*.[2]

Christianity had to form the foundation of America's republican national and state governments, in Webster's new view, or they would rest on sand. He made this point repeatedly, both in private letters and in the public prints. To James Madison, years after that gentleman had stepped out of public life, Webster confided, "I know not whether I am singular in the opinion, but it is my decided opinion, that the christian religion, in its purity, is the basis or rather the source of all genuine freedom in government." The Christian religion he was referring to, he added, was not one imposed by the state, but was that "which was preached by Christ & his apostles, which breathes love to God & love to man. And I am persuaded that no civil government of a republican form can exist & be durable, in which the principles of that religion have not a controlling influence."[3]

Webster also defined true Christianity in a letter to another acquaintance. He said,

> When I speak of the Christian religion as the basis of government, I do not mean an ecclesiastical establishment, a creed, or rites, forms, and ceremonies, or any compulsion of conscience. I mean primitive Christianity in its simplicity as taught by Christ and His apostles, consisting in a belief in the being, perfections, and moral government of God; in the revelation of His will to men, as their supreme rule of action; in man's accountability to God for his conduct in this life; and in the indispensable obligation of all men to yield entire obedience to God's commands in the moral law and in the Gospel.[4]

In his 1832 American history text, Webster went to great lengths to explain the connection between Christianity and republican government. The "genuine source of correct republican principles," he maintained, was to be found in the Bible, "particularly the New Testament or the Christian religion."[5] Civil liberty, properly understood as a benefit derived from responsible behavior and the rejection of licentiousness, was the fruit of Christianity. "Almost all the civil liberty now enjoyed in the world owes its origin to the principles of the Christian religion," Webster believed. "Men began to understand their natural rights, as soon as the reformation from popery began to dawn in the sixteenth century; and civil liberty has been gradually advancing and improving, as genuine Christianity has prevailed." Again, he was careful to point out the precise nature of the Christianity he was exalting. It was not a religion based on "the decisions of ecclesiastical councils," nor was it one narrowed down to a "particular church established by law." Further, it did not consist "in a round of forms, and in pompous rites and ceremonies." Instead, it was the religion that had "introduced civil liberty," and that "enjoins humility, piety, and benevolence; which acknowledges in every person a brother, or a sister, and a citizen with equal rights. This is genuine Christianity, and to this we owe our free constitutions of government."[6]

Webster pointed to the Puritans as the true founders of American civil liberty. While noting their shortcomings, he praised their strengths. "They were not without their failings and errors," he readily acknowledged. "Emerging from the darkness of despotism, they did not at once see the full light of Christian liberty; their notions of civil and religious rights were narrow and confined, and their principles and behavior were too rigid." Yet their faith and character outweighed such defects because "they were pious and devout; they endeavored to model their conduct by the principles of the Bible and by the example of Christ and his apostles." Neither did they regard "distinctions among men, which are not warranted by the scriptures, or which are created by power or policy, to exalt one class of men over another, in rights or property." These Puritans "established institutions on republican principles" and "formed churches on the plan of the independence of each church." Land was distributed "among all persons, in free hold, by which every man, lord of his own soil, enjoyed independence of opinion and of rights." And governments were founded "on the principle that the people are the sources of power; the representatives being elected annually, and of course responsible to their constituents."[7] If they erred in some ways, at least their errors "were the effects of their firm and conscientious attachment to the scriptures, as the oracles, of God."[8] The real strength of the Puritans, for Webster, was that the Bible was their guide in the establishment of their institutions. They might not have fully understood the parameters of liberty, but they had started at the proper point and were headed in the right direction. The motivation of their hearts could not be faulted, and, as a result, God blessed their endeavors with a continuation of their principles through the American Revolution.

Biblical principles, then, were dominant in the formation of the

American nation, and a continued adherence to Scripture was essential to the maintenance of a free society. The problem, Webster further noted, was man's desire to rule by reason alone, without the benefit of God's Word. "The scriptures," he remarked, "were intended by God to be the *guide of human reason*."[9] Webster's early training in Common Sense had not abrogated the need for God's guidance, but it had placed a lot more emphasis on the ability of the rational powers God had given man. The more disillusioned Webster became with man's use of his reason, the more receptive he became to the idea that man needed some sort of outside rudder and guide to direct his reason. Even before his conversion, Webster's disillusionment with his fellow Americans had been evident. The conversion cemented his pessimism about human nature and gave him a rationale for why man did not use his reason properly. Man's sinful nature was at odds with God. Left to itself, it would degenerate. "The creator of man," Webster explained, "established the moral order of the Universe; knowing that *human reason*, left without a divine guide or rule of action, would fill the world with *disorder, crime & misery*."

> A great portion of mankind, ignorant of this guide or rejecting its authority, have verified the fact; and the history of three thousand years is a tissue of proof that human reason left to itself can neither preserve morals nor give duration to a free government. Human reason never has been, and unquestionably never will be, a match for the *ambition, selfishness* and other *evil passions* of man.[10]

How different from the statements of his early years when the dissemination of knowledge was all that was necessary to secure liberty. Now Webster was saying, "No truth is more evident to my mind than that the Christian religion must be the basis of any government intended to secure the rights and privileges of a free people." He lambasted the foolish opinion "that *human reason*, left without the constant control of divine laws and commands, will preserve a just administration, secure freedom and other rights, restrain men from violations of laws and constitutions, and give duration to a popular government." Only a maniac would hold to such a view. "The history of the whole world refutes the opinion;

the Bible refutes it; our own melancholy experience refutes it."[11]

His attacks on unguided human reason in government and public affairs extended even to the Constitution. "The citizens of the U. S. profess to constitute a *christian* nation; but they have attempted to establish a government solely by the help of *human reason*." "Our constitution," he contended, "recognizes no Supreme Being, & expresses no dependence on divine aid for support & success. In this respect, the framers of the constitution are rebuked, not only by the scriptures, but by heathen sages."[12] Never was this idea broached in Webster's pre-conversion days. Certainly his *Examination into the Leading Principles of the Constitution*, written in 1787, gave no hint of such an attitude. Once again the example of the Puritans was cited—and the religious and moral degeneracy of the times hinted at:

> The little band of pious christians who settled on this spot . . . little thought of the mighty changes which a revolution, and a confederation of their descendants with communities of a different character would produce in the principles and policy on which their institutions were founded. They never conceived that not two centuries would pass, before attempts would be made to substitute human reason and philosophy, in the place of the Bible, as furnishing sufficient rules of life, and policy. But this being the fact, every christian and every descendant of the Puritans, who venerates the memory of his ancestors, is to buckle on his armor, and defend his faith; for certain it is that if we abandon the God of our fathers, the God of our fathers will abandon their children.[13]

Character and Principle

Indispensable for the maintenance of a Christian republic, according to Webster, was the placing of men with sound Christian principles into public office. One year after his conversion, in a letter to President-elect Madison, Webster wrote, "The great body of our respectable men, in New England, are believers in the Christian religion, & warmly attached to its support; and they have more confidence in men who adhere to that religion, than in those who reject it." Webster continued with a warning: "The Chief Magistrate who disregards this consideration, in his appointments, in these states, will very much impair the public confidence in his administration."[14] The rule of the righteous was now the cornerstone of his political message. Principle and character become the watchwords. "In selecting men for office, let principles be your guide," he wrote in one of his post-conversion treatises. "Regard not the particular sect or denomination of the candidate—look to his character as a man of known principle, of tried integrity, and undoubted ability for the office." Although "men of loose principles" might allege "that religion and morality are not necessary or important qualifications for political stations," they are quite mistaken. The Scriptures teach differently. "They direct that rulers should be men *who rule in the fear of God, able men, such as fear God, men of truth, hating covetousness.*" Even if the Scriptural admonition had been absent, "our own interest would demand of us a strict observance of the principle of these injunctions. And it is to the neglect of this rule of conduct in our citizens," he preached, "that we must ascribe the multiplied frauds, breaches of trust, peculations and embezzlements of public property which astonish even ourselves; which tarnish the character of our country; which disgrace a republican government; and which will tend to reconcile men to monarchy in other countries and even in our own."[15] Both Scripture and self-interest, in Webster's formulation, demand officeholders of high religious and moral character. To have otherwise would be to invite an onset of political horrors, some of which Webster already could see.

In *Value of the Bible*, one of his lesser-known works, published in 1834, he expounded more fully on the Biblical basis for righteous rulers, and pressed for greater fidelity to this principle. "Among the last words of David," Webster wrote, "were the following 'He that ruleth over men must be just, ruling in the fear of God.'" The neglect of this divine precept had brought "war, oppression, and misery upon the human race," and man's lack of consideration of "piety, religion or moral worth as indispensable qualifications in rulers" had been the cause.[16] This was especially true in a republic where the people choose their rulers. In representative governments, Webster admonished, "if rulers are bad men, it is generally the fault of the people." They might simply be deceived (Webster's prevailing viewpoint at the inception of his disillusionment in the 1790s), but it would be more likely that they were not heeding the words of David:

> They choose men, not because they are just men, men of religion and integrity, but solely for the sake of supporting a party. This is a fruitful source of public evils. But as surely as there is a God in heaven, who exercises a moral government over the affairs of this world, so certainly will the neglect of the divine command, in the choice of rulers, be followed by bad laws and as bad administration; by laws unjust or partial, by corruption, tyranny, impunity of crimes, waste of public money, and a thousand other evils. Men may desire and adopt a new form of government; they may amend old forms, repair breaches and punish violators of the constitution; but there *is*, there *can be* no effectual remedy, but obedience to the divine law.[17]

The remedy would not be external; a mere alteration of forms would not bring effective change. Rather, men had to obey God's law and be certain that human governments and laws did not deviate from God's standard. "As the will of God is our only rule of action, and that will can be fully known only from revelation," Webster advised, "the Bible must be considered as the great source of all the truths by which men are to be guided in government, as well as in all social transactions." What did this mean for other sources? "Other books," he continued, "if in accordance with the Bible, may be read with advantage. But a large proportion of the books which fill our libraries have little or no bearing on the sound principles of morals and religion."[18] The post-conversion Webster analyzed all other claimants to knowledge, understanding, and wisdom in light of the Bible. Only those in agreement with basic scriptural tenets could be considered worthy of serious scrutiny. The hold his orthodoxy had on him led Webster to include in his proposed amendments to the Constitution the following: "Every person before being admitted to Congress or to other civil office must subscribe to the following declaration—'I believe in the existence & providence of one God, to whom I am accountable for my conduct. I believe in the principles of the Christian religion & hold myself bound to obey its injunctions.'"[19]

Webster's concern for the connection between Christianity and American government was not just an abstract principle. It was a living axiom that what a man believes in his heart translates into outward practice, and that only a firm reliance on the God revealed in the Bible can offset the evil in man's heart—evil that would cause untold misery if it found its way into public office. No longer could Webster trust in a man of knowledge or undisputed talent if that man did not adhere to right moral and political principles and did not possess a pure heart. "Knowledge, learning, talents are not necessarily connected with sound moral and political principles," he admonished in an 1814 Fourth of July oration. "And eminent abilities, accompanied with depravity of heart, render the possessor tenfold more dangerous in a community."[20]

In *Letters to a Young Gentleman Commencing His Education*, Webster was explicit on the need for moral integrity in individuals, and for people to act on principle, not expedience. "Nothing can be more false than the opinion that *honor* can exist without *moral rectitude*," he taught. "Every violation of moral duty . . . implies a disposition to offend or treat with contempt the greatest and best Being in the Universe, or a disposition to injure a fellow citizen, or both." Real honor consisted in "a disposition to promote the best interests of the human family," which meant "an exact conformity of heart and life to the divine precepts. Whatever voluntary conduct in man impairs human happiness or introduces disorder into society, manifests a defect of character, a destitution of honorable principles."[21]

He then delved into greater detail on the nature of false honor and corrupt principles. "One of the first efforts of an ingenuous mind, is to disabuse itself of the prejudice, that the *laws of honor* may *require* or *justify* what the *laws of God and man forbid*." But, he counseled, "Amidst the corrupt maxims of fashionable life, no young man is safe, whose mind is not elevated to that pitch of moral heroism, which enables him to combat successfully with vicious principles disguised under the garb of *honor*." So-called laws of honor were "derived from pagans and barbarians: they hang on half civilized men, as the tawdry trappings of savage ancestors—they deform the manners and debase the character of the age." Weak minds, "less under the influence of principle, than of fashion," would not find it easy to resist them. "But let it be deeply impressed on your mind, that no person is duly fortified against their entice-ments, who is not convinced, and who does not habitually act from the conviction that *moral principle and practice are essential to the character of a gentleman.*" He concluded,

> Whatever may be a man's external deportment, his polite-ness, or his hospitality, if he will seduce my wife, my sister or my daughter; if he will take my money from me at the gaming table, or my life in a duel, he is destitute of the *first requisites of a gentleman—justice, humanity, benevolence and real dignity of mind.* Under a polished exterior, he conceals the heart of a barbarian.[22]

Webster directed attention to the internal character of men rather than to their exterior behavior. This was another aspect of the change brought about by his conversion. Previously, he placed greater emphasis on politeness and correct manners; post-conver-sion, he was aware that genteel action might conceal a depraved heart. Only someone who was resolute in correct principles could develop the character requisite for social happiness and order. And such principles could be found only in religious conviction, or true faith. He stressed, "Both in government and religion, form your opinions with deliberation, and when you have settled your opin-ions, adhere to them with firmness." Particularly in religion, "when you have attached yourself to any system, from deliberate convic-tion, do not rashly and for light causes, abandon it. When satisfied that you have embraced an error, conscience will direct you to renounce it." One must be careful of constant changes that give evidence of a "want of principle or want of firmness and stability, neither of which is compatible with true dignity of character."[23] Beliefs are not to be either appropriated or tossed away like new and old clothes, Webster was saying. They are too important to be treated cavalierly. Convictions must be internalized by careful deliberation and not changed unless conscience demands it. People who readily discard beliefs do not possess a clear understanding of principle, and have not developed "true dignity of character."

Probably the most galling aspect of the American political scene, in Webster's view, was that a partisan press abused men of sound principles and unsullied character. This was particularly the case, Webster believed, of the Republican presses. His conversion had not changed his political alignment; rather, it had confirmed for him the correctness of the Federalist viewpoint, understood now in the light of Scripture instead of human reason. Webster was one of the most active promoters of the Hartford Convention, summoned during the War of 1812 to recommend amendments to the Constitution.[24] When Republicans attacked that gathering as a traitorous plot to sever the Union, Federalism was badly discredited. Twenty years after the event, Webster still was indignant over the Republicans' attack. To Daniel Webster he reminisced about the Convention and concluded, "The object of the people & the measures of the convention were in my view, as *lawful*, as *constitutional* & as *honorable*, as any that ever characterized the councils of any public body in this country." Furthermore, he commented, "I knew *all* the gentlemen who first met to consult on the subject. I knew *most* of the members of the convention, & with many of them I had been intimately acquainted for twenty or thirty years." No body of men, he remonstrated, had "combined more talents, purer integrity, sounder patriotism & republican principles, or more firm attachment to the constitution of the United States, than the gentlemen who composed the convention."[25]

Attacks of this type, Webster charged, had been employed "for more than half a century, to discredit the best men that ever adorned the councils of the United States." He had examined for many years the motives and effects of "this spirit of calumny & misrepresentation," he informed the other Webster, and had concluded that "instead of deriving any hopes of reformation from the supposed increasing intelligence of the people, recent facts continually occurring have confirmed my apprehensions that evil admits of no effectual remedy."[26] Increase of knowledge was not the answer; the nature of man had to be changed.

Webster tried to be optimistic about America's political future. He wrote to his daughter Harriet in 1835, "But it is not only *useless* but *criminal* to indulge great anxiety, for the same God who made the world still governs it; and those of us who put our trust in Him He will not abandon. Let us, my Dear Harriet, confide in Him and not anticipate evil."[27] Yet anticipation of the people's continued degeneracy haunted his mind. The loss of principle and character seemed so obvious that his trust in God was sorely tested. It was the newspapers, time and again, that bore the brunt of his assaults. "It is an observation which I have often made," he wrote Charles Chauncey, a leading Pennsylvania Federalist, in 1837, "that the character of our public papers has been much changed since the establishment of the present constitution." He discerned that "neither in pamphlets nor newspapers, have we any (or very few) discussions of the general principles of government. And I think it capable of proof that most of our leading men entirely mistake the principles & the inherent tendency of our democratic institutions to disorder & oppression; & they mistake the remedy."[28]

Later the same year, Webster again wrote Chauncey:

> *Principles*, Sir, are becoming corrupt, deeply corrupt; & unless the progress of corruption, & perversion of truth can be arrested, neither liberty nor property, will long be secure in this country. And a great evil is, that men of the first distinction seem, to a great extent, to be ignorant of the real, original causes of our public distresses. Many of our greatest men are making vigorous efforts to *remove present evils*, but not an effort is made to correct the radical cause of our political calamities. . . .
>
> I can do nothing of value in attempts to arrest public evils, except occasionally to use my pen. But I was educated in the Washington School, the principles of which have been abandoned by a large portion of our citizens; but which *must be revived*, as the basis of public policy, or our republic is destined to ruin.[29]

The principles of the Washington School, as Webster styled them, were Federalist, and were based on moral integrity, a quality that seemed to him to be diminishing in the country with each new year. Especially upsetting was the large number of Federalists who had abandoned the cause and taken shelter in one of the two new parties of the 1830s, either the Democrats or the Whigs. The principles of Andrew Jackson and the Democrats, in particular, were the very antitheses of tried and true Federalist principles. As one scholar has shown, many ex-Federalists attached themselves to Jackson for the opportunity to regain prominent positions in the government, in the hope that a three-decade long proscription would be terminated.[30] Such an abandonment of principle was anathema to Webster, and it must have been a hard blow to witness lifelong acquaintances such as Timothy Pickering suddenly sing the praises of the Tennessee General. Webster had a greater affinity for the Whigs, but he took them to task for compromising and abandoning principle. Thus, to Rufus Dawes, son of Webster's brother-in-law and, in 1838, the editor of a Whig newspaper, he wrote:

> I cannot enter into a particular statement of my views & opinions, in regard to our country. It would require too much labor for a man in his *eightieth year*. But I will from time to time give you my opinions. I am of the old Washington School. I have found reason every year to be confirmed in my principles; . . . And it irritates me to see men calling themselves *Whigs*, join with the profligate adherents of Jackson & Van Buren in railing at *federalists*. The truth is this govt cannot stand, or at least it cannot answer the objects of govt, till our citizens administer it upon the principles of Washington. But there is no necessity of insisting on the use of *names—principles* we must have that are just & practicable, or we cannot sustain the govt.[31]

The Whigs he again decried in a letter to his eldest daughter, Emily: "Jefferson's principles have so corrupted the public mind, & tainted the opinions of the *Whigs*, so called, that four fifths of them are about as wrong, in *general principles*, as their opposers." He concluded with the verbal equivalent of a plague on the houses of both Whigs and Democrats:

> I look with disgust & contempt on the electioneering management of both parties. Their conventions, their

> dinner speakers, their vituperations in the papers, their
> log-cabin-building. . . . Oh, it is all folly, & meanness &
> degradation. But I have a short time only to witness these
> scenes, & all I can say is, I wish well to my country, &
> pray for its prosperity.[32]

Phony electioneering practices drew his ire primarily for two
reasons: first, they attempted to flatter the common man and
promoted a leveling spirit; and second, they grasped at power. On
this latter point, he minced no words. Speaking of America's first
president, Webster declared, "That virtuous man did not seek the
suffrages of his fellow-citizens; he employed no arts to *obtain* the
office of President; he had no selfish views in *accepting* it. Such a
man, and such only can be safely trusted with the public welfare."[33]

Letters to a Young Gentleman further expounded this theme. "One
of the surest tests of a man's real worth, is the esteem & confidence
of those who have long known him, and his conduct in domestic and
social life," Webster held. He believed it was generally true "that
respect spontaneously attaches itself to real worth; and the man of
respectable virtues, never has occasion to run after respect." How
would one run after respect? "Whenever a man is known to seek
promotion by intrigue, by temporizing, or by resorting to the haunts
of vulgarity and vice for support, it may be inferred, with moral
certainty, that he is not a man of real respectability, nor is he entitled
to public confidence." As a general rule, he affirmed "that the man
who never *intrigues* for office, may be most safely *entrusted* with
office; for the same noble qualities, his pride, or his integrity and
sense of dignity, which make him disdain the mean arts of flattery
and intrigue, will restrain him from debasing himself by betraying
his trust." This would be a man who "cannot desire promotion,
unless he receives it from the respectable part of the community; for
he considers no other promotion to be honorable."[34] In 1834, he
looked back to the glory days of Federalist ascendancy and invoked
the names of those in the Federalist pantheon:

> A Washington and a Jay would sooner have cut off a right
> hand than *bribe a press*, or *promise an office*, or *remove a*
> *faithful officer*, to gratify a partisan, or secure a vote.

Such men never employ agents to sneak into every nook and corner of a country for votes. Men of worth enjoy respect, but it comes without their seeking it. And let it be remarked, that no man who is obliged to resort to grog-shops, and secret combinations of the *people*, for his election, is worthy of any public trust whatever.[35]

Parties and Equality

Closely allied with Webster's concern for morality and principle was his contempt for political parties and their techniques. He perceived Party men to be in pursuit of only one thing—political office—usually at the expense of moral principle and moral practice. His conversion only sharpened and strengthened his objections. His heightened sense of morality, based upon Biblical standards, was more easily offended than before when confronted with parties and their methods for securing the vote. Truth, he remarked to Daniel Webster, is sacrificed by a party spirit that can "impose misrepresentations upon a *whole people*, & mislead a great portion of them into opinions directly contrary to facts."[36]

Because Webster never reconciled himself to the existence of parties, he never saw himself as a member of one. Regardless how vociferous he was in favor of Federalist policies, he preferred to consider himself, and all Federalists, as merely good citizens who placed principle and statesmanship above party allegiances. Perhaps modern readers, scrutinizing for the first time Webster's denunciation of parties, might feel he was hypocritical because of his Federalist loyalties. In fact, though, he honestly felt that he was simply supporting the views of those who established the country, and his attacks against Jeffersonian Republicanism were attacks against a foreign (presumably French) influence that had wormed its way into the American system.[37] Therefore, he could write the following instructions and feel no sense of hypocrisy:

> When we consider that men are all brethren of the same family, all created with similar capacities, and vested with the same natural rights; and in this country, all enjoying equal civil and religious rights, under the protection of law; all equally entitled to security and public privileges;

all placed under the same moral discipline, and all destined to the same end—how disgusting is it to see one party or one sect arrogating to itself superior merit, or proud distinction, and saying to others, *"stand by thyself—come not near me, for I am holier than thou!"* Yet such is the language of parties; often in religion—always in government. When the fundamental principles of government or our holy religion are assaulted, good men must unite to defend them. But the most numerous and most violent parties that trouble society, spring from private ambition and interest, when no principles are in jeopardy—or from an undue attachment to speculative opinions in politics, or to the externals of religion; and in such parties, the human character is displayed in all its depravity and degradation. In the tranquil condition of affairs in this country, when our citizens enjoy all the privileges which good men can desire, and more than many can enjoy without abuse, a disposition to exalt one class of citizens and to depress another, is a foul reproach to men—a fouler reproach to Christians.[38]

The "depressed" citizens, from Webster's perspective, were Federalists who, as a body, had been proscribed by a succession of Republican administrations. Regarding men as members of a party is wrong, he asserted, and counseled, "Accustom yourself from your youth to consider all men as your brethren, and know no distinction between fellow citizens, except that which they make themselves, by their *virtues* or their *vices*; by their *worth* or their *meanness.*"[39] A man's character, represented by his virtues or vices, was the real issue.

Webster considered party spirit an active agent in the destruction of character. The lust for political office overshadowed all concern for moral integrity. Candidates for offices, he commented in the *Commercial Advertiser* in 1834, "establish printing presses to secure their election," praising themselves and vilifying their opponents "at the expense of truth."

In this way, the candidates are represented as having qualifications for office of which they are wholly destitute—while the best and purest characters in the land, if opposed to the candidates, are slandered and exposed to popular odium. This practice of slandering good men has had a most deleterious effect on public morals, by encouraging a contempt for character, and exciting the evil passions of envy, jealousy, and hatred. It is doubtful whether the world can present another example of a people so notorious for slander and contempt for moral worth, as the supporters of party spirit in the United States.[40]

When Webster stated this opinion, he was not taking aim at one party only, because both parties, he explained to his son, William, had "abandoned the true republican principle of *public good*, & occupy their time & exertions in scrambling for offices." The mania for party had created a new type of monarchy: "It is supposed that our govt is secure because it rests on the *will of the people*, but a few millions of dollars bestowed in offices & in supporting party presses will control the *will of the people*," he lamented, "& we have now a *monarchy in essence*, executed by the *will of the people*."[41]

Both parties' new fascination with an abstract concept of "the people" worried Webster. Bowing and scraping to the common man, in order to obtain office, betrayed again a lack of principle and firm moral foundations. Courageous leadership was in short supply as politicians sought to determine what the people would accept, whether or not the people were correct in their views of good policy. He winced when prominent Whigs conformed to the practice. "When H. Clay & D. Webster utter opinions, which I deem *radicalism*, opposition will do no good," he moaned to Charles Chauncey in 1838. "Mr. Clay, in two instances, the last session, said he should be in favor of a National Bank, *if the people* wished it. When such men resort to the *people*, indefinitely, for direction on such questions, our case is hopeless."[42]

Webster believed in an equality of rights and in each man's equality before the law. But he objected to a broad use of the term without a proper definition. "It seems to be a political axiom," he acknowledged, "that republics should be founded on an equality of rights, or so constructed as to preserve that equality." It also was undeniable that all men had an equal right to "the protection of their persons, their reputation and their property." But, he queried, "has a man who has no property to defend, and none to support the expenses of government, an *equal right* to legislate upon property, as a man who has property to guard and to apply to the support and defense of his country?" This reasoning led to a hypothetical scenario:

> May it not be true in a republic, that a *majority* of the citizens may possess a *minority* of the property, and may it not happen that the *minor* interest may govern the *major interest*? And in this case, what becomes of the *equality of rights*, on which we profess to found a republican government? When the sober, industrious citizen, who, by his toil and economy, collects a moderate estate, brings up a family in good habits, and pays his taxes to the government, finds that his property and virtue give him no influence or advantage as a member of the government, over the idle pennyless lounger, who earns little and spends that little in vice, paying nothing to government, what attachment can this good citizen feel to the government? What confidence can he place in its administration? What expectation can he entertain of its durability? And what sort of government is that in which the *owners* of the country do not govern it?[43]

This was a plea for property ownership to remain a qualification for the privilege of suffrage. Webster the Federalist was not necessarily against an extension of the suffrage per se, but did oppose an indiscriminate extension that would include the "idle pennyless lounger" who would then cancel the influence of an industrious, solid citizen.

Perhaps his most expansive treatment of the subject of equality is found in a letter to the well-known jurist, James Kent, written just three months before Webster's death in 1843. In this letter, the aged Federalist explained in full his understanding of that controversial concept. After noting statements of equality and freedom found in state bills of rights and in the national Declaration of Independence, Webster proceeded to interpret the words "free" and "equal" in the light of his now-established Biblical foundations.

"In the first place," he declared, "no person is born *free*, in an unrestricted sense of the word; for all children are born subject to their parents, & this by the express command of God. And this provision of divine authority is for the benefit of the child; as well as of the parent & of society." A second restriction on freedom, also by divine command, consisted in subjection to the government of the country into which each person happens to be born. "The word *free* then," he maintained, "applied to persons in society can mean only that they are born *free* to do what when minors, their parents or guardians permit, & in their adult years, they are *free* to do what the laws of the country, & the laws of God permit."[44]

Turning to equality, he remarked, "That all men are equal in an unqualified sense of the word, can not be true. So far is this from the truth, that no two persons are born *equal*, either in the powers of body or mind; & rarely indeed are any two persons born in equal condition." There is only one sense in which citizens are equal—in the possession and enjoyment of equal personal rights, particularly the right to protection of person and property, and the right to "the free use of his powers & faculties for his own benefit, without any restraint," except, of course, for the laws of God and society. "To secure every member of society in the enjoyment of these rights, is the great object of government," declared Webster.[45]

Men are unequal in their faculties and abilities, and in their circumstances, Webster reasoned, because it is the will of God—not an arbitrary, cruel will, but a will specifically designed to bring benefit to everyone. He then outlined the possibilities:

> Suppose all men to be in an equal condition, & all poor; then in sickness & distress or long continued calamity, who could furnish relief? One poor man could not give his time or his labor for the relief of his neighbor. . . .
>
> And if all men were rich & in equal condition, their case would be little better than if they were all poor, so far as assistance in distress should be required. One rich man would not perform the labor of another gratuitously, nor could he be hired to perform it. . . . Occasional & temporary services might be rendered from kindness; but

no great sacrifices to assist each other would proceed from favor. . . .

Nothing can be more obvious than that by the appointment of the Creator, in the constitution of man, & of human society, the conditions of men must be different & *unequal*. Mutual wants produce a dependence of one man upon another, & mutual dependence, resulting from different circumstances & inequality of conditions, is the common tie that binds man to man, uniting the members of society by a common *necessity*, & a common *interest*.[46]

Webster obviously held to a belief in a hierarchical society, yet not one in which differences were a source of frustration and resentment; rather, they were a divinely inspired policy to promote unity and union. He explained further: "The rich depend on the poor for labor & services; the poor depend on the rich for employment & the means of subsistence. The parent depends on the child for assistance in his business, & for support in old age; the child depends on the parent for food & raiment; for protection & instruction. These dependencies," Webster felt, were "essential to the welfare of society," and "result from diversities in conditions; from *inequality* in age & experience; *inequality* of strength; *inequality* of knowledge & skill; & *inequality* of wealth." Yet these dependencies

provide harmony in society; mutual dependences produce mutual attachments, which an entire independence or equality of condition would destroy. Mutual attachments, resulting from reciprocal wants, are the guaranty for the exercise of humanity, justice & kindness of the rich to the poor, & of integrity & fidelity of the poor to the rich. It is this mutual dependence which counteracts selfishness, haughtiness & insolence, & subjects both the rich & the poor to the laws of humanity, justice, benevolence & social decorum. Remove these dependences arising from different & unequal conditions, & we should derange or wholly interrupt the employments, & the order of society, & to a great degree, the very civilities of life. This inequality of conditions, which political dreamers stigmatize as injustice, is, in reality, the support of the social system; the basis of all subordination in families & in govt.[47]

God's plan was not inscrutable, but could be clearly understood. God knew how depraved men (this includes all mankind) would act and react to differing circumstances, that they "would not perform the necessary duties & services of social life, from the mere impulse of good principles or from favor." God therefore allowed a diversity of conditions that would "make *necessity* a substitute for *principles*, & compel men by their *wants* & their *interests*, mutually to aid each other."[48] Left to himself, man will exalt self; God intervenes to turn man toward unselfishness by ensuring that men need one another.

Webster also explored the exact meaning of the sovereignty, or will, of the people. There can be no doubt, he reasoned, that a majority of citizens have the right to form governments and make laws. But in a country as large as the United States, it was essential to delegate the legislative powers to representatives, and have them determine policy. The representative assembly, freely elected by the people, constitutes the sovereign power until the next election. Any attempt to disrupt the sovereignty of elected representatives is usurpation. Binding instructions to representatives, therefore, would be inappropriate. A representative is under obligation to collect facts and opinions from the deliberations of the representative assembly, and then form his conclusions and vote accordingly. To do otherwise would be a violation of his oath and a dereliction of duty. "Hence it results that a representative has not right to pledge his vote before his election, nor after his election, till he has the benefit of consulting the representatives in the council of the whole confederacy, which is to be affected by his vote. All such pledges," Webster deduced, "are judgments formed before the hearing of a cause. The contrary practice proceeds from one of the most palpable & mischievous errors that can, in any way, affect legislation." Near the end of his letter to Kent, Webster concluded that the exaltation of the "people," without a clear definition of the term, leads the "people" to mistake their powers, assume an unconscionable control over the laws, and destroy the public will. "The law must be sovereign," he insisted, "or there is no regular government."[49]

Webster's conversion did not change his Federalist stance on matters of public policy; he was a Federalist before the experience, and he remained a steadfast Federalist to his last breath. It did, however, transform his Federalism because he now believed it to have Biblical sanction. The Federalist outlook in such matters as a society with a definite hierarchy was confirmed by the Biblical worldview he had accepted. A new basis for his Federalism was provided: no longer would he have to resort to man's reason as the authority for his political beliefs; he now could speak with the authority of the Word of God.

Other studies have made much of Webster's pessimistic prognostications for American politics. It is true that he soured on America's future with each passing year. His concept of a Christian republic seemed to recede further from reality with each new turn of events. Yet it would be a mistake to translate that pessimism into outright hopelessness, for, since his conversion, Webster had a new hope. This hope was primarily personal, but it also impinged on his political thoughts. As he expressed to his daughter, Emily, late in his life, "Our political condition is woefully bad, & were it not that I see the influences of divine grace in reforming my fellow citizens, I should abandon all hope of the future welfare of the country."[50] There remained a spark of hope for America, and it lay in the intervention of God in the lives of individuals. What Webster eventually forsook was the hope of changing the outward structures and institutions in a way that would brighten future prospects. He never gave up on the inward transformation that God might perform on certain individuals. He hoped the Righteous Judge would withhold the full force of His judgments on America if enough of the regenerate were present to act as a preservative in society. If it had happened in his life, he speculated, it could happen in the lives of others also.

---

[1] Webster to David McClure, 25 October 1836, in Warfel, *Letters*, 457.

[2] Webster to Elijah Steele, 31 January 1809, Miscellaneous Manuscripts 237, Yale.

[3] Webster to James Madison, 16 October 1829, Madison Papers, Series 2, Library of Congress.

[4] Webster to David McClure, 25 October 1836, in Warfel, *Letters*, 454.

[5] Webster, *History of the United States* (New Haven: Durrie & Peck, 1832), v.

[6] Ibid., 273-74.

[7] Ibid., 274-75.

[8] Webster, speech to the Connecticut Historical Society (1840), Webster Papers, NYPL, Box 8.

[9] Webster, letter to the editor, New York *Commercial Advertiser*, 22 October 1836.

[10] Ibid.

[11] Webster to David McClure, 25 October 1836, in Warfel, *Letters*, 453-54.

[12] Webster, unpublished manuscript, "Origin of Parties," (ca. 1840), 38, Webster Papers, NYPL, Box 8.

[13] Webster, speech to the Connecticut Historical Society (1840).

[14] Webster to James Madison, 20 February 1809, Madison Papers, Series 1, Library of Congress.

[15] Webster, *Letters to a Young Gentleman Commencing His Education* (1823) in Verna M. Hall & Rosalie J. Slater, *Rudiments of America's Christian History and Government* (San Francisco: Foundation for American Christian Education, 1968), 26.

[16] Webster, *Value of the Bible, and Excellence of the Christian Religion* (New Haven: Durrie & Peck, 1834), from manuscript copy, 127-28, Beinecke Rare Book and Manuscript Library, Yale.

[17] Ibid., 219-20.

[18] Ibid., 221.

[19] Webster, proposed amendments to the U.S. Constitution, n.d., Webster Papers, NYPL, Box 8.

[20] Webster, *An Oration, Pronounced before the Knox and Warren Branches of the Washington Benevolent Society, at Amherst, on the Celebration of the Anniversary of the Declaration of Independence, July 4, 1814* (Northampton, MA: William Butler, 1814), 6.

[21] Webster, *Letters to a Young Gentleman*, in Hall & Slater, *Rudiments*, 17-18.

[22] Ibid., 18.

[23] Ibid., 27.

[24] Webster, "Memoir," 51.

25 Webster to Daniel Webster, 6 September 1834, Daniel Webster Papers, Library of Congress. Noah had written the other Webster in sympathy for a newspaper's misrepresentation of a comment made by Daniel Webster. "I am mortified," he consoled him, "that the propagation of such a calumny, & its reception by a portion of the people should make it necessary for a gentleman of your character to deny the charge. I am mortified that men can be found, in this country, *weak* enough to suppose you, or any respectable man, capable of the meanness which could dictate such a declaration, or *wicked* enough to propagate it, knowing it to be false. Yet it is not improbable our country contains multitudes of persons who may fall under both descriptions."

26 Ibid.

27 Webster to Harriet Webster Fowler, 7 January 1835, in Warfel, *Letters*, 446.

28 Webster to Charles Chauncey, 27 February 1837, Chauncey Family Papers, Yale. On the subject of newspapers and the misinformation they contain, Webster related to Daniel Webster, 6 September 1834, "The freedom of the press is a valuable privilege; but the abuse of it, in this country, . . . is a frightful evil. The licentiousness of the press is a deep stain upon the character of the country; & in addition to the evil of calumniating good men, & giving a wrong direction to public measures, it corrupts the people by rendering them insensible to the value of truth & of reputation."

To Horace Greeley, editor of the *New Yorker*, ca. 20 December 1838, Webster Papers, NYPL, Box 1, Webster lamented, "Errors propagated through the press can not be recalled, & rarely or never can the injurious impressions which they make, be wholly effaced. This, Sir, is a great public evil."

29 Webster to Charles Chauncey, 17 October 1837, Chauncey Family Papers, Yale.

30 See Shaw Livermore, *The Twilight of Federalism* (New York: Gordian Press, 1972), particularly chapter XII, "The Emancipation of a Numerous Class."

31 Webster to Rufus Dawes, 9 March 1838, Webster Papers, NYPL, Box 1.

32 Webster to Emily Webster Ellsworth, 29 April 1840, Webster Papers, CHS. In another letter to Emily, 3 July 1840, Webster Papers, CHS, Webster echoed his earlier distress, "But the *Log Cabin*—Oh how our country is degraded, when even men of respectability resort to such means to secure an election! I struggled, in the days of Washington, to sustain good principles—but since Jefferson's principles have prostrated the popular respect for sound principles, further efforts would be useless—And I quit the contest forever."

33 Webster, *1814 Oration*, 4.

34 Webster, *Letters to a Young Gentleman*, in Hall & Slater, *Rudiments*, 26-27.

35 Webster, article signed "A Whig of '76" in the New York *Commercial Advertiser*, 14 February 1834.

36 Webster to Daniel Webster, 6 September 1834, Daniel Webster Papers, Library of Congress.

37 A striking example of how Webster lay the blame for American political evils at Jefferson's feet is found in a letter to his daughter Emily, 6 December 1839, Webster

Papers, CHS, in which he expresses disbelief in her tardy recognition of just how wrong Jefferson had been: "I have received your long & good letter, in which the very first sentence surprises me. Why really have you just made the discovery that Thomas Jefferson was a very bad man? I am afraid I have not been faithful in my instructions to my children. I have known & published for forty years that Jefferson's principles have been the primary causes of all our public evils—not merely commercial evils, which are bad enough, but the evil of *erroneous opinions, corrupt opinions*, which infest the great body of our citizens & which render it impossible to rectify disorders during this generation. . . . The evil is too deep-rooted to be cured for a long time."

38 Webster, *Letters to a Young Gentleman*, in Hall & Slater, *Rudiments*, 22.

39 Ibid., 23.

40 Webster, article signed "A Whig of '76" in the New York *Commercial Advertiser*, 14 February 1834.

41 Webster to William Webster, 25 March 1836, Webster Papers, Yale.

42 Webster to Charles Chauncey, 4 January 1838, Chauncey Family Papers, Yale.

43 Webster, *Letters to a Young Gentleman*, in Hall & Slater, *Rudiments*, 24.

44 Webster to James Kent, 7 February 1843, Webster Papers, NYPL, Box 1.

45 Ibid.

46 Ibid.

47 Ibid.

48 Ibid.

49 Ibid. Concerning pledges by representatives to vote a certain way while campaigning for election, Webster wrote to his son, William, 8 April 1838, Webster Papers, NYPL, Box 1: "Abolition too is taking a high tone in New England, & the anti-slavery society in Hartford, I am told, have demanded of the candidates for our Senate, a *pledge* that they will favor the cause. This is a degree of effrontery which was hardly to be expected in Connecticut. I look on our public affairs with alarm."

50 Webster to Emily Webster Ellsworth, 25 April 1838, Webster Papers, CHS.

CHAPTER 9

Christian Foundations:
Education Revisited

Webster's 1808 conversion strongly affected not only his views of government and public policy, but of education also. But whereas conversion primarily authenticated long-held views of government and politics, the conversion's application to Webster's educational views involved a more profound change. Biblical truth became the channel through which the intellect was strengthened and expanded. "The Christian religion exalts the intellect and perfects the human character," became his new outlook. Although the main objective of religion was "to correct the heart and purify it from whatever is wrong and inconsistent with the enjoyment of God," it nonetheless was true that "the sublime views of God and of his works, which the scriptures exhibit have a wonderful effect in strengthening the intellect and expanding its powers." Further,

> This purity of mind and this elevation and expansion of intellect are the beginnings of that ever increasing holiness and that boundless enlargement of knowledge which are to complete the character and the felicity of the children of God, in another world.[1]

No longer was Webster eager to downplay the use of the Bible in the classroom. Instead, he felt that "the first principle to be established in the human mind, is reverence for the character and laws of God. *The fear of God is the beginning of wisdom.*"[2] He began to believe that "any system of education, therefore, which limits instruction to the arts and sciences, and rejects the aids of religion in forming the characters of citizens, is essentially defective."[3] His own early education, in light of his new criteria, also had been defective. "I read books without system, and embraced theories which misled me, or diverted my mind from a due attention to facts and common sense, the basis of practical knowledge," he lamented in a letter to the *Genesee Farmer and Gardener's Journal*. Most important, he "neglected to imitate the example of Christ and his apostles, in attempting to be *great* rather than *good*." This was an admission that his motivation in the early years was self-aggrandizement. He continued,

> I devoted more time and attention to human literature, than to the acquisition of that knowledge which ought to be the first and principal business of life—a knowledge of my Maker's will, and of the means of benefiting myself and my fellow men, by correcting vices, erroneous opinions, and evil habits, and thus exalting the human character to the dignity of christians.[4]

In his quest for immediate greatness, Webster confessed in his *Manual of Useful Studies*, he had published his opinions prematurely. "Possibly this example," he hoped, "may operate as a caution to young men, ambitious of authorship, not to hazard the publication of their opinions, till time, long study, observation and experience, have matured their judgment."[5] Perhaps his regrets over his own past helped prompt a thorough reexamination of his philosophy of education.

The first twenty years of Webster's life after his conversion were devoted to the compilation of his dictionary. Yet even with all his attention drawn to that great work, he could not help thinking about education and airing his views on the proper mode of education. In 1812, he moved his family to Amherst, Massachusetts, to enable him "to subsist my family at a less expense."[6] In the ensuing years, he helped establish both an academy and a college in that town. He was a charter member of the Amherst Academy's Board of Trustees, and later became its president. Moreover, as a member of the

Massachusetts General Court (to which he was elected in 1814, 1815, and 1817), he proposed that a school fund be established in his new state similar to that of Connecticut's.

In 1822, Webster removed once again to New Haven, where he resided for the rest of his life. The removal did not interrupt other attempts to further his new educational agenda. Shortly after his return to Connecticut, he published *Letters to a Young Gentleman Commencing His Education* and, after a major revision of his Speller in 1829, he offered the nation a series of instructional books, for use both in schools and in the home. In 1830, he published *A Biography for the Use of Schools*. He followed this with an *Elementary Primer* and *An Improved Grammar* in 1831, and his *History of the United States* one year later. In 1833, he came out with an amended version of the Bible, to his mind an educational as well as a religious endeavor, and one that he called "the most important enterprise of my life, & as important as any benevolent design now on foot."[7] Webster introduced a revised reader, *Instructive and Entertaining Lessons for Youth*, in 1835, followed by a supplement to his Speller, entitled *The Teacher*, in 1836. *The Little Franklin*, also published in 1836, was a shorter reader intended for younger children; *A Manual of Useful Studies*, 1839, was an attempt to put in one book all the essentials of a basic education for young people. Webster's final publication, which appeared at about the same time as his death in May 1843, was *A Collection of Papers on Political, Literary, and Moral Subjects*, comprised of what he considered to be the best of all his previous writings.[8]

Education Defined

Definition of terms is made easy when dealing with a lexicographer who compiled every word of his dictionary himself. Webster's understanding of education, already quoted in the introduction to this study, is worth repeating:

> The bringing up, as of a child; instruction; formation of manners. Education comprehends all that series of instruction and discipline which is intended to enlighten the understanding, correct the temper, and form the manners and habits of youth, and fit them for usefulness

in their future stations. To give children a good *education* in manners, arts and science, is important; to give them a religious *education* is indispensable; and an immense responsibility rests on parents and guardians who neglect these duties.[9]

The emphasis on the indispensability of religious education at the end of Webster's definition confirms that Webster's conversion made a dramatic alteration in his views of education. Priority is given to religious instruction, and those who fail to take their children's education seriously are derelict in duty.

Webster, in all his post-conversion comments on educational theory, held true to his definition. He found it hard not to include thoughts on education in most of his writings, even those not directly related to the subject. In a formal address delivered before an agricultural society, for instance, he made a connection between husbandry and intellectual improvement. "The rational powers of men," he reminded his audience, "are talents entrusted to them by their Creator, for the purpose of use and improvement—and we are not authorized to keep them in a napkin."[10] He concluded the address with an affirmation of the crucial role of religion in education. and counseled obedience to God as essential to the welfare of the country:

> The proper business of man is to enlarge the powers of his mind by knowledge, and refine it by the culture of moral habits; to increase the means of subsistence and comfort; to supply the wants and alleviate the distresses of his brethren; to cherish the virtues and restrain the vices of society; to multiply the rational enjoyments of life; to diffuse the means of education, and the blessings of religion; and to extend his benevolence and charities to the whole human family. In a word, the duty, the whole business, of man is, to yield obedience to his Maker; and just in proportion to that obedience, will be the private happiness, and the public prosperity of a nation.[11]

Amherst College
Possibly one of the most satisfying educational experiences of

Webster's life was the founding of both an academy and college in Amherst, Massachusetts. The Amherst Academy was founded in 1814 and incorporated in 1816 by the Massachusetts legislature, largely through Webster's efforts. Webster himself, as a member of the Board of Trustees, spent considerable time at the school speaking to the students, and even offered his home for school functions. By 1817, there was interest in the establishment of a college to train indigent young men for the ministry. One reason for agitation for a new college was the dissatisfaction of evangelicals with the Harvard drift toward Unitarianism. As Webster wrote to Jedidiah Morse in 1820: "Is it not probable that the institution we are founding may have a college annexed to it, & become a large & respectable seminary which shall attract round it all the evangelical people of the commonwealth; & ultimately circumscribe the influence of Cambridge? If so, what is the duty of all the friends of truth & piety?"[12] And to another compatriot he confided, "We do hope that this infant institution will grow up to a size which will contribute to check the progress of errors which are propagated from Cambridge. The influence of the University of Cambridge, supported by great wealth and talents, seems to call on all the friends of truth to unite in circumscribing it."[13]

When the cornerstone for Amherst College was laid on 9 August 1820, Webster gave the opening remarks:

> The object of this institution, that of educating for the gospel ministry young men in indigent circumstances, but of hopeful piety and promising talents, is one of the noblest which can occupy the attention and claim the contributions of the public. It is to second the efforts of the apostles themselves, in extending and establishing the Redeemer's empire—the empire of truth. It is to aid in the important works of raising the human race from ignorance and debasement; to enlighten their minds; to exalt their character; and to teach them the way to happiness and glory. . . . We live to see a new era in the history of man—an era when reason and religion begin to resume their sway, and to impress the heavenly truth, that the appropriate business of men, is to imitate the Savior; to serve their God; and

bless their fellow-men.[14]

Furthering the Christian faith, raising the human race out of ignorance, and promoting individual piety and righteous living were Webster's goals. It is interesting to note again that he countenanced no dichotomy between the intellectual and religious realms; "reason and religion" would work together to inaugurate a new era.

A year later, when Amherst officially opened, Webster again gave the introductory remarks, directed to the new president, Zephaniah Swift Moore. In his remarks, he expressed the hope that "the fostering patronage of the Christian public" would raise the new college "to distinction among the literary institutions of the American Republic." Religious values received the greatest emphasis:

> By your precepts and example may virtue be honored and piety encouraged, among the youth of the Seminary; while every species of immorality shall be discountenanced and repressed. May your instructions enlarge the sphere of intellectual improvement, and circumscribe the dominion of error. In yonder Edifice may the youth of America be richly furnished with the science and erudition which shall qualify them for eminent usefulness in Church and State. There may they be instructed in the principles of our Holy Religion, and armed with fortitude and grace to defend and maintain its doctrines in their Apostolic purity.
>
> And while your labors contribute to exalt the moral, religious and literary character of your own country, may there issue from this Seminary some beams of the light of civilization and of heavenly truth, to illuminate the "dark places of the earth which are full of the habitations of cruelty."[15]

The college was to be a place where Christian morality and literary achievement would coexist; where young men would be fit for usefulness, not only in the Christian ministry, but in business and government positions. Webster hoped the new college would contribute to a moral America and to the furthering of American literary achievements.

Webster's Post-Conversion Educational Philosophy

In 1823, Webster wrote *Letters to a Young Gentleman Commencing His Education*. The first "letter" to this hypothetical young gentleman dealt at length with educational concerns and deserves more attention than it has received from scholars. While it does not go into detail on curriculum development, it does offer a fascinating glimpse into Webster's understanding of what makes education truly educative. Already this work has been cited to document the lexicographer's governmental philosophy; it also must be considered a prime source for his post-conversion educational philosophy.

Webster began with an empathetic discourse designed to connect the younger generation with the older. "As you are now commencing a course of classical education, and need the guidance of those who have preceded you in the same course," he wrote to the unspecified gentleman, "you cannot but receive with kindness, and treat with attention, the remarks of a friend, whose affection for you, excites in him a deep solicitude for your future reputation and happiness." Further, he confided, "I feel the more desirous to furnish you with some hints for the direction of your studies, for I have experienced the want of such helps myself; no small portions of my life having been spent in correcting the errors of my early education."[16]

His exposition of an educational philosophy began where it logically should—with the first stages of learning:

> It has been often remarked, that men are the creatures of habit. The rudiments of knowledge we receive by tradition; and our first actions are, in a good degree, modelled by imitation. Nor ought it to be other wise. The respect which young persons feel for their parents, superiors and predecessors is no less the dictate of reason, than the requirement of heaven; and the propensity to imitation, is no less natural, than it may be useful.[17]

Habit, tradition, and imitation are the heaven-directed modes of early education, according to Webster. The reasoning powers have not yet developed to the point of critical examination and under-standing, and children learn primarily by following the example of parents and others in authority. These modes also were beneficial in the early development of respect for those who wield authority. But Webster was no slave to imitation or habit. He also stressed the development of independent reasoning powers and the need for verification of truth:

> These principles however, like many others, when pursued or indulged to an extreme, produce evil effects; as they often lead the young to embrace error as well as truth. Some degree of confidence in the opinions of those whom we respect, is always a duty—in the first stages of life, our confidence in parents must be explicit—and our obedience to their will, complete and unreserved. In later stages of life, as the intellectual faculties expand and the reasoning power gains strength, implicit confidence in the opinions even of the most distinguished men, ceases to be a duty. We are to regard their opinions only as *probably* correct; but refer the ultimate decision of this point to evidence to be collected from our own reasoning or researches. All men are liable to err; and a knowledge of this fact should excite in us constant solicitude to obtain satisfactory reasons for every opinion we embrace.[18]

What may be correct for one stage of life may be wrong for another. Imitation and unquestioning obedience should be the norm until the ability to reason independently develops. This will be a gradual development. Yet independent reason, in Webster's Biblical understanding, also has its limitations. "As men are furnished with powers of reason," he deduced, "it is obviously the design of the creator, that reason should be employed as their guide, in every stage of life." The problem, though, was that reason "without culti-vation, without experience and without the aids of revelation, is a miserable guide," a guide that "often errs from ignorance, and more often from the impulse of passion."[19]

Common Sense philosophy, with its emphasis on reason and control of the passions, still was present in Webster's thought. But it was now a Common Sense with a foundation in revelation. Independent, unguided reason might ask the right questions, but it could not answer them without the aid of revelation. "The first questions a rational being should ask himself," Webster instructed, "are, *Who made me? Why was I made? What is my duty?* The proper answers to these questions, and the practical results, constitute, my dear friend, the whole business of life."

> Now reason, unaided by revelation, cannot answer these questions. The experience of the Pagan World has long since determined this point. Revelation alone furnishes satisfactory information on these subjects. Let it then be the first study that occupies your mind, to learn from the scriptures the character and will of your maker; the end or purpose for which he gave you being and intellectual powers, and the duties he requires you to perform. In all that regards faith and practice, the scriptures furnish the principles, precepts and rules, by which you are to be guided. Your reputation among men; your own tranquillity of mind in this life; and all rational hope of future happiness, depend on an exact conformity of conduct to the commands of God revealed in the sacred oracles.[20]

Webster assumed that any rational being would begin to wonder about life's purpose and would try to find the answers. The first two questions he catalogued—*who made me* and *why was I made*—were theological, exploring the purpose of the universe and man's place in it; the third—*what is my duty*—was ethical in its orientation, inquiring into the nature of good and evil. The answers, he concluded, could *only* be found in God's revelation. This being the case, the Bible becomes the answer-book for all of life's questions.

The letter continued with an exposition on the full meaning of the Ten Commandments, and then an appeal to know the Person—God Himself—behind the commandments. "Let it then be the first study of your early years, to learn in what consists *real worth* or *dignity of character*. To ascertain this important point, consider the character and attributes of the Supreme Being." Since God is "the only perfect Being in the Universe," it followed that "his character, consisting of all that is good and great, must be the model of all human excellence; and his laws must of course be the only rules of conduct by which his rational creatures can reach any portion of like excellence." God's character is the standard by which a man is judged. "In the very nature of things then a man is exalted in proportion to his conformity to the divine standard of worth; and degraded in proportion to his want of conformity to that standard." It also followed that "Nothing can be *really honorable* and *dignified* which is not in *exact accordance with rectitude*. Let this be imprinted on your mind as the first principle of moral science." If a violation of human laws "impairs the reputation and lessens the moral worth of the offender—much more does a transgression of the Divine Law, imply want of dignity and self-respect as well as contempt for the Supreme Lawgiver—it sinks a man in his own estimation and debases him in the opinion of his fellow-men."[21]

Rational men, desirous of developing true "dignity of character" naturally should look to the character of "the only perfect Being" and conscientiously follow that example as revealed in the Scriptures. To do less, to settle for less, to base character on any source other than God, could not be acceptable. More than that, if a man's conduct did not square with the Biblical standard, not only was it wicked, but a degradation of what man was supposed to be. Webster always had been concerned about character. He now had a higher source for judging proper character, independent of philosophies that he felt were grounded in man's reason alone. As Webster commented in a letter to a newspaper in 1840, "The general preference given to instruction in human science and literature, in our Seminaries, while the subjects of ethics and religion, which constitute the basis of all social and durable happiness, are neglected, I have long lamented, not merely as an *error*, but as a *sin*." He then made a comparison: "I have often thought how different was the conduct of Christ and his Apostles, who, in their efforts to reform the world, never mentioned human learning or the sciences, among the means of effecting their purpose." Instead, "They knew, what we may all know, that reformation is to be effected through the *heart*, and not through the *head*."[22]

Character and education could not be separated. Fully one-half of Webster's definition of education—correcting the temper, forming manners and habits—was devoted to the development of character. Since character is influenced by far more than classroom experience, and education is not just a classroom phenomenon, Webster next turned his attention to the education a young man receives in general society, and he offered guidance and warnings commensurate with his post-conversion worldview:

> In selecting books for reading, be careful to choose such as furnish the best helps to improvement in morals, literature, arts and science; preferring profit to pleasure, and instruction to amusement. A small portion of time may be devoted to such reading as tends to relax the mind, and to such bodily amusements as serve to invigorate muscular strength and the vital functions. But the greatest part of life is to be employed in useful labors, and in various indispensable duties, private, social and public. Man has but little time to spare for the gratification of the senses and the imagination. I would therefore caution you against the fascinations of plays, novels, romances, and that species of descriptive writing which is employed to embellish common objects, without much enlarging the bounds of knowledge, or to paint imaginary scenes, which only excite curiosity, and a temporary interest; and then vanish in empty air.[23]

According to Webster, a man should realize that the major portion of his time should be spent in productive labor. Webster himself always had been an indefatigable worker. His conversion only strengthened his natural bent toward industry. Time must be spent profitably because all time is a gift from God, and God expects man to be continually employed in the improvement of society's moral health and in its advances in learning. Pleasure and amusement are fine in small doses, but profit and instruction are to be preferred. On the division between amusement and instruction, and the superiority of the latter, he was quite emphatic. "The readers of books may be comprehended in two classes—those who read chiefly for amusement, and those who read for instruction. The first, and far the more numerous class, give their money and their time for private gratification; the second employ both for the acquisition of knowledge, which they expect to apply to some useful purpose." The comparison continued: "The first, gain subjects of conversation and social entertainment; the second, acquire the means of public usefulness, and of private elevation of character." However,

> the readers of the first class are so numerous, and the thirst for novelty so insatiable, that the country must be deluged with tales and fiction; and if you suffer yourself to be hurried along with the current of popular feeling, not only your *time*, but your *mind* will be dissipated; your native faculties, instead of growing into masculine vigor, will languish into imbecility. Bacon and Newton did not read tales and novels; their great minds were nourished with very different aliment.[24]

Undue attention to books of amusement would then, in his view, undermine an individual, rendering him unfit for usefulness in society and depriving him of the strength of character that could be imparted through proper reading.

Webster's solicitudes were not limited to frivolous books a young man might read, but extended also to other morally questionable activities. Stage plays were of special concern to the educator because they had "strong attractions, especially for the young and the thoughtless." "They are vindicated," he explained, "as a rational and instructive amusement," and although men "of sober judgment and sound morals" sometimes attended them, he believed pure entertainment must be their only rationale. It could not be because the attendees actually believed the plays would somehow impart useful knowledge. He then focused on the real problem:

> Very few plays, however, are free from sentiments which are offensive to moral purity. Many of them abound with ribaldry and vulgarity, too gross for exhibition before persons of delicacy and refined manners. Before I can believe the stage to be a school of virtue, I must demand proof that a single profligate has ever been reformed, or a

single man or woman made a christian by its influence.[25]

Webster's criteria for judging the worth of any activity was whether it led the viewer or participant into the Christian faith, or at least made people think seriously about a more virtuous life. If an activity did not promote these purposes, it was a waste of time and effort, and even morally degrading.

Young men also are educated through the acquaintances they make. These companions can have a determining influence on character. Webster therefore cautioned his young gentleman to choose his associates carefully, with utmost attention given to their piety and character. In picking friends, one must be careful to select "young men of good breeding, and of virtuous principles and habits. The company of the profligate and irreligious is to be shunned as poison." Of course, "You cannot always avoid some intercourse with men of dissolute lives; but you can always select, for your intimate associates, men of good principles and unimpeachable character." Above all, "Never maintain a familiar intercourse with the profane, the lewd, the intemperate, the gamester, or the scoffer at religion. Towards men of such character, the common civilities of life are to be observed—beyond these," Webster felt, "nothing is required of men who reverence the divine precepts, and who desire to 'keep themselves unspotted from the world.' "[26] Webster's advice was not a prohibition against all relationships that do not have a basis in Christian convictions and character, but a warning against too close an association with those who have chosen to disregard the ways of God, as evidenced by the dissoluteness of their character. Men actuated by principle and devoted to the development of good character were the ideal companions.

Near the end of his treatise, Webster turned back to the classroom and touched upon the proper deportment of a serious student. "On entering an Academy or a College, adopt the firm resolution, to yield obedience to all the officers of the Institution, and to all its laws and regulations," he advised. "You are not too young to know, though you may not be able to realize, in all its extent, the importance of entire subordination in such institutions." Was this an attempt at social control? To an extent, yes, but not solely out of concern for external domination by a societal institution. Rather,

Webster's concerns began with the internal motivations of each person and the deterioration of character that would result from a rejection of proper authority. His admonitions stemmed from a firm Biblical conviction concerning the nature of man. Man, he believed, by virtue of a sinful nature, was in opposition to God, an opposition that not only disrupts society, but ruins one's own character as well. Webster feared not only for society, but also for each individual who chose a life of resistance to authority. The entire human race had "an instinctive reluctance to obedience—a disposition to resist control." This attitude was usually more prevalent in the young, "who have had little experience of the necessity of restraint, to preserve order and peace in society." Often they "set their own will and pleasure in opposition to authority," or "claim privileges and exemptions which are inconsistent with the general regulations of the institution." They sometimes disturb studies and cause problems with the administration, thereby bringing disrepute on both the institution and themselves. "Never be ambitious of proving yourself a *stout fellow* in defiance of authority. Never indulge the pride of insulting the officers by little vexations, boyish tricks, and petty mischiefs," Webster warned. "If young men think such things heroic and manly, all the world besides, think them mean, cowardly and degrading to the offender, and what is more, he will afterwards think so himself, and blush for the folly of his youth."[27]

Webster's final admonition concerned the importance of mastering the subjects one is studying. "In the prosecution of your studies, endeavor to make yourself master of whatever you learn," he stressed. "Understand well the rudiments or first principles of every branch of study, whether in literature or in science. The first principles are often difficult to beginners; but when you have overcome the first difficulties, your progress will be more easy and pleasant."[28] A good foundation is essential to success: first principles, or general truths, the source or origin of subordinate truths, had to be incorporated into every branch of learning. To attempt to gain knowledge piecemeal, or from a purely inductive approach, without resort to basic truths handed to man by God, was to attempt the impossible. If mastery, rather than mere competence, was the goal, first principles would have to be mastered before anything else. Once they were effectively internalized, progress would be swift and sure.

The educational philosophy found in the *Letters* formed the bedrock of all that Webster said, after his conversion, about education's purposes. He did not contradict the *Letters* in his remaining years, but on occasion he was able to amplify his concepts or express them in another fashion. His *History of the United States* included an addendum entitled, "Advice to the Young," which consisted of fifty-six rules of conduct, principles by which to live, and duties that man should perform. In his preface to the <u>History</u>, Webster described his purpose in attaching the "Advice":

> The Advice to the Young . . . will be useful in enlightening the minds of youth in religious and moral principles, and serve, in a degree, to restrain some of the common vices of our country. Republican government loses one-half of its value, where the moral and social duties are imperfectly understood, or negligently practiced. To exterminate our popular vices is a work of far more importance to the character and happiness of our citizens, than any other improvements in our system of education.[29]

The purpose of his *History* was to reveal republican government as Biblical in origin and to extol the United States as a Christian republic. "Almost all the civil liberty now enjoyed in the world," Webster declared, "owes its origin to the principles of the Christian religion." It is to Christianity that "we owe our free constitutions of government," and to the Puritans in particular, whose "wise institutions . . . have been the foundation of our republican governments."[30] It was only natural for him to add the extra pages of moral advice because the future status of the Christian republic rested on the soundness of the religious and moral principles of its young people.

A reworking of his reader, *Instructive and Entertaining Lessons for Youth*, published in 1835, echoed themes of the earlier *Letters*. "In the selection of compositions in this book, regard has been had to *entertainment* as well as *utility*," he informed readers. "But," he clarified, "it has been my aim to make *useful instruction* the *prominent* object; *amusement* being a *secondary* consideration." Going to the heart of the matter, he told them, "The main purpose of education is, to instill into the minds of youth *practical truth*, and *sound*

principles in religion, morals, in social relations, in law and government, as well as in arts and sciences." These principles, he believed,
could be applied in all branches of education and would further the
progress and happiness of a people. The problem with Europe was
the Europeans' attachment to "branches of knowledge which serve
only for *ornament*, and *distinction* in the present life," and their lack
of attention or disdain for correct "principles of the heart."
Americans were in danger of going the same direction because of
their "rage for books of mere amusement," a rage that already had
banished, in some measure, "the love of solid learning," and had
"condemned to neglect, not only the Bible, but the most excellent of
all human writings." Webster acknowledged that some of the
amusement books attempted to "furnish the mind with good principles," but he worried that men seem to forget that "*truth* in such a
form is presented to the mind *without a divine sanction*—the only
authority that can effectually restrain the passions, and subject the
will to the influence of truth and correct principles." His intellectual
reorientation, through his conversion, was so thorough, that even
truths presented without a "Thus saith the Lord" were deemed
insufficient for their stated goals.

After declaring a total dependence on Biblical authority, Webster
lamented the decline of Bible-based authority in America and its
replacement with human authority. If this continued, he prophesied,
America would experience a rapid descent into depravity, degradation of character, and certain ruin:

> This general disposition to subject the *slight* and *fleeting
> influence of human example and opinions*, for the
> *controlling authority of divine commands*, is among the
> most gloomy presages of the present times. Without a
> great change of public taste . . . the progress of deprav-
> ity will be as *rapid*, as the ultimate loss of morals, of reli-
> gion, and of civil liberty, is *certain*. God has provided but
> *one* way, by which nations can secure their rights and
> privileges . . . *by obedience to his laws*. Without this, a
> nation may be *great* in population, *great* in wealth, and
> *great* in military strength; but it must be *corrupt in
> morals, degraded in character*, and *distracted with*

factions. This is the order of God's moral government, as firm as his throne, and unchangeable as his purpose; and nations, disregarding this order, are doomed to incessant internal evils, and ultimately to ruin.[31]

Man's attempt to forge his own moral system independent of God's divine commands was the subject of another lesson, a short essay entitled, "Human Ignorance." In it, Webster stated succinctly, "'The fear of God is the beginning of wisdom;' and without this fear of God, or true religion, all the arts, and science, and knowledge in the world, do not constitute *true wisdom*."[32]

Webster no longer was a utopian who believed progress was possible through the secular development of human faculties. His beliefs in the nature of man, transformed by his conversion, now prevented the easy acceptance of inevitable progress that had permeated his early works. Although a champion of the enlargement and improvement of the common schools, Webster did not succumb to the enthusiasm for the Prussian educational system that became prevalent in the 1830s.[33] Unitarians and Protestant evangelicals viewed that system, which rested on statist control of all education, as a model for future American educational development, although for different reasons. Unitarians sought to wrest education from what they considered to be erring or misguided sectarian forces, i.e., the church denominations; many evangelicals, meanwhile, searched for a system that would bring uniformity to curriculum and defend Protestantism against the Catholicism carried by the new wave of Catholic immigration during the 1830s.[34] They formed an odd alliance, especially when the words of the eventual leader of the Unitarian forces, Horace Mann, are considered. Contrary to the dominant evangelical view, Mann declared,

> *The Common School is the greatest discovery ever made by man* . . . Other social organizations are curative and remedial; this is a preventive and an antidote; they come to heal diseases and wounds; this to make the physical and moral frame invulnerable to them. Let the Common School be expanded to its capabilities, let it be worked with the efficiency of which it is susceptible, and nine-tenths of the

crimes in the penal code would become obsolete; the long catalogue of human ills would be abridged; men would walk more safely by day; every pillow would be more inviolable by night; property, life and character held by a stronger tenure; all rational hopes respecting the future brightened.[35]

Webster believed in the efficacy of a sound, appropriate education. Yet he did not share the enthusiasm for such "visionary schemes, which can never be carried into effect."[36] "In correcting public evils, great reliance is placed on schools," he commented in an unpublished manuscript. "But schools no more make statesmen than human learning makes christians. Literature & scientific attainments have never prevented the corruption of government. Knowledge derived from experience & from the evils of bad measures," he added, "may produce a change of measures to correct a particular evil. But learning & sciences have no material effect in subduing ambition & selfishness, reconciling parties or subjecting private interest to the influence of a ruling preference of public good."[37] Again, he cannot escape the logic of his conversion. As he stated in his last published textbook, *A Manual of Useful Studies*,

> *Practical truths* in religion, morals, and in all civil and social concerns, ought to be among the first and most prominent objects of instruction. Without a competent knowledge of legal and social rights and duties, persons are often liable to suffer in property or reputation, by neglect or mistakes. Without religious and moral principles deeply impressed on the mind, and controlling the whole conduct, science and literature will not make men what the laws of God require them to be; and without both kinds of knowledge, citizens can not enjoy the blessings which they seek, and which a strict conformity to rules of duty will enable them to obtain.[38]

Webster's devotion to the Christian religion and God's commands as the fundamental basis of education appears again in a comment to a correspondent: "In my view," he wrote, "the Christian religion is the *most important and one of the first things* in which *all* children, under a free government, ought to be instructed."[39] Webster's philosophy of education, after 1808, was thoroughly Christian in its concepts. When Webster changed, his educational views changed with him.

---

[1] Webster, *Value of the Bible*, manuscript copy, 225-26.

[2] Webster, *A Manual of Useful Studies: For the Instruction of Young Persons of Both Sexes in Families and Schools* (New Haven: S. Babcock, 1839), 70.

[3] Webster to David McClure, 25 October 1836, in Warfel, *Letters*, 456.

[4] Webster, letter to the editor of *The Genesee Farmer and Gardener's Journal* 2, no. 9, 3 March 1832, 70-71.

[5] Webster, *Manual of Useful Studies*, v.

[6] Webster diary, 2 July 1812, in Ford, 2: 174.

[7] Webster to Sidney E. Morse, 24 February 1834, Webster Papers, NYPL, Box 1. Webster commented in the preface to the amended version, "The Bible is the chief moral cause of all that is *good*, and the best corrector of all that is *evil*, in human society; the *best* book for regulating the temporal concerns of men, and the *only book* that can serve as an infallible guide to future felicity." *The Holy Bible*, with amendments of the language, by Noah Webster, LL.D. (New Haven: Durrie & Peck, 1833; reprint ed., Grand Rapids: Baker Book House, 1987).

[8] In view of this prolific outpouring of literary efforts, especially after the publication of his dictionary, it is hard to know how to comment on Rollins's remark, 120, when he states, "Webster's concern with education slowly disappeared around the turn of the century. It was of relatively little importance to him even after his conversion, and in fact he mentioned it only rarely." Rollins obviously is wrong. Not only did Webster continue to write and publish textbooks, but also his observations on educational theory and practice did not decrease with time.

[9] Webster, *1828 Dictionary*.

[10] Webster, *An Address, Delivered before the Hampshire, Franklin and Hampden Agricultural Society, at their Annual Meeting in Northampton, October 14, 1818* (Northampton, MA: Thomas W. Shepard, 1818), 25.

[11] Ibid., 28.

[12] Webster to Jedidiah Morse, 27 September 1820, Beinecke Library, Yale.

[13] Webster to William Leffingwell, 27 September 1820, in Warfel, *Noah Webster*, 340.

[14] Webster, *An Address, Delivered at the Laying of the Corner Stone of the Building Erected for the Charity Institution in Amherst, Massachusetts, August 9, 1820* (Boston:

Ezra Lincoln, 1820), 7-8. Webster's address preceded a sermon entitled *A Plea for a Miserable World*, preached by the Rev. Daniel A. Clark. The pamphlet was issued with the sermon title as its main component.

[15] Webster, address at the building dedication and induction of new officers of Amherst College, 18 September 1821, manuscript copy, Webster Papers, NYPL, Box 10.

[16] Webster, *Letters to a Young Gentleman*, in Hall & Slater, *Rudiments*, 7.

[17] Ibid.

[18] Ibid.

[19] Ibid., 8.

[20] Ibid.

[21] Ibid., 17.

[22] Webster, letter to the editor, *Vermont Chronicle*, 8 April 1840.

[23] Webster, *Letters to a Young Gentleman*, in Hall & Slater, *Rudiments*, 19-20. Webster's eldest daughter, Emily Webster Ellsworth, published a book of short stories, *Wild Flowers*, which was published in 1837. In Webster's response to its publication, 27 May 1837, Webster Papers, CHS, he reveals once again that he is not overly fond of fiction, yet recognizes its value if written for a sound purpose:
"Of the merit of this book, I am not as good a judge as many others; as I am not a reader of books of fiction of any kind. I hear those who are much better judges than myself speak of it with much commendation. Of the style I can better judge, & can freely say that it is very good. If a second edition should be called for, a few slight alterations would improve the language; but as it is, it will do you credit.
"Only think. NW's eldest daughter commenced authoress! It stands you in hand to write pretty well, because the public will expect it.
"Your mother & myself are very much gratified by your *motive* in writing & publishing. For this reason as well as others we feel much interest in the book is to recommend religion, & it may be considered as a mite thrown into the treasury of the Lord."

[24] Webster, *Letters to a Young Gentleman*, in Hall & Slater, *Rudiments*, 20.

[25] Ibid.

[26] Ibid., 21.

[27] Ibid., 29.

[28] Ibid.

[29] Webster, *History of the United States*, v-vi.

[30] Ibid., 273-75.

[31] Webster, *Lessons for Youth*, 9-10.

[32] Ibid., 182.

[33] Webster, in a review of a book by J. Orville Taylor, entitled *The District School*, remarked in the *Commercial Advertiser*, 25 November 1834, "Our primary schools may, doubtless, be improved, and I trust they will be. But you will permit a man, probably older than yourself, to remark, that in the *modern schemes of improvement*, many projects will be found to be *visionary*. The perfection sought is not attainable; and if it was, the results would disappoint expectation."

[34] For an excellent revisionist history of the beginnings of the public school movement, see Samuel L. Blumenfeld, *Is Public Education Necessary?* (Boise, ID: The Paradigm Co., 1981.)

[35] Horace Mann, introduction, *The Common School Journal* 3 (1 January 1841): 15, cited in Rousas J. Rushdoony, *The Messianic Character of American Education* (Nutley, NJ: The Craig Press, 1979), 29.

[36] Webster to William Ellsworth, 26 March 1839, Webster Papers, CHS.

[37] Webster, "On Suffrage," n.d., Webster Papers, NYPL, Box 8.

[38] Webster, *Manual of Useful Studies*, v.

[39] Webster to David McClure, 25 October 1836, in Warfel, *Letters*, 453.

CHAPTER 10

Christian Foundations: Language and the Dictionary

Webster's concern that appropriate morality and principles be upheld and promoted, both in government and in education, was often stated and strongly worded. If he had had no other means of expression than fulminations in the newspapers of his day, those historians who characterize him as a dour, sour old Puritan might be excused for their interpretation. But Webster did have a vehicle for the positive promulgation of his beliefs. This was his *American Dictionary of the English Language*, first published in 1828, the crowning achievement of his very productive life. This dictionary provided the Yankee lexicographer with a vehicle for furthering his prescriptions for the moral, political, and intellectual improvement of his country. The 1828 version, especially, incorporated all his views on morality, principles, government, and education, and it became a testimony to the Christian convictions that first gripped him in 1808.

As early as 1806, when he had just completed his first dictionary, the *Compendious*, Webster already was planning a more extensive and thorough work. He knew his *Compendious* was only a preliminary step. He hoped to amplify his definitions and produce a dictionary that would be the standard work for America. The time and expense he projected for this new project led him to solicit funds from gentlemen who could appreciate the finished product. He was sorely disappointed by the response. He wrote to Oliver Wolcott, Jr., in 1807, that Rufus King had informed him that there was "little hope" of receiving "any pecuniary aid in the prosecution of my great design." Webster estimated that the entire cost might be $10,000—beyond his means—but added, "I would not ask men of property to aid me for my *own sake*. The design is the most interesting to literature of any ever undertaken in America—as I can certainly throw more light on the formation of the languages of Europe & on its early history, than any writer of the last century has done." He was astonished, he claimed, "to see the vast sums of money expended in donations to support a party or a despicable newspaper—when not a cent can be obtained for very valuable purposes."[1]

Initial setbacks in obtaining financial support did not discourage Webster enough to refrain from asking again, periodically, over the next fifteen years, but the result always was the same. To Josiah Quincy he wrote, in 1811, "But what can I do? My own resources are almost exhausted & in a few days I shall sell my house to get bread for my children. All the assurances of aid which I recd in Boston, N York & c have failed & I am soon to retire to a humble cottage in the country."[2] The prophecy proved true as Webster, the next year, moved from New Haven to Amherst, Massachusetts, to reduce living expenses. By 1813, he was confiding to John Jay,

> I shall pursue my design, if kind providence shall permit. But the disappointments I have experienced, lead me to place no dependence on my fellow citizens. Some few of my friends would do all in their power to encourage me, but literary men in the large towns appear to be opposed to *me* or my *design* and their pointed opposition has had no small effect in preventing me from receiving encouragement. If I live to finish my proposed work, it is probable, I shall go to England to revise and publish it, and as my own country furnishes no patron, I may find one in Great Britain. I am so well satisfied that my researches will open an unexplored field and throw more light on the origin and history of language than all that has before been written as well as lead to important illustrations of

ancient History, sacred and profane, that I think it my
duty to pursue the subject, unless absolutely compelled to
relinquish it.[3]

By 1821, as he related to Stephen Van Rensselaer, he had "already
consumed about fifteen years," and his original projection of the
$10,000 necessary to complete the task he revised to more than
$25,000. "I hope to complete the work in 4 or 5 years," he added.[4]
For once, he was ahead of his timetable; Webster finished the actual
research and writing in January 1825.

Webster in Linguistic History

Lack of funding was not the only reason for such an extended
period of labor; near the beginning of the project, Webster came face
to face with an immense problem. His original research plans had to
be extended because of his lack of knowledge of the origin of words.
He chronicled the problem in the completed dictionary's preface:

> My original design did not extend to an investigation of
> the origin and progress of our language; much less of
> other languages. I limited my views to the correcting of
> certain errors in the best English Dictionaries, and to the
> supplying of words in which they are deficient. But after
> writing through two letters of the alphabet, I determined
> to change my plan. I found myself embarrassed, at every
> step, for want of a knowledge of the origin of words. . . .
> Then laying aside my manuscripts, and all books treating
> of language, except lexicons and dictionaries, I endeav-
> ored, by a diligent comparison of words, having the same
> or cognate radical letters, in about twenty languages, to
> obtain a more correct knowledge of the primary sense of
> original words, of the affinities between the English and
> many other languages, and thus to enable myself to trace
> words to their source.
>
> I had not pursued this course more than three or four
> years, before I discovered that I had to unlearn a great
> deal that I had spent years in learning, and that it was
> necessary for me to go back to the first rudiments of a

branch of erudition, which I had before cultivated, as I had supposed, with success.

I spent ten years in this comparison of radical words, and in forming a synopsis of the principal words in twenty languages, arranged in classes, under their primary elements or letters. The result has been to open what are to me new views of language, and to unfold what appear to be the genuine principles on which these languages are constructed.[5]

To understand better the problems Webster confronted and the solution he adopted, one must see his work in light of the history of linguistics. From this perspective, it should be obvious that the dictionary was far more than a simple accumulation of definitions.

Eighteenth-century linguistic studies, while not systematic, formed a foundation for the work of the nineteenth century. Interest in linguistic research had developed in a number of countries—particularly England, Germany, and France—independently of each other throughout the century. The French school was headed by E. B. de Condillac and Rousseau; the Germans, through essay competitions conducted by the Berlin Academy in Prussia, provided the world with the works of Pierre Louis Moreau de Maupertuis, Johann David Michaelis, and Johann Gottfried Herder; and the English contributed to the linguistic potpourri through James Harris, Horne Tooke, James Burnett (Lord Monboddo), and Sir William Jones.[6]

Although it is likely that Webster was familiar with the French works, he made reference particularly to the German and English theorists. One theorist was Johann David Michaelis, who wrote the *Dissertation on the Influence of Opinions on Language and of Language on Opinions* (1760). This work made such an impression on Webster in his early years that one of the articles he published in the *American Magazine* of 1788 and reprinted in his *Collection of Essays and Fugitiv Writings*, took its title and main ideas straight from Michaelis, as he acknowledged in a footnote.[7]

Michaelis was a strong German nationalist, in much the same way as Webster was a fervent American nationalist. This nationalism led Michaelis to support distinct German names for fields such as botany. He also declared, "Language is a democracy where use or custom is the supreme law."[8] This was a concept Webster adopted in his 1789 *Dissertations*. The problem with Michaelis's linguistic nationalism, though, was its relativistic basis that denied universal concepts applicable to all languages. Each people's perception of the world and its objects was unique, so unique that the ideas behind the words used to describe the world meant quite different things to each national group. Webster, until his conversion, held to two contradictory ideas—the relativism of nationalistic language and the desire to find the universals that tied all languages together. It seems that he did not understand the inherent incompatibility of the two positions until he had to face the task of tracing word origins.

Another premise upon which Michaelis's theories rested was a naturalistic, materialistic philosophy to explain the growth and development of language.[9] Webster, in all his pre-conversion writings on language, echoed Michaelis's naturalism and materialism. His anthropology was wholly naturalistic, despite his ties to a Puritan heritage. In his early writings there was no hint of an original man and woman created by God upon whom language was bestowed. Instead, as Webster wrote in his 1789 *Dissertations*, "We first hear of men in the mild climate of Asia Minor and about the head of the Mediterranean."[10] He expounded further:

> The invention and progress of articulate sounds must have been extremely slow. Rude savages have originally no method of conveying ideas, but by looks, signs, and those inarticulate sounds, called by grammarians, *Interjections*. These are probably the first beginnings of language. They are produced by the passions, and are perhaps very little superior, in point of articulation or significancy, to the sounds which express the wants of the brutes.[11]

The materialism was evident in Webster's belief that the noun was the primary basis for language. It was materialistic because it emphasized objects or things over ideas and concepts in a wholly naturalistic way:

But the first sounds, which, by being often repeated, would become articulate, would be those which savages use to convey their ideas of certain visible objects, which first employ their attention. These sounds, by constant application to the same things, would gradually become the *names* of those objects, and thus acquire a permanent signification. In this manner, rivers, mountains, trees, and such animals as afford food for savages, would first acquire names; and next to them, such other objects as can be noticed or perceived by the senses. Those names which are given to ideas called *abstract* and *complex*, or, to speak more correctly, those names which express a combination of ideas, are invented much later in the progress of language. Such are the words, faith, hope, virtue, genius, &c.[12]

The relativism, naturalism, and materialism of Webster's youth would be rooted out of his thought upon reexamination of his philological foundations after his conversion.

Another strong tie to Michaelis was the German's belief that language influences a people's thought.[13] Webster, in his essay based on Michaelis's ideas, explained,

The design of this dissertation is to show how far truth and accuracy of thinking are concerned in a clear understanding of *words*. I am sensible that in the eye of prejudice and ignorance, grammatical researches are the business of school boys; and hence we may deduce the reason why philosophers have generally been so inattentiv to this subject. But if it can be proved that the *mere use of words* has led nations into error, and still continues the delusion, we cannot hesitate a moment to conclude, that grammatical enquiries are worthy of the labor of *men*.[14]

The "mere use of words" upon which Webster focused was not meant to imply that words, standing by themselves without definitional content, have an impact on people's opinions. Definitions always are the key to how language can be an influence on men.

Webster sought to understand first how a people's concepts led to the use of certain words; and second, how the use of these words with a certain definitional content led people to think and act in a particular way. For example, Webster, in discussing the various names for deity, noted,

> The Greek name of the Supreme Being, *Theos*, is derived from *Theo, to run, or move one's self.* Hence we discover the ideas which the Greeks originally entertained of God, viz. that he was the *great principle of motion.* . . .
>
> The English word *God*, is merely the old Saxon adjectiv *god*, now spelt and pronounced *good*.
>
> The German *Gott* is from the same root. The words *God* and *good* therefore are synonimous. The derivation of the word leads us to the notions which our ancestors entertained of the Supreme Being; supposing him to be the principle or author of good, they called him, by way of eminence, *Good*, or *the Good*. By long use and the progress of knowledge, the word is become the name of the great Creator, and we have added to it ideas of other attributes, as justice, power, immutability, &c. Had our heathen ancestors entertained different ideas of the Deity; had they, for instance, supposed justice to have been his leading attribute, if I may use the term, they would have called him *the just*; and this appellation, by being uniformly appropriated to a certain invisible being, or supposed cause of certain events, would in time have lost the article *the*, and *just* would have become the name of the Deity. Such is the influence of opinion in the formation of language.[15]

Even as opinion could influence the formation of language, so language could influence opinion and lead into errors of understanding. Webster cited a number of examples:

> For want of attending to the true etymology of the word *glory*, false opinions have gained an establishment

in the world, and it may be hazardous to dispute them. It
is said that the *glory* of God does not depend on his creatures, and that the glory of the good man depends not on
the opinion of others. But what is glory? The Greek word
doxe explains it. It is derived from *dokeo, to think*; and
signifies the *good opinion of others*. This is its *true* original meaning; a man's glory therefore consists in having
the good opinion of men, and this cannot generally be
obtained, but by meritorious actions. The *glory* of God
consists in the exalted ideas which his creatures entertain
of his being and perfections. His *glory* therefore depends
wholly on his creatures. . . .

 We have been accustomed from childhood to hear the
expressions, *the dew falls; the dews of heaven*; and it is
probable that nine people out of ten, have never suspected
the inaccuracy of the phrases. But *dew* is merely the
perspiration of the earth; it *rises* instead of *falling*, and
rises during the night.[16]

Webster's essay was short and limited in its scope, yet it stoked
his natural desire to make words his occupation. As he concluded:

 This is a fruitful theme, and would lead an ingenious
inquirer into a wide field of investigation. But I have
neither the time nor talents to do it justice; the few hints
here suggested may have some effect in convincing my
readers of the importance and utility of all candid
researches into the origin and structure of speech; and
pave the way for further investigations, which may assist
us in correcting our ideas and ascertaining the force and
beauty of our own language.[17]

Webster affected modesty in his abilities and claimed the task
was beyond him, but when the time afforded, he entered into the
project with his distinctive diligence and industry.

 As discussed in a previous chapter, Webster also owed a debt to
the English theorist, Horne Tooke, who convinced him of the direct
relationship of Anglo-Saxon to English. Yet it was Sir William

Jones who, in 1786—a watershed year in terms of linguistic study—opened the way for a new approach in linguistics that became Webster's methodological cornerstone. In that year, Jones read a paper to the Royal Asiatic Society that proved beyond any doubt of linguists, both then and now, that Sanskrit, an early Indian language, was closely related to Latin, Greek, and the Germanic languages. For Jones, this meant that languages had stronger common affinities than before supposed, and that all languages might perhaps be traced back to a common language that no longer existed. Jones's hypothesis launched the first systematic growth of comparative and historical linguistics, a discipline that became Webster's sole occupation for approximately ten years. One scholar calls Webster "America's first comparative philologist," who "shared the view that had developed by the eighteenth century that there was an 'affinity' among the languages that we now call the Indo-European family."[18]

Michaelis, although he had posited that language could affect thought and action, also had noted that the effects were almost entirely negative. Language, rather than being the channel through which truth and guidance could be obtained, more often than not, because of the nationalistic biases of man, had created schisms between men. This created a dilemma for Webster. He desired to promote stability through the development of universal perceptions in language, yet the relativism of his nationalistic beliefs presaged failure. Stability could not be achieved if each people's perceptions and the words by which their perceptions were shared were too different. How could one be a great nationalist, as Webster was, and still believe that perceptions were universal and language could be the medium through which men could create stable societies?

Webster found a solution, but it came only after he had set aside his definitions, had devoted himself to original research, and had experienced his conversion. His new religious commitment and outlook clothed his studies in a theological, rather than a rationalistic, epistemology. All the problems others labored over, he could dismiss because he found the answer in God. When they worried about how to prove universality in perception, Webster merely turned to his belief that absolute truth, as exemplified in the Bible, existed, and his questions were satisfied. His new Christian faith led to a rejection of the materialistic philosophy and an embrace of language as the immediate gift of God in the Garden of Eden. He stated, in his *Observations on Language and Commerce,* "Language, in man, is, next to reason, the grand characteristic by which he is distinguished from the brutes." He finished his thought:

> Its origin is buried in obscurity, although there is strong reason to believe it had its origin in divine communications. The structure of the human organs of speech, by which four or five different parts of the mouth and throat are made to utter voices and modulations of sound to an indefinite extent, is a most wonderful contrivance, indicating both the wisdom and the benevolent design of the Creator.[19]

The goal of his research now was to prove that language could be traced back to the original pair created by God. Again, in his *Observations,* he commented, "The affinity of the languages of Asia and Europe, furnishes a strong argument in favor of the scriptural doctrine, that all nations have descended from a single pair, Adam and Eve."[20] And in the notes of one of his speeches, he further affirmed that the "affinity between the principal languages of the earth . . . illustrate and confirm the Scriptural account of the common origin of the human species."[21]

When Webster concluded that the linguistic beliefs that he had promulgated for twenty years were erroneous and that he had been wrong in promoting them, he showed a remarkable willingness to alter those beliefs. It would have been easier and far more profitable for him to have continued his labor with the more restrictive goal of correcting previous English dictionaries, yet his integrity and desire to ferret out the truth on language led him into a ten-year detour, the fruits of which he compiled in a manuscript that still remains unpublished in his personal papers.

Where did his ten-year study, influenced by his new religious faith, lead Webster linguistically? First, he became convinced that the original language that God had bestowed on Adam, a language Webster called "Chaldee," was a language simple in structure and limited in vocabulary. Although it grew and developed variants, it remained the one language that all mankind at that time understood. Then, he surmised, God divided this one language into a variety of dialects in the Biblical incident known as the Tower of Babel. When man sought to exalt himself and build a monument to his own glory, God intervened and confused the language. The original Chaldee no longer existed, but remnants of it could be found in all the new dialects. The descendants of Noah's three sons, Japheth, Shem, and Ham, developed an even greater variety of dialects but, in Webster's scheme, they all still had a resemblance to the original Chaldee.

The descendants of Japheth, Webster believed, populated Russia and Europe and, thus separated from the descendants of the other brothers, created greater differences between the branches. Webster also surmised a late introduction of a written language, thereby assuring that "common sounds used as symbols of ideas among the immediate descendants of Noah, must have been liable to incessant changes, which could not fail materially to diversify their language, & in many instances, to obliterate the evidences of its original affinity."[22] Yet it still was possible to find affinities between certain words of Japhetic and Shemitic stock. These affinities would be the closest to the original Chaldee. English was a late branch of the Japhetic dialect and based most directly on Saxon, its mother tongue. In order to find the correct definition of an English word, Webster presumed that he must discover all of an English word's cognates in the other languages—Saxon principally, but not exclusively.[23] Words that could be linked directly to an affinity with Shemitic (Semitic) roots offered, he felt, a clue to the original meaning of the word in ancient Chaldee. These were the "primary" meanings Webster sought for as many words as possible.

Another conclusion he reached was that almost all primitive words in Chaldee were verbs, from which had sprung all other parts of speech. "The most important observation," he wrote in *Observations on Language*, "is, that original words express physical action, or properties. No term in language, expressing a moral or abstract idea, is original." Rather, he continued, "The principal word, in all known languages, is the *verb*; and it is a quest not yet settled, whether *all* other words are not derived from verbs. The *most* of them are certainly thus derived."[24] This conclusion was radically different from his earlier view that the noun was the most ancient aspect of language. Moreover, Webster decided that of all the possible verbs, "move" was the most primitive of all because of all the types of general actions its derivatives could denote.

These discoveries excited Webster. His excitement was more than a wordsmith's natural joy over philological inquiries. He believed he had discovered a key to the spiritual rejuvenation of America. He retained his pre-conversion belief that language influences opinion, which, in turn, determines the political, educational, and moral parameters of a nation. "From more than fifty years' observation," he wrote, "I am convinced that *words* or *names* often have more influence on the mass of men than *things*, and that the abuse and misapplication of terms may counteract the *best*, and promote the *worst*, political measures."[25] He felt that these insights, which were based on his religious beliefs, could help keep America on course politically (Federalism), educationally (with Biblical truths as the foundation), and morally.

For Webster, the linguistic experience was essentially a religious experience, made possible only by the new light he had received in his conversion. Webster felt he had found an exciting and stimulating link with one of God's original endowments. It was as though he were reaching back into the Garden, before the fall of man, and grasping the essence of what God had made, and the intent of the original creation. If man could understand the original meanings of the words given by God, these words could introduce the very thoughts of God into society and provide man with another undeniable link to the intents and purposes of creation, the Bible itself being the first link. This bond with the original order of things could introduce a semblance of that order into his contemporary world, provided men would use words with their God-ordained "primary" definitions. Proper definitions, then, could help provide America with what one scholar calls an "internal gyroscope for self-regulating order." Through the words they spoke, Americans could have "direct access to a stable ontological order, an order that texts of any kind, political or literary, could express."[26]

Webster believed he had achieved a signal breakthrough in etymological understanding. So certain was he of the correctness of the path of research he had chosen that he did not draw from contemporary works of German linguists such as Jacob Grimm.

The nature of the German studies bothered him. Webster was engaged in tracing words to their primary sense; the Germans were not concerned with this, and to Webster that revealed a profound misdirection. "In this branch of etymology," he wrote, "even the German scholars, the most accurate philologists in Europe, appear to be wholly deficient."[27] Whereas Webster operated on a closed system based upon Biblical foundations, German studies assumed there was no original language, focused strictly on particular languages and their history of phonetic changes, and considered history as an "open system with no definite beginning or ending." They were process-oriented, unconcerned with any connection of word usage and definitions with the original God-created order. As one scholar of Webster's writings acknowledges,

> The new philology had great value for a history of the evolution of ideas. But its meticulous record of the evolution of usages provided no clear unity and limits in the meanings of words. It sacrificed a clear sense of stability and permanence, of unity and limits in the meanings of words. These were the very qualities which Webster, with his emphasis on prescriptive standards, sought in definition. No longer are we provided with a primary sense that unites a word's meanings at its source and offers precise limits in the proper use of the word.[28]

Webster's contemporary critics charged him with vanity and pride in his rejection of the theories of other philologists. Webster tried to explain his position in letters to newspaper critics. "When I claim to understand etymology better than English and German writers, I am charged with vanity"; but, he remonstrated, "however my claims may appear to the world, I know that I am actuated by higher and more laudable motives, a consciousness of which buoys me above my regard to such charges."[29] Besides knowledge of his own motivations, he offered the following rationale for rejection of German authority, based on the divergent approaches he and the Germans were taking:

In this country great reliance is placed on German

authors, particularly in philology; and it is probably a correct opinion that among the Germans are the most profound philological scholars. But my researches render it certain that in etymology the Germans are in darkness; and from such samples as I have seen of their derivations, it seems improbable that they can arrive at correct principles on that subject.[30]

He was quite willing to give the Germans credit where he felt it was due, but his Christian worldview could not countenance what he considered to be improper foundations in their etymological work.[31] He had a different purpose: "The great object of all my labors in philology has been to ascertain *truth*, to restore the language to purity, & to check the progress of corruption."[32]

Completion of the Great Work

"I am now proceeding with the Dictionary," Webster penned to John Jay in 1821. "I am engaged in the letter H. Making my past progress the basis of calculation, it must require the constant labor of *four years*, to complete the work even if my health should be continued." On that count he was unsure, although quick to ascribe his hopes of future health to God:

> For this blessing, I rely tranquilly on the goodness and forbearance of that Being whose favor I desire to seek in the way which he has prescribed and which I trust I value above any temporal good. But I did not begin my studies early enough. I am 63 years of age, and after this age a small portion only of active life remains. If however, I should not be permitted to finish the work begun, the synopsis will enable some other person to pursue the plan with advantage, so that my labor will not be wholly lost to my country.[33]

Webster's method for compiling the dictionary was systematic. In his study, the industrious lexicographer set up a table built in the shape of a horseshoe. As his granddaughter, Emily Ellsworth Fowler Ford, described the arrangement:

Dictionaries and grammars of all obtainable languages were laid in successive order upon its surface. Webster would take the word under investigation, and standing at the right end of the lexicographer's table, look it up in the first dictionary which lay at that end. He made a note, examined a grammar, considered some kindred word, and then passed to the next dictionary of some other tongue. He took each word through the twenty or thirty dictionaries, making notes of his discoveries, and passing around his table many times in the course of a day's labor of minute and careful study.[34]

In this way, Webster traced all 70,000 of the words in his original work. As he neared its completion, he decided it would be necessary to visit libraries in France and England to gain access to material unavailable in America. So, in June 1824, with son William at his side, he set sail for France.

Paris was not his favorite city; he often was offended by the callousness he perceived toward religion and by the moral habits of the people.[35] He devoted himself to his work in the hope of moving on to England as soon as possible. "Papa has not yet seen any of the *great lords of France*," young William wrote his sister Emily. "He confines himself more closely than ever to study, too closely, I fear. But his health was never better & his spirits are always good. He talks a great deal of home."[36]

Webster's completed his work in the Parisian libraries in early September, and he traveled immediately to England, staying at Cambridge through the remainder of 1824 and into 1825. Shortly after the beginning of the new year, the goal was achieved, but not without some last-second anxiety. As Webster related,

> I finished writing my dictionary in January 1825, at my lodgings in Cambridge, England. When I had come to the last word, I was seized with a trembling, which made it somewhat difficult to hold my pen steady for writing. The cause seems to have been the thought that I might not then live to finish the work, or the thought that I was so near the end of my labors. But I summoned strength to

finish the last word, & then walking about the room, a few minutes, I recovered.[37]

The mental labor had concluded, but the labor of finding a publisher had only begun. Webster had been confident he could find someone in England willing to publish the work and he used his American connections in England, including the American minister, Richard Rush, to attempt to secure publication. To a man, the English publishers and booksellers refused the honor. No one had the time or interest to promote an "American" dictionary. Webster had to pack his valuable commodity and once again subject it to the dangers of a transatlantic voyage. He arrived back in New Haven almost one year from the day he left, greeted by the Yale faculty and townsmen who hailed their homegrown scholar. It was not until early 1826 that a publisher was contracted—Sherman Converse of New York; the last pages came from the printer, Hezekiah Howe of New Haven, in 1828, and *An American Dictionary of the English Language*, 2,500 copies selling for twenty dollars each, came into existence the same year.

The American Christian Dictionary

Webster's original dictionary—the 1828—was unique in its approach and in its purpose. It provided, in his view, a firm anchor for language in the original God-bestowed, Edenic language. He also designed it to stabilize the deterioration, or corruption, of the English language as he perceived it. But, most importantly, it could serve as a force for educating Americans in the principles of the Christian faith, principles that could remake government, schools, and other pertinent social institutions into Webster's Christian ideal. "Webster's great dictionary," notes a student of the work, "was a personal document expressing social values and views that Webster fervently hoped to impress on the minds of future generations of Americans." The dictionary was "a one-man equivalent of the American Bible Society, the American Tract Society, the American Sunday School Union, the American Society for the Promotion of Temperance, or the American Home Missionary Society." The same scholar concludes:

Webster inveighed against pauperism, deism, the slave trade, indebtedness, dueling, gambling, and immorality, and he used his word illustrations to convey his moral and political lessons. Every copy of the *American Dictionary* carried the evangelical crusade into the classroom, library, and college, and Webster hoped that his dictionary would hold in every American home a place of honor beside the Bible.[38]

Shaping America into a more Christian republic was Webster's primary aim. But he had not forgotten the desire, which he stated first in the 1780s and never repudiated, to create an American literature culturally independent of Britain. In the dictionary's preface, he argued on behalf of a distinctly American dictionary:

It is not only important, but, in a degree necessary, that the people of this country, should have an *American Dictionary* of the English Language; for, although the body of the language is the same as in England, and it is desirable to perpetuate that sameness, yet some differences must exist. Language is the expression of ideas; and if the people of one country cannot preserve an identity of ideas, they cannot retain an identity of language.[39]

America needed its own distinct identity in ideas and language, Webster contended. There were many differences in the ideas and language of Britain and America, and those differences had to be identified and noted. Most of the differences, he instructed, "arise from different forms of government, different laws, institutions, and customs." Many British terms were unknown or had fallen into disuse in the New World. Even in the case of words that the two countries both used, meanings often were quite dissimilar. To aid in the Americanization, Webster employed quotations from American authors to be used side by side with the best of British writers. This did not lower the quality of the work, he urged, but, in some instances, actually elevated its character and gave it even greater stature:

A life devoted to reading and to an investigation of the origin and principles of our vernacular language, and especially a particular examination of the best English writers, with a view to a comparison of their style and phraseology, with those of the best American writers, and with our colloquial usage, enables me to affirm with confidence, that the genuine English idiom is as well preserved by the unmixed English of this country, as it is by the best *English* writers. . . . But I may go farther, and affirm, with truth, that our country has produced some of the best models of composition. The style of President Smith; of the authors of the Federalist; of Mr. Ames; of Dr. Mason; of Mr. Harper; of Chancellor Kent; [the prose] of Mr. Barlow; of the legal decisions of the Supreme Court of the United States; of the reports of legal decisions in some of the particular states; and many other writings; in purity, in elegance and in technical precision, is equaled only by that of the best British authors, and surpassed by that of no English compositions of a similar kind.[40]

Webster's attempt to Americanize the dictionary included bows to American history in his illustrations. He also could not resist the temptation to add personal notes. In a letter to daughter Emily shortly after the dictionary's publication, he confided,

I suppose you must have noticed that I have not forgotten my own country & friends under the words *endowment, oak, elm, isthmus, prospect, scenery, commemoration, settle, beaming, celebrity, antiquity, gin*—& especially *embalm*. I hope my observation under the latter, if a weakness, will be pardoned. I know my children will pardon it.[41]

The reference to embalm was the illustrative sentence, "The memory of my beloved daughter is *embalmed* in my heart," a clear reference to Mary, Webster's favorite daughter, who died during childbirth. He referred to Jay, Ellsworth, and Hamilton—sturdy

Federalists all—as Americans who "possessed uncommon *endowments* of mind," and utilized quotations from his beloved brother-in-law, Thomas Dawes, to illustrate *beaming, celebrity,* and *antiquity.* Most of the other words incorporated New England sites and historical events, i.e., Hartford's *oak* tree in which had been hidden the royal charter when it was threatened with recision under the Dominion of New England in the late seventeenth century, and the Pilgrims' landing at Plymouth (*commemoration*).

Webster's Americanization project in the dictionary worked in tandem with his primary goal of shaping the way in which Americans understood words, and in promoting his views respecting their origins and proper uses. His definitions and illustrations were rooted in his Biblical worldview, a way of thinking still dominant at the time of the dictionary's publication. One Webster scholar concedes, "Though controversy raged over Webster's etymology system and his spelling reforms, most critics agreed that Webster's definitions were peerless. None questioned his illustrations or objected to the messages they carried."[42] The entire work, as one biographer notes, had a distinctively "religious tone"[43] that began in the preface when Webster declared:

> To that great and benevolent Being, who, during the preparation of this work, has sustained a feeble constitution, amidst obstacles and toils, disappointments, infirmities and depression; who has twice borne me and my manuscripts in safety across the Atlantic, and given me strength and resolution to bring the work to a close, I would present the tribute of my most grateful acknowledgments. And if the talent which he entrusted to my care, has not been put to the most profitable use in his service, I hope it has not been "kept laid up in a napkin," and that any misapplication of it may be graciously forgiven.[44]

Webster also included in the preface an outline of what he hoped the dictionary could accomplish for the country:

> If the language can be improved in regularity, so as to

be more easily acquired by our own citizens, and by foreigners, and thus be rendered a more useful instrument for the propagation of science, arts, civilization and christianity; if it can be rescued from the mischievous influence of sciolists and that dabbling spirit of innovation which is perpetually disturbing its settled usages and filling it with anomalies; if, in short, our vernacular language can be redeemed from corruptions, and our philology and literature from degradation; it would be a source of great satisfaction to me to be one among the instruments of promoting these valuable objects. . . .

. . . I present it to my fellow citizens, not with frigid indifference, but with my ardent wishes for their improvement and their happiness; and for the continued increase of the wealth, the learning, the moral and religious elevation of character, and the glory of my country.[45]

Webster's dictionary thus had two related, intertwined purposes. First, it would stabilize the English language and ground it in the language God had bestowed on men in Eden. Second, it would enable Americans to improve in religious devotion, moral character, and intellectual achievement. Proper definitions would shape the opinions and the character of future generations.

Webster's Christian orientation throughout the work was evident. His definitions and definitional illustrations abounded with Biblical references. Often, short sermons were incorporated into the definitions themselves. When he defined *religion*, he assumed the true religion to be Christianity. The first three definitions of the word applied to Christianity; only the last accommodated other religious beliefs. Even then he was careful to add a comment on the distinction between true and false religion. Illustrations included a quote from Washington's "Farewell Address," in which the first president declared, "Let us with caution indulge the supposition, that morality can be maintained without religion." A *Christian*, according to the strongest of the definitions, is a "real disciple of Christ; one who believes in the truth of the christian religion, and studies to follow the example, and obey the precepts, of Christ; a believer in Christ who is characterized by real piety." This was to distinguish the *true* Christian from the one who merely professed to believe, or the one who happened to be born in a "christian country or of christian parents." For Webster, real Christianity was predicated on a conversion experience and the inner transformation of character that was to follow the experience.

God was the God of the Bible; all others were false gods or idols. *Providence*, in its theological definition, again assumed the Judeo-Christian God as the embodiment of the term. It was the "care and superintendence which God exercises over his creatures." Webster continued with an admonition:

> He that acknowledges a creation and denies a *providence*, involves himself in a palpable contradiction; for the same power which caused a thing to exist is necessary to continue its existence. Some persons admit a *general providence*, but deny a *particular providence*, not considering that a *general providence* consists of *particulars*. A belief in divine *providence*, is a source of great consolation to good men.

This is not standard dictionary fare. Webster was on a mission to direct and guide the thinking and attitudes of a nation in an evangelical Christian direction.

The same assumption reigned in definitions of other theological terms. *Revelation* was that which God communicated to man in the Old and New Testaments, and Scriptural quotations were employed as illustrations of the word. *Doctrine* had a general sense, meaning whatever is taught, but there were also Biblical connotations—"the truths of the gospel in general" and "instruction and confirmation in the truths of the gospel." Meanwhile, rivals of the Christian faith came under attack. The definition of *atheism* was straightforward, but the quoted illustration for the word was taken from Robert Hall's *Modern Infidelity Considered with Respect to its Influence on Society* (1800): "*Atheism* is a ferocious system that leaves nothing above us to excite awe, nor around us, to awaken tenderness." *Deism* received the same treatment in a quote from William Wirt's biography of Patrick Henry: "The view which the rising greatness of our country presents to my eyes, is greatly tarnished by the general prevalence of *deism*, which, with me, is but another name for vice and depravity." It is obvious that although Webster was utilizing other people's comments, he was promulgating the truth as he saw it.

Other words that Webster defined from his theological perspective were *moral, morality, love, rectitude, reverence, selfishness, and happy.* "The word *moral*," Webster wrote, "is applicable to actions that are good or evil, virtuous or vicious, and has reference to the law of God as the standard by which their character is to be determined." "The system of *morality* to be gathered from the writings of ancient sages," he quoted from Jonathan Swift, "falls very short of that delivered in the gospel." *Love* had many applications in Webster's perspective, but in his explanation of the verb form of the word, he rhapsodized over the Biblical application:

> The christian *loves* his Bible. In short, we *love* whatever gives us pleasure and delight, whether animal or intellectual; and if our hearts are right, we *love* God above all things, as the sum of all excellence and all the attributes which can communicate happiness to intelligent beings. In other words, the christian *loves* God with the love of complacency in his attributes, the love of benevolence towards the interests of his kingdom, and the love of gratitude for favors received.

The noun form also offered an opportunity to spread his message:

> The *love* of God is the first duty of man, and this springs from just views of his attributes or excellencies of character, which afford the highest delight to the sanctified heart. Esteem and reverence constitute ingredients in this affection, and a fear of offending him is its inseparable effect.

In the definition of *rectitude*, Webster reminded the dictionary-user that "*Perfect rectitude* belongs only to the Supreme Being. The more nearly the *rectitude* of men approaches to the standard of the divine law, the more exalted and dignified is their character. Want of *rectitude* is not only sinful, but debasing." And *reverence* became an occasion to make a connection between the attitude owed to God and to earthly authorities as well:

> We *reverence* superiors for their age, their authority and their virtues. We ought to *reverence* parents and upright judges and magistrates. We ought to *reverence* the Supreme Being, his word and his ordinances.

The examples are too many to enumerate, as can be shown in the letter "I" alone: "It is the duty, as it is the desire of a good man, to *improve* in grace and piety"; "We are *indebted* to God for life. We are *indebted* to the christian religion for many of the advantages, and much of the refinement of modern times"; "The distribution of the Scriptures may be the *instrument* of a vastly extensive reformation in morals and religion"; "The *internal* evidence of the divine origin of the Scriptures, is the evidence which arises from the excellence of its precepts and their adaptation to the condition of man, or from other peculiarities."

A direct reference to the role of Christ is found in the term *meritorious*: "We rely for salvation on the *meritorious* obedience and sufferings of Christ." *Selfishness*, for Webster, "in its worst or unqualified sense, is the very essence of human depravity, and stands in direct opposition to *benevolence*, which is the essence of the divine character. As God is *love*, so man, in his natural state, is *selfishness*." And a selfish person can never be truly *happy*, because "the pleasurable sensations derived from the gratification of sensual appetites render a person temporarily *happy*; but he only can be esteemed really and permanently *happy*, who enjoys peace of mind in the favor of God." Perhaps the best indication of how thoroughly Webster Christianized the dictionary can be seen in his inclusion of a theological pronouncement in the most ordinary words. Consider his rumination on the *potato*: "In the British dominions and in the United States, it has proved one of the greatest blessings bestowed on man by the Creator."

With his Christian convictions as the foundation, Webster also used the dictionary to prescribe—and proscribe—certain political theories and beliefs. His firm Federalism, which he held before his conversion, but which received divine sanction after conversion, formed the framework for definition of political terms. A *Federalist*, for example, was "An appellation in America, given to the friends of the constitution of the United States, at its formation and adoption, and to the political party which favored the administration of President Washington." This angered Republicans [Democrats by 1828] because they felt it gave the impression that Republicans had been opposed to both the Constitution and Washington. Yet Webster did not cast opprobrium on the word *Republican*, simply stating that a republican was "one who favors or prefers a republican form of government." After all, Webster considered himself a prime example of true republicanism.

Where he did make a distinction was in the definitions of two types of government—a democracy and a republic. Whereas a *democracy* was "a form of government, in which the supreme power is lodged in the hands of the people collectively, or in which the people exercise the powers of legislation," a *republic* lodged the sovereign power in the hands of "representatives elected by the people."" The two were not the same. In the first, there were dangers of mob rule and chaos; the latter promoted order while maintaining a voice for the people through their representatives. The people had the privilege of *suffrage*, or "the choice of a man for an office or trust. Nothing can be more grateful to a good man," Webster added, "than to be elevated to office by the unbiased *suffrages* of free enlightened citizens."

Other definitions shed more light on Webster's political convictions. *Free* and *freedom* were subject to frequent misunderstanding, he believed, so proper definitions of the terms could check potential evils resulting from such misunderstandings. To be *free* was not to be "under necessity or restraint, physical or moral," and not to be enslaved or "in a state of vassalage or dependence." Yet to be truly *free* did not denote a state of total irresponsibility. Man still was subject to "fixed laws, made by consent, and to a regular administration of such laws." To be free was not to be "licentious; unrestrained." *Freedom* was not synonymous with *license*, which was "freedom abused, or used in contempt of law or decorum." In the definition of *freedom*, Webster issued this warning: "Beware of what are called innocent *freedoms*." The perfect example of licentious behavior for Webster was drawn from the turmoil of the 1790s:

> The *Jacobins*, in France, during the late revolution, were a society of violent revolutionists, who held secret meetings in which measures were concerted to direct the proceedings of the National Assembly. Hence, a Jacobin is the member of a club, or other person, who opposes government in a secret and unlawful manner or by violent means; a turbulent demagogue.

A *demagogue*, meanwhile, was a man not to be trusted, "an orator who pleases the populace and influences them to adhere to him. . . . Any factious man who has great influence with the great body of people in a city or community." The key to the definition was the term *factious*. Webster's lifelong disgust with political parties and their effects—particularly the tendency toward blind loyalty without regard to reflection on the issues—was vented forcefully when he described *factious* as "addicted to form parties and raise dissensions, in opposition to government; turbulent; prone to clamor against public measures or men. No state is free from *factious* citizens." *Politician* does not come off much better; Webster's second definition of that word is "a man of artifice or deep contrivance."

What Webster sought was a society in proper *order*, not in an aristocratic sense, but in a sense that signified a "regular disposition or methodical arrangement of things. . . . Regular government or discipline." He commented, "It is necessary for society that good *order* should be observed." In an ordered society, there was a proper respect for *property*, or "the exclusive right of possessing, enjoying and disposing of a thing; ownership." Webster then continued with an exposition on the origins of man's claim to property:

> In the beginning of the world, the Creator gave to man dominion over the earth, over the fish of the sea and the fowls of the air, and over every living thing. This is the foundation of man's *property* in the earth and in all its productions.

Once again, a theological observation served as the main support for the complete understanding of a word's meaning. For this ordered society to function properly, man had to do his *duty*": "That which a person owes to another; that which a person is bound, by any natural, moral or legal obligation, to pay, do or perform." To be more specific:

> Obedience to princes, magistrates and the laws is the *duty* of every citizen and subject; obedience, respect and kindness to parents are *duties* of children; fidelity to friends is a *duty*; reverence, obedience and prayer to God are indispensable *duties*; the government and religious instruction of children are *duties* of parents which they cannot neglect without guilt.

Educational concerns also figured prominently in the dictionary. His educational philosophy, after 1808, was decidedly evangelical. *Philosophy* he defined as "an explanation of the reasons of things; or an investigation of the causes of all phenomena both of mind and matter." It comprised, in each field of knowledge, "the collection of general laws or principles under which all the subordinate phenomena or facts relating to that subject, are comprehended." Webster possessed, through his conversion, a comprehensive philosophy that touched upon every aspect of knowledge. Consequently, he was able to continue, "The objects of philosophy are . . . to enlarge our views of God and his works, and to render our knowledge of both practically useful and subservient to human happiness." A quote from Samuel Stanhope Smith was appended, which stated, "True religion and true *philosophy* must ultimately arrive at the same principle."

No matter where one turns in the dictionary, one finds Webster the teacher—enlightening, correcting, admonishing, instructing, and exhorting. He constantly imparts *knowledge*, "a clear and certain perception of that which exists, or of truth and fact; the perception of the connection and agreement, or disagreement and repugnancy of our ideas." He incessantly combines the pursuit of knowledge with his conception of spiritual illumination. He encourages the *cultivation* of the intellect and the spirit, the "study, care and practice directed to improvement, correction, enlargement or increase; . . .

men may grow wiser by the *cultivation* of talents; they may grow better by the *cultivation* of the mind, of virtue, and of piety."

The Success of the Dictionary

Webster revised his great work for republication in 1841. Three thousand copies were printed, selling from thirteen to fifteen dollars each. The economy still was recovering from the depression of 1837, and at Webster's death in 1843, 1,420 copies still were on hand.[46] By 1845, George and Charles Merriam, printers and booksellers based in Springfield, Massachusetts, had secured the rights to the dictionary from the Webster family. The first revision under the Merriams, with the help of Webster's son-in-law, Chauncey Goodrich, was offered to the public in 1847. Webster dictionaries, published by the Merriam company, have been a staple of American education ever since.[47]

A great dictionary war with the competing Worcester's dictionary began during Webster's lifetime. Joseph E. Worcester was more of a philological conservative whose ideas of language were closer to the British standards that Webster castigated. Worcester appealed to the highly educated who preferred a "more refined type of pronunciation."[48] The battle waged for decades after Webster himself had passed from the scene, but Worcester eventually lost the war. Right from the start of the criticisms, Webster defended his crowning achievement. To the editors of one newspaper he responded with great vigor:

> As some of your correspondents are disposed to find what
> I have *not* done, in making a dictionary, I will thank them
> to tell your readers what I *have* done. If they are not satis-
> fied with the book I have published, they have perfect
> liberty to make a better one. I am sure, that before they
> have collected thirty or forty thousand words, the number
> I have added to the English vocabularies, traced them to
> their origin, as far as they can & defined them; & after
> they have spent thirty thousand dollars in the work; they
> will regret the undertaking.[49]

These words echo the preface to Samuel Johnson's 1755

Dictionary:

> In this work, when it shall be found that much is omitted,
> let it not be forgotten that much likewise is performed; and
> though no book was ever spared out of tenderness to the
> authour, and the world is little solicitous to know whence
> proceeded the faults of that which it condemns; yet it may
> gratify curiosity to inform it, that the *English Dictionary*
> was written with little assistance of the learned, and with-
> out any patronage of the great; not in the soft obscurities
> of retirement, or under the shelter of academick bowers,
> but amidst inconvenience and distraction, in sickness and
> in sorrow: and it may repress the triumph of malignant
> criticism to observe, that if our language is not here fully
> displayed, I have only failed in an attempt which no
> human powers have hitherto completed.[50]

Like Johnson, it is understandable that Webster would take pains
to point out the labor involved in his work, and emphasize the inap-
propriateness of the ease with which others could criticize a project
that had engulfed twenty years of a person's life.

Webster visited Washington, D. C., in 1830-1831 to lobby for a
better copyright law. Congress received him warmly; he gave an
hour's discourse on the English language in the House of Representatives, and even dined with President Jackson. To his daughter,
Harriet, Webster wrote of his delight at being so warmly embraced:

> They had learned in my books—they were glad to see me,
> and ready to do me any kindness in their power. They all
> seemed to think also that my great labors deserve some
> uncommon reward. Indeed, I know of nothing that has
> given me more pleasure in my journeys, the last summer
> and this winter, than the respect and kindness manifested
> towards me in consequence of the use of my books. It
> convinces me that my fellow citizens consider me as their
> benefactor and the benefactor of my country.[51]

In February 1831, Congress passed a new copyright law that

gave authors exclusive rights to their works for twenty-eight years. Widows and children were entitled to renew the rights for another fourteen. Webster had succeeded in the object of his visit.

He had another object in mind as he visited the nation's capital. While speaking with Congressmen and Senators, Webster urged them to sign a recommendation for the dictionary. The recommendation called for adoption of the Webster dictionary as a standard for all Americans. Seventy-three Congressmen and thirty-one Senators affixed their signatures to the document. Although it was purely a promotional endeavor and not an official act of Congress, it nevertheless, by the weight of the names attached, gave an aura of authority to Webster's great work.[52] By the 1850s, people were beginning to refer to Webster's dictionary as the national standard.

Regardless of the critics, there were those who grasped the scope and size of what Webster had accomplished. As one correspondent acknowledged:

> The labor indispensable to such an enterprise, has been, I presume, the chief cause why it has not been attempted; for few there are, how gifted soever with talents and industry, who would be willing, like Johnson, to venture alone and unassisted into the mazes of lexicography, lest their success, in surmounting difficulties, should not be as eminent as was his. . . .
>
> The work in which you are engaged, is almost too much to be accomplished by an individual: it should be enterprised by many, from whose united efforts it would be reasonable to expect what the industry of the longest single life can never achieve. Let me not be understood to doubt, Sir, either your acquirements or your capacity; all that one can perform I feel persuaded will be done by yourself; and I sincerely hope that the result of your labors of twenty years, will not only be delivered to the world "with the spirit of a man who has endeavoured well," but will also add to the literary reputation of our country.[53]

A single individual never again duplicated Webster's effort. Later editions expunged the individual characteristics that had made it

Webster's dictionary: "Though modern editors of Webster's magnificent work have revised and modified his vigorously asserted beliefs," one scholar opines, "Webster performed a task that matched his era and expressed its values."[54] The sciences of philology and lexicography soon turned away permanently from the Biblically based evangelical approach that had been Webster's personal imprint on his labor of love. The dictionary continued under the Webster name and most American households know what it means to "look it up in Webster," but the Webster who penned the dictionary is largely unknown. Forgotten is the evangelical and moral basis of the original edition; forgotten also are the hopes of the man who sought to establish the American nation on a firm Christian foundation for government, education, and morality.

---

[1] Webster to Oliver Wolcott, Jr., 18 June 1807, Wolcott Papers, CHS.

[2] Webster to Josiah Quincy, 12 February 1811, in Ford, 2: 102.

[3] Webster to John Jay, 19 May 1813, in Ford, 2: 119.

[4] Webster to Stephen Van Rensselaer, 5 November 1821, Webster Papers, HSP.

[5] Webster, *1828 Dictionary*, preface.

[6] This overview of linguistic history is drawn from Robert H. Robins, *A Short History of Linguistics* (Bloomington: Indiana University Press, 1968) and Vincent Paul Bynack, "Language and the Order of the World: Noah Webster and the Idea of an American Culture" (Ph.D. dissertation, Yale University, 1978).

[7] Webster, "A Dissertation Concerning the Influence of Language on Opinions, and of Opinions on Language," in *Collection of Essays*, 222-28.

[8] Johann David Michaelis, *A Dissertation on the Influence of Opinions on Language and of Language on Opinions* (English translation, London, 1769), 2.

[9] Bynack, 104-105.

[10] Webster, *Dissertations*, 318.

[11] Ibid., 182.

[12] Ibid., 183.

[13] Bynack, 86-87.

[14] Webster, "Influence of Language," in *Collection of Essays*, 222.

[15] Ibid., 222-23.

[16] Ibid., 225-27.

[17] Ibid., 228.

[18] Allen Walker Read, "The Spread of German Linguistic Learning in New England During the Lifetime of Noah Webster," *American Speech* 41:3 (1966), 163-64.

[19] Webster, *Observations on Language and Commerce* (New Haven: S. Babcock, 1839), 3.

[20] Ibid., 7.

[21] Webster, "A Discourse Pronounced before the Connecticut Academy of Arts and Sciences, at their Annual Meeting, on the Fourth Sunday of October, 1808," 7, Webster Papers, NYPL, Box 7.

[22] Ibid., 4.

[23] Webster established a pattern of tracing words through approximately twenty languages. As he wrote to Oliver Wolcott, Jr., 26 September 1810, Wolcott Papers, CHS: "I have lately finished an examination of the Oriental languages of the Assyrian stock—the Chaldaic, Syriac, Samaritan, Hebrew, Ethiopic, Persian & Arabic. This examination has been attended with much advantage, & will produce results wholly new, & I believe, unknown even in Europe. I think it probable that every radical word now in use in Europe, if not in Arabic & the east, was invented before the dispersion of men—for they are the same in about eighteen languages or rather dialects which I have examined. In the progress of this investigation, some facts will appear to illustrate the history of man & of society."

[24] Webster, *Observations on Language*, 3.

[25] Webster to David McClure, in *Religious Intelligencer* 21 (3 December 1836): 417, in Webster Papers, NYPL, Box 5.

[26] Bynack, 22.

[27] Webster, *Observations on Language*, 5.

[28] Dennis Patrick Rusche, "An Empire of Reason: A Study of the Writings of Noah Webster" (Ph.D. dissertation, University of Iowa, 1975), 423.

[29] Webster, "A Letter to a Gentleman in Andover," in the *New England Puritan*, 3 March 1842.

[30] Webster, letter to the New Haven *Daily Herald*, 10 October 1842, quoted in Read, 180.

[31] Even people with the same evangelical Christian foundation upon which Webster rested would have to accept his basic premise as a prerequisite for approval of his entire etymological system. That is, they would have to believe with him that the confusion of languages at Babel resulted in mere dialectic changes rather than a complete restructuring of all language. The Biblical account gives no clear exposition

on the extent of the language alteration, but the dominant view among evangelical scholars is that more than dialectical changes were effected."

[32] Webster, "A Brief Sketch of the Errors Contained in Certain Elementary Books," manuscript, n.d., Webster Papers, NYPL, Box 7.

[33] Webster to John Jay, November 1821, in Ford, 2: 162.

[34] Ford, 2: 116.

[35] Webster to Rebecca Webster, 21 July 1824, Webster Papers, NYPL, Box 1: " This [Sunday] is not a day of *rest* in France—at least not universally. Before my eyes now, the masons are at work on the walls of a new house & I am within the sound of the hammer, the adze or other instruments. Some shops are shut—but others not. Little regard is had to the Sabbath. The Catholics generally have no bibles—& the Sabbath is a day of amusement for the rich & the gay. The theaters are open every night—& one of the greatest inconveniences I experience is the noise of carriages at the breaking up of plays, about 12 at night. I must submit to be thus annoyed at present, in every way imaginable; but I think these things may shorten my stay in France."

[36] William G. Webster to Emily Webster Ellsworth, 23 August 1824, Webster Papers, CHS.

[37] Webster, note at the bottom of a manuscript page in which he strongly denied borrowing from another English dictionary, July 1833, Webster Papers, NYPL, Box 7.

[38] P. Staudenraus, "Mr. Webster's Dictionary: A Personal Document of the Age of Benevolence," *Mid-America* 45:3 (1963): 193-95.

[39] Webster, *1828 Dictionary*, preface.

[40] Ibid.

[41] Webster to Emily Webster Ellsworth, 4 February 1829, Webster Papers, CHS.

[42] Staudenraus, "Mr. Webster's Dictionary," 195-96.

[43] Moss, 104.

[44] Webster, *1828 Dictionary*, preface.

[45] Ibid.

[46] E.E.F. Skeel, comp., and Carpenter, ed., *Bibliography*, 238.

[47] James Root Hulbert, *Dictionaries: British and American* (London: Andre Deutsch, 1955), 28-30.

[48] Ibid., 31-32.

[49] Undated manuscript, Noah Webster Papers, New Haven Colony Historical Society, New Haven, CT. A reference to the "Herald" in the postscript indicates that it might be a letter that appeared in the New York *Commercial Advertiser*, 26 August 1829, and

again in the New York *Spectator*, 28 August 1829.

50 Samuel Johnson, *Johnson's Dictionary: A Modern Selection*, eds. E.L. McAdam, Jr., and George Milne (New York: Pantheon Books, 1963), 28-29. In the same preface, 3, Johnson gives his view of the lot of lexicographers:

"It is the fate of those who toil at the lower employments of life, to be rather driven by the fear of evil, than attracted by the prospect of good; to be exposed to censure, without hope of praise; to be disgraced by miscarriage, or punished for neglect, where success would have been without applause, and diligence without reward.

"Among these unhappy mortals is the writer of dictionaries."

And among his definitions, one finds the following under *lexicographer*: "A writer of dictionaries; a harmless drudge, that busies himself in tracing the original, and detailing the signification of words."

51 Webster to Harriet Webster Fowler, December 1830, in Warfel, *Noah Webster*, 391-92.

52 Monaghan, 145-46.

53 George Ord to Webster, 30 January 1827, Webster Papers, NYPL, Box 5.

54 Staudenraus, "Mr. Webster's Dictionary," 201.

CONCLUSION

Noah Webster Defined

An undated manuscript in Webster's handwriting, buried within the thousands of sheets of personal papers in the New York Public Library's Webster Collection, probably sums up the life of this industrious scholar better than anything else he ever wrote. In the manuscript, Webster said simply,

> *Truth* is the end to which all learning should be directed. We want *truth* in literature; we want *truth* in science; we want *truth* in politics; we want *truth* in morals; we want *truth* in religion; we want *truth* in everything. To gain *truth* in learning & science, we want accurate scholars for teachers; to gain *truth* in politics, we want great statesmen, & men of pure integrity; to gain *truth* in religion, we want the scriptures in language that conveys the exact sense of the inspired writers, & which every reader can understand.
>
> In short, *truth* is everything that is valuable in theory or practice; & without it, nothing either in theory or practice, is of any value.[1]

Noah Webster's version of his own life was that it was an attempt to apply truth in every intellectual and moral sphere—to make truth the bedrock for every societal improvement. He found truth where he did not expect to find it. For nearly fifty years he philosophized and theorized until he came face to face with his religious heritage. Once he capitulated to the God of the Bible, he set out on a quest to make Scriptural principles the foundation of government, education, and language, thereby improving America and making it more conformable to Biblical standards. It was a holy quest, actuated by a sense of divine mission. It was a battle against the forces of error and deception. And the warrior fought the good fight until he became an ancient warrior, knowing that the battle, for him, was nearing an end.

Webster began to scale down the war as he sensed his days drawing to a close. In 1837, he began to dismantle his library, perhaps his greatest treasure besides his family. Emily Webster Ellsworth wrote to her seventy-nine year old father, "Your trunks came several days since. . . . I was sorry your library was dissolved. Many long years I trust, are yet before you my dear father & I fear you will sometimes miss your old companions the wonted volumes."[2] Webster responded to her concerns with a tenderness that many of his critics would have thought impossible for him:

> If the books I have sent you serve to revive the remembrance of early days, spent under a paternal roof, & to recall the image of your father & of his toils, one of my objects will be obtained. The recollection of such things serves to sustain that kindly feeling of family nearness, which is among the best affections of the human heart.[3]

Noah Webster toiled for a long time in a life that spanned the colonial, revolutionary, early republic, and Jacksonian eras. He was well known to most of the men who framed the Constitution and still was breathing Federalist principles after most of the Founding Fathers had breathed their last. He was trained in Puritan doctrines as a child. His parents, pious Congregationalists, hoped to instill in the young Webster the same spiritual values, and a love and respect for family and tradition. His lineage could be traced back to the Pilgrim father, William Bradford, and one of his Puritan ancestors joined in the original migration to Connecticut. Religious duties and family tradition were hallmarks of his early education.

The senior Webster thought his son would follow in his footsteps and be a farmer. But the younger Webster, although he always appreciated husbandry, had a different bent. His desire for book-learning led him to Yale one month before his sixteenth birthday, and opened up to him a world of intellectual ferment that fanned his natural tendencies. Although he remained a nominal churchgoer and maintained the basic Puritan moral beliefs, theologically he began to drift. Webster became a disciple of the Enlightenment's conservative Common Sense philosophy. Common Sense was not antithetical to a rational Christian explanation of the nature of the universe, but it offered an intellectual foundation to which he could cling, rather than the Puritan theological framework with which he felt uncomfortable.

The one constant in Webster's life was his ambition to elevate the moral character and the literary endeavors of his countrymen. Throughout his long life, he sought means to accomplish this objective. He was a schoolteacher, a lawyer, an editor of a magazine and then a newspaper, a town councilman, a state legislator and, finally, a lexicographer. At every stage of his career, no matter how many twists it took, his aim remained unchanged. Only the approaches differed.

Initially an unknown and penniless schoolteacher, Webster nevertheless felt that a single individual could make an impact on his society. This he proved with the astounding success of his Speller. The educator graduated into a public man, letting his views be known on every subject imaginable, whether through published essays, in the first original American magazine, or as a newspaper editor and columnist. He championed educational reform, the literary independence of the new American nation, and a society established on civility and decorum, governed by republican principles. His ambition was great, and so, at times, was his ego. When he traveled the country giving lectures on language, he earned both respect for his views and lack of respect for his vanity, simultaneously. The cocksure Webster often hurt his cause by his attitudes. Yet when Federalists sought a man to state their position in a fledgling newspaper, Webster was chosen for the task.

New York City's *American Minerva* was Webster's organ for the promulgation of Federalist wisdom. He na(vely assumed that all America needed was a greater dissemination of the knowledge he offered and the nation would stay on course politically, educationally, and morally. Youthful optimism was shaken by the excesses of the French Revolution and the receptiveness of many of his fellow citizens to what he considered the licentious and chaotic actions of the French in the 1790s. The destruction of his illusions led to a reexamination of human nature and the place of man in the order of the world.

Ultimately, through the instrumentality of a religious revival in New Haven, his reexamination of man and society finally led to a dramatic Christian conversion. This conversion was thorough enough to undermine all his previous philosophical conceptions and form the basis for reworked theories of government, education, and language. The moral underpinnings for each became decisively Christian.

Christianity became the basis for politics and republican government. Indeed, Webster became convinced that no government could long remain free unless Christian principles formed its cornerstone. Civil liberty, he concluded, was the fruit of Christianity, and to attack the Christian religion was to endanger the happiness and stability of the nation. Man could not rule by reason alone, but had to allow the Bible to be the guide for human reason. Character, always a prime concern for Webster, became even more important. Men of sound Christian principles should be elected to office, he believed; and the men who elected them had to be of good character also. He became a firmer Federalist than ever, buoyed by the belief that he now had divine precepts to support his views.

Webster's educational concepts also underwent transformation. Prior to his conversion, he had frowned upon what he called the overuse of the Bible in schools. But the internal change brought a new outlook. Biblical truth became the bedrock for all real education. He often quoted the Biblical admonition that the fear of God was the beginning of wisdom. While residing in Amherst, Massachusetts, from 1812 to 1822, he was a leader in educational initiatives. He helped establish an academy in the town, and then assumed leadership in the founding of Amherst College, designed to be an institution that would train indigent young men for the ministry.

Webster also added a number of educational textbooks to the Speller, Grammar, and Reader of his early years. Among these were a book of biographies of worthy men (with an emphasis on character) and a history of the United States, written to show the Christian foundations of the nation and the need for republican government to rest on a Biblical basis. His revised edition of the Bible, published in 1833, he considered to be an educational endeavor, and considered it the greatest contribution he could make to his country.

The most prominent change of direction was in his philological labors. Ten years of intensive study opened up to him a theory of language that traced words back to their original meanings, recapturing elements of the language that God had bestowed on the first humans. This connection with the Edenic creation, as Webster perceived it, also was a link with God himself and the order that He had ordained in the world. The closer man could get to that original order and purpose, Webster believed, the more contemporary society would reflect God's intentions. The dictionary, finally published in 1828, after more than twenty years of labor, was, for him, a means of restoring the language God had given. If men would use words as they originally were intended to be used, Webster had faith that society could continue to progress in the sciences, in the arts, and in the true knowledge of God.

Both the similarities and differences between Webster and Samuel Johnson, the renowned English lexicographer, are worthy of note.[4] Both men engaged in dictionary work as a symbol of national pride. Johnson wanted to produce something that would rival the national dictionaries of the Italians and the French; Webster sought to promote American literary achievement through publication of the first major American dictionary of the English language. Both used copious quotations from the best writers of the English language to illustrate word usage. Webster even copied a great number of his quotations directly from Johnson. And both felt they had labored against great odds with virtually no support, either of an emotional or monetary nature.

Yet the differences were even more pronounced. While Johnson used quotes and tried to provide philosophical content through them, he never was as determined as Webster was to promote a particular view of the world. Neither was Johnson systematic in his treatment of the origin and development of language. Webster's ten-year detour into the maze of comparative linguistics was not an arena Johnson wished to enter. And Webster's belief that proper definitions could help shape men's thinking and practices was a doctrine Johnson never claimed for himself. Webster obviously had a grander vision and a clearer purpose for his work.

But perhaps the greatest single difference between the two men was in their characters and temperaments. Johnson always had trouble focusing on his projects; he entertained "rebellious fits of indolence," followed by spurts of energy designed to get the work over with as soon as possible.[5] When his dictionary finally was completed and sent to the printer, he had a terrible time preparing the history and grammar of the language that was to be part of the introduction to the work. He stayed five weeks at Oxford for that purpose, yet did not collect any materials or write a single word on the subject. He put it off until the last possible minute.[6] Nothing could have been further from the nature of Noah Webster.

In contrast to Johnson, who made last-minute deadlines a habit, the most obvious personal character trait that Webster brought to his labors, and indeed every aspect of his life, was his ceaseless industry. He was a tireless worker who produced prodigiously. Another aspect of his character was perseverance, his ability to see a project through to completion, no matter what odds he faced. Although his *American Magazine* had to fold for lack of subscriptions, he had initiated the first truly original American magazine. He may have had to retire from the newspaper business from exhaustion, but while he was editor of the *Minerva*, he was the most effective Federalist voice in the country. And no one matched the vast reservoir of energy and determination he called upon to complete the research and writing of his greatest achievement, the *American Dictionary of the English Language*. It remains a monument to his diligence, perseverance, and Christian worldview.

This study has been an intellectual biography and has touched only briefly on Webster's personal life. His character has been remarked upon in the context of his views of government, education, and lexicography, yet much of the character displayed in everyday life has been omitted for the sake of a narrower focus. One question remains, however, for those who might be disturbed by Webster's disdain for the "idle lounger." Did Webster's conversion lead him to act on behalf of the poor, or was he merely all talk when he spoke constantly of the love of God?

In 1803, during Webster's transition years just prior to his conversion, he made a public appeal for the establishment of a charitable society in New Haven, designed specifically to help those who, through no fault of their own, had come upon hard times. "The poor of this class," he commented, "seem to stand on different ground from those who, by their vices and laziness, fall into indigence and contempt."[7] There was a clear distinction in Webster's mind between the deserving and the undeserving poor. Those who truly were needy, and who had not been put in their distressful situation because of laziness, he felt should be the recipients of the benevolence of their fellow citizens. Although no society was founded at that time, his appeal helped keep the idea before the people of New Haven who did, after Webster moved to Amherst, establish a fund for the types of people Webster sought to aid.

Webster's philippics against laziness stemmed from his own devotion to labor. Yet his personal distaste for "idle loungers" did not keep him from trying to redeem such people from their indolent habits. Webster's granddaughter, Emily Ellsworth Fowler Ford, related how if her grandfather found a boy loitering in the neighborhood, he would ask him to do some work in the yard or garden, and then pay him a wage much higher than the usual rate. As a result, boys often would show up at the Webster home seeking work, and while they worked, Webster would instruct them about plants, trees, grafting, and budding. The true educator never ceases to be an educator.[8]

Neither did Webster's strict Sabbatarianism, which regarded Sunday as a day of rest from labor, transform itself into a harsh legalism, at least when the needs of others were concerned. Daughter Julia tells of the time when she discovered a child in Amherst who had no shoes or stockings in winter. She went to her father and asked if it would be acceptable to knit something for the needy child on Sunday. His reply, according to his daughter, was "Certainly my child. It is a work of necessity and mercy."[9]

Webster also remained firmly committed, in his post-conversion days, to the eventual abolition of slavery. He did, however, have sharp tactical differences with the radical abolitionists. "I believe the measures of the abolitionists to be wrong, extremely wrong," he wrote. "The anti-slavery societies have no right . . . to pursue any measures, which tend directly to disturb society in the north, where there is no slavery. If slavery is a sin, that sin rests on the south; we, in the north, are not answerable for it."[10] That disavowal of Northern responsibility for Southern sins did not mean that Webster's individual responsibility to help alleviate the circumstances of blacks in America had been abrogated. It was discovered in his will that he had been putting aside twenty dollars a year in the bank to the account of a black woman, Lucy Griffin, who had been a domestic servant in the Webster home. This yearly gift, awarded to her after his death, made her much wealthier than other blacks in town and enabled her to buy her own home.[11] This was Webster putting his faith into practice.

Webster always protested, once his dictionary was published, that he was near the completion of his labors, but there always was just one more project that had to be finished first. Probably his most honest comment on the subject was in a letter to daughter Emily when he said, "One thing I desire & that is, to be relieved from the toil of study, & business, & yet I am so accustomed to action, that I presume inaction would be tedious & perhaps not salutary."[12] An inactive Noah Webster would have been oxymoronic—the two could not have coexisted. In the last month of his life, he wrote to an acquaintance, "I have published a small volume of papers, containing my own writings, & accounts of transactions in which I had an agency. The last article contains a brief account of the errors in our language & in school books. And here I close my literary labors."[13] For once, he was right about his oft-expressed opinion that his labors were at an end.

On 22 May 1843, Webster walked twice to the post office. When he returned from the second trip, he had a chill. It soon turned into pleurisy. By the next Sunday, it was obvious that he was fatally ill. The thoroughness of his conversion carried forward to his last day. Rev. Nathaniel Taylor visited him in his final hours and Webster's daughter, Eliza Webster Jones, penned an account of the meeting:

> Father remarked, "I am very sick this afternoon, but I have no pain, and I think I may recover." Dr. Taylor kindly answered, "You are an old man Dr. Webster, and it is well to be prepared for the result whatever it may be." Father looked expressively. He understood him and folding his hands, said, "I'm ready to go; my work is all done, I know in whom I have believed." He then went on to speak of the past. "I have struggled with many difficulties. Some I have

been able to overcome, and by some I have been overcome. I have made many mistakes, but I love my country,
and have labored for the youth of my country and I trust
no precept of mine, has taught any dear youth to sin."[14]

Modern historians are prone to treat familial accounts of the
passing of a loved one with some skepticism, and often it is wise to
do so. Yet the account related above is faithful to the whole realm of
thought and action in which Webster lived and moved in his last
thirty-five years. Everything he did after 1808, whether political
essays and letters, the promotion of education, even the great dictionary, was done for the advancement of an American Christian
republic—a portion of God's visible kingdom on earth. At five
minutes before eight, Sunday evening, 28 May 1843, Noah
Webster's literary labors ended.

---

[1] Webster, address to an unnamed audience, "Investigations into the Origins and Principles of the English Language, and How This Investigation Throws Light on Our Ancestors," n.d., 25, Webster Papers, NYPL, Box 7.

[2] Emily Webster Ellsworth to Webster, 19 October 1837, Webster Papers, NYPL, Box 6.

[3] Webster to Emily Webster Ellsworth, 27 November 1837, Webster Papers, CHS.

[4] Information on Samuel Johnson is culled from the following sources: Walter Jackson Bate, *Samuel Johnson* (London: Chatto & Windus, 1978); Walter Jackson Bate, *The Achievement of Samuel Johnson* (New York: Oxford University Press, 1955); and James H. Sledd and Gwin J. Kolb, "Johnson's *Dictionary* and Lexicographical Tradition," in Donald J. Greene, ed., *Samuel Johnson: A Collection of Critical Essays* (Englewood Cliffs, NJ: Prentice-Hall, 1965), 114-23.

[5] Bate, *Samuel Johnson*, 242.

[6] Ibid., 255.

[7] Webster, "Memoir," 40.

[8] Ford, 2: 169.

[9] Ibid., 170.

[10] Webster to Rev. Dr. Hawes, n.d., Webster Papers, NYPL, Box 1.

[11] Ford, 2: 512-13.

12 Webster to Emily Webster Ellsworth, 8 August 1840, Webster Papers, CHS.

13 Webster to Mr. Parker, 11 May 1843, Webster Papers, Pierpont Morgan Library, New York City.

14 Account by Eliza Webster Jones, "For My Little Boy," in Ford, 2: 367.

Bibliography

Manuscript Collections

Hartford, Connecticut. Connecticut Historical Society. Noah Webster Papers. Oliver Wolcott, Jr., Papers.

New Haven, Connecticut. New Haven Colony Historical Society. Noah Webster Papers.

New Haven, Connecticut. Manuscript Vault Shelves. Beinecke Rare Book and Manuscript Library. Yale University.

New Haven, Connecticut. Manuscripts and Archives. Yale University Library. Webster Family Papers. Baldwin Family Papers. Chauncey Family Papers. David Humphreys Papers. Miscellaneous Manuscripts 237.

New York City, New York. Rare Books and Manuscripts Division. New York Public Library. Astor, Lenox, and Tilden Foundations. Noah Webster Papers.

New York City, New York. Pierpont Morgan Library. Noah Webster Papers.

Philadelphia, Pennsylvania. Historical Society of Pennsylvania. Noah Webster Papers.

Washington, D. C. Library of Congress. James Madison Papers. Daniel Webster Papers.

Noah Webster: Selected Published Works

Webster, Noah. *An Address, Delivered at the Laying of the Corner Stone of the Building Erected for the Charity Institution in Amherst, Massachusetts, August 9, 1820.* Boston: Ezra Lincoln, 1820.

_____. *An Address, Delivered before the Hampshire, Franklin and Hampden Agricultural Society, at their Annual Meeting in Northampton, October 14, 1818.* Northampton, Massachusetts: Thomas W. Shepard, 1818.

_____. *An Address to the Citizens of Connecticut.* New Haven: J. Walter, 1803.

_____. *An American Dictionary of the English Language.* New York: Sherman Converse, 1828; reprint ed., Anaheim, California: Foundation for American Christian Education, 1967.

_____. *An American Selection of Reading and Speaking.* Philadelphia: Young and M'Culloch, 1787.

_____. *A Brief History of Epidemic and Pestilential Diseases.* 2 vols. Hartford: Hudson and Goodwin, 1799.

_____. *A Collection of Essays and Fugitiv Writings. On Moral, Historical, Political and Literary Subjects.* Boston: Thomas and Andrews, 1790; reprint ed., Delmar, New York: Scholars' Facsimiles and Reprints, 1977.

_____. *A Compendious Dictionary of the English Language.* Hartford: Hudson and Goodwin, 1806.

_____. *Dissertation in English on the universal diffusion of literature as introductory to the universal diffusion of Christianity.* Prepared for Master of Arts degree, 1781. Published in the *Gazette of the United States*, Philadelphia, 2-16 June 1790.

_____. *Dissertations on the English Language.* Boston: Isaiah Thomas and Company, 1789.

_____. *Effects of Slavery, on Morals and Industry.* Hartford: Hudson and Goodwin, 1793.

_____. *Elements of Useful Knowledge.* 2 vols. Hartford: Hudson and Goodwin, 1806.

_____. *An Examination into the Leading Principles of the Federal Constitution Proposed by the Late Convention Held at Philadelphia.* Philadelphia: Prichard and Hall, 1787.

_____. *A Grammatical Institute of the English Language, Part I.* Hartford: Hudson and Goodwin, 1783.

_____. *A Grammatical Institute of the English Language, Part II.* Hartford: Hudson and Goodwin, 1784.

_____. *A Grammatical Institute of the English Language, Part III.* Hartford: Barlow and Babcock, 1785.

_____. *History of the United States.* New Haven: Durrie and Peck, 1832.

_____, ed. *The Holy Bible, Containing the Old and New Testaments, in the Common Version. With Amendments of the Language by Noah Webster, LL.D.* New Haven: Durrie and Peck, 1833; reprint ed., Grand Rapids, Michigan: Baker Book House, 1987.

_____. *Instructive and Entertaining Lessons for Youth.* New Haven: S. Babcock and Durrie and Peck, 1835.

_____. *Letters to a Young Gentleman Commencing His Education.* New Haven: Sherman Converse, 1823.

_____. *A Manual for Useful Studies: For the Instruction of*

Young Persons of Both Sexes, in Families and Schools. New Haven: S. Babcock, 1839.

_____. *Miscellaneous Papers, on Political and Commercial Subjects*. New York: E. Belden and Company, 1802.

_____. *Observations on Language and Commerce*. New Haven: S. Babcock, 1839.

_____. *An Oration, Pronounced before the Citizens of New Haven, on the Anniversary of the Declaration of Independence; July 1802*. New Haven: William W. Morse, 1802.

_____. *An Oration, Pronounced before the Knox and Warren Branches of the Washington Benevolent Society, at Amherst, on the Celebration of the Anniversary of the Declaration of Independence, July 4, 1814*. Northampton, Massachusetts: William Butler, 1814.

_____. *Peculiar Doctrines of the Gospel*. Poughkeepsie: Joseph Nelson, for Chester Parsons and Company, 1809.

_____. *A Philosophical and Practical Grammar*. New Haven: Oliver Steele and Company, 1807.

_____. *The Prompter; or A Commentary on Common Sayings and Subjects, which are Full of Common Sense, the Best Sense in the World*. Hartford: Hudson and Goodwin, 1791.

_____. *The Revolution in France, Considered in Respect to its Progress and Effects*. New York: George Bunce and Company, 1794.

_____. *A Rod for the Fool's Back*. New Haven: Read and Morse, 1800.

_____. *Sketches of American Policy*. Hartford: Hudson and Goodwin, 1785.

————. *Ten Letters to Dr. Joseph Priestley*. New Haven: Read and Morse, 1800.

————. *Value of the Bible, and Excellence of the Christian Religion*. New Haven: Durrie and Peck, 1834. Quoted from manuscript copy in Beinecke Library, Yale University.

Newspapers and Periodicals

The American Magazine, December 1787-November 1788.

The American Minerva (New York), 9 December 1793-18 March 1794.

The American Minerva and the New York (Evening) Commercial Advertiser, 19 March 1794-5 May 1795.

The American Minerva and Evening Advertiser (New York), 6 May 1795-30 April 1796.

The Commercial Advertiser (New York), 2 October 1797-24 July 1798; 14 February 1834; 25 November 1834; 22 October 1836.

The Connecticut Courant, 26 August-2 September 1783; 20 November 1786.

The Genesee Farmer and Gardener's Journal 2, no. 9, 3 March 1832.

The Minerva and Mercantile Evening Advertiser (New York), 2 May 1796-1 October 1797.
The New England Puritan, 3 March 1842.

The New York Packet, 17 January-7 February 1782.

The Vermont Chronicle, 8 April 1840.

Secondary Sources – Books

Aulard, A. *Christianity and the French Revolution*. Benn, 1927; reprint ed., Fertig, 1966.

Babbidge, Homer D., Jr., ed. *Noah Webster: On Being American*. New York: Frederick A. Praeger, 1967.

Banner, James M. *To the Hartford Convention: The Federalists and the Origins of Party Politics in Massachusetts*. New York: Alfred A. Knopf, 1970.

Banning, Lance. *The Jeffersonian Persuasion: Evolution of a Party Ideology*. Ithaca: Cornell University Press, 1978.

Bate, Walter Jackson. *The Achievement of Samuel Johnson*. New York: Oxford University Press, 1955.

_____. *Samuel Johnson*. London: Chatto and Windus, 1978.

Beattie, James. *An Essay on the Nature and Immutability of Truth*. Edinburgh, 1770; reprint ed., New York: Garland, 1983.

Blumenfeld, Samuel L. *Is Public Education Necessary?* Boise, Idaho: The Paradigm Company, 1981.

Brinton, Crane. *The Jacobins: An Essay in the New History*. 1930; reprint ed., New York: Russell and Russell, 1961.

Burkett, Eva Mae. *American Dictionaries of the English Language Before 1861*. Metuchen, New Jersey: The Scarecrow Press, 1979.

Cremin, Lawrence A. *American Education: The Colonial Experience, 1607-1783*. New York: Harper and Row, 1970.

Cunningham, Charles E. *Timothy Dwight, 1752-1817: A Biography*. New York: Macmillan, 1942.

Curry, Thomas J. *The First Freedoms: Church and State in America to the Passage of the First Amendment.* New York: Oxford University Press, 1986.

Dilworth, Thomas. *A New Guide to the English Tongue.* Philadelphia: T. and W. Bradford, 1793; reprint ed., Delmar, New York: Scholars' Facsimiles and Reprints, 1978.

Elliott, Emory. *Revolutionary Writers: Literature and Authority in the New Republic, 1725-1810.* New York: Oxford University Press, 1982.

Fay, Bernard. *The Revolutionary Spirit in France and America.* Harcourt, Brace, and World, 1927; reprint ed., New York: Cooper Square, 1966.

Fennelly, Catherine. *Town Schooling in Early New England, 1790-1840.* Old Sturbridge Village, Sturbridge, Massachusetts: The Meriden Gravure Company, Meriden, Connecticut, 1962.

Ford, Emily Ellsworth Fowler, comp. Skeel, Emily Ellsworth Ford, ed. *Notes on the Life of Noah Webster.* 2 vols. New York: Burt Franklin, 1912; reprint ed., 1971.

Friend, Joseph H. *The Development of American Lexicography, 1798-1864.* The Hague and Paris: Mouton, 1967.

Frost, William. *Connecticut Education in the Revolutionary Era.* Chester, Connecticut: Pequot Press, 1974.

Green, Donald J. *Samuel Johnson: A Collection of Critical Essays.* Englewood Cliffs, New Jersey: Prentice-Hall, 1965.

Hall, Verna and Slater, Rosalie. *Rudiments of America's Christian History and Government.* San Francisco: Foundation for American Christian Education, 1968.

Hamilton, Sir William, ed. *The Works of Thomas Reid, D. D.* 2 vols.

Edinburgh: Maclachlan and Stewart, 1872.

Hartmann, R. R. K., ed. *The History of Lexicography*. Amsterdam and Philadelphia: John Benjamins Publishing Company, 1986.

Hazen, Charles D. *Contemporary American Opinion of the French Revolution*. Johns Hopkins Press, 1897; reprint ed., Gloucester, Massachusetts: Peter Smith, 1964.

Hindle, Brook. *The Pursuit of Science in Revolutionary America, 1735-1789*. Chapel Hill: University of North Carolina Press, 1956.

Hulbert, James Root. *Dictionaries: British and American*. London: Andre Deutsch, 1955.

Johnson, Samuel. *Essays from the Rambler, Adventurer, and Idler*. Walter Jackson Bate, ed. New Haven: Yale University Press, 1968.

_____. *Johnson's Dictionary*. Edited by E. L. McAdam, Jr., and George Milne. New York: Pantheon Books, 1963.

Kafker, Frank A. and Laux, James A. *The French Revolution: Conflicting Interpretations*. New York: Random House, 1968.

Kaplan, Lawrence S. *Jefferson and France*. New Haven: Yale University Press, 1967.

Kelley, Brooks Mather. *Yale: A History*. New Haven: Yale University Press, 1974.

Link, Eugene Perry. *Democratic-Republican Societies, 1790-1800*. New York: Columbia University Press, 1942.

Livermore, Shaw. *The Twilight of Federalism*. New York: Gordian Press, 1972.

McDonald, Forrest. *Novus Ordo Seclorum*. Lawrence, Kansas: University Press of Kansas, 1985.

McManners, John. *The French Revolution and the Church*. New York: Harper and Row, 1969.

McMaster, John Bach. *A History of the People of the United States*. 8 vols. New York: Appleton, 1891.

Madsen, David L. *Early National Education, 1776-1830*. Wiley, 1974.

May, Henry F. *The Enlightenment in America*. New York: Oxford University Press, 1976.

Michaelis, Johann David. *A Dissertation on the Influence of Opinions on Language and of Language on Opinions*. London, 1769.

Monaghan, E. Jennifer. *A Common Heritage: Noah Webster's Blue-Back Speller*. Hamden, Connecticut: Archon Books, 1983.

Morse, Jedidiah. *A Sermon, Exhibiting the Present Dangers*. Charlestown, Massachusetts: Etheridge, 1799.

Moss, Richard J. *Noah Webster*. Boston: Twayne Publishers, 1984.
Palmer, Robert R. *The World of the French Revolution*. New York: Harper and Row, 1971.

Robins, Robert H. *A Short History of Linguistics*. Bloomington, Indiana: Indiana University Press, 1968.

Rollins, Richard M. *The Long Journey of Noah Webster*. University of Pennsylvania Press, 1980.

Rushdoony, Rousas J. *The Messianic Character of American Education*. Nutley, New Jersey: The Craig Press, 1979.

Scudder, Horace E. *Noah Webster*. Boston: Houghton Mifflin Company, 1883.

Skeel, Emily Ellsworth Ford, comp. Carpenter, Edwin H., ed. *A Bibliography of the Writings of Noah Webster*. New York: New York Public Library and Arno Press, 1958; reprint ed., 1971.

Small, Walter Herbert. *Early New England Schools*. Columbia University Teachers College series on *American Education: Its Men, Ideas, and Institutions*. Boston: Ginn and Company, 1914; reprint ed., New York: Arno Press and *The New York Times*, 1969.

Unger, Harlow Giles. *Noah Webster: The Life and Times of an American Patriot*. New York: John Wiley And Sons, 1998.

Warfel, Harry R. *Letters of Noah Webster*. New York: Library Publishers, 1953.

_____. *Noah Webster: Schoolmaster to America*. Macmillan, 1936; reprint ed., New York: Octagon, 1966.

Witherspoon, John. *Lectures on Moral Philosophy*. Princeton: Princeton University Library, 1912.

Secondary Sources - Periodicals

Ahlstrom, Sydney E. "The Scottish Philosophy and American Theology." *Church History* 24:3 (September 1955):257-271.

Good, Douglas L. "The Christian Nation in the Mind of Timothy Dwight." *Fides et Historia* 7:1 (1974):1-18.

Howe, Daniel W. "The Political Psychology of *The Federalist*." *William and Mary Quarterly*. 3rd series. 44:3 (July 1987):485-509.

Howe, John R., Jr. "Republican Thought and the Political Violence of the 1790s." *American Quarterly* 19:2, Pt. 1 (1967):147-165.

McAllister, James L., Jr. "Francis Alison and John Witherspoon: Political Philosophers and Revolutionaries." *Journal of Presbyterian History* 54:1 (1976):33-58.

Read, Allen Walker. "The Spread of German Linguistic Learning in New England During the Lifetime of Noah Webster." *American Speech* 41:3 (1966):163-181.

Staudenraus, P. J. "Mr. Webster's Dictionary: A Personal Document of the Age of Benevolence." *Mid-America* 45:3 (1963): 193-201.

Secondary Sources - Doctoral Dissertations

Bynack, Vincent Paul. "Language and the Order of the World: Noah Webster and the Idea of an American Culture." Ph.D. dissertation. Yale University, 1978.

Coll, Gary R. "Noah Webster, Journalist, 1783-1803." Ph.D. dissertation. University of Southern Illinois, 1971.

Rusche, Dennis Patrick. "An Empire of Reason: A Study of the Writings of Noah Webster." Ph.D. dissertation. University of Iowa, 1975.

Name Index